# Orsch
## ...Cutting the Edge in Education

Lessons Learned from an Innovative Lab School

Jackie Burt

Copyright © 2013 Jackie Burt
Authored by Jackie Burt
Edited by Shelley Read
Contributions by Ashley Burt
Cover design or artwork by Samuel Burt
All rights reserved.

ISBN: 0988609002
ISBN 13: 9780988609006

Library of Congress Control Number: 2013918946
Stone Press, Gunnison, CO

## *Dedications*

This book is dedicated, first, to my mom and Glenny,
also known as Gramma and Pa-dilla or Glom-n-men.
Thank you for allowing me to be a creative individual,
encouraging all of the innovative ideas and silly inventions.
You believed in the person I am and encouraged me to follow
my dreams.
And, especially significant to this project,
thank you for all of the experiences and travel;
you showed me the world and its many perspectives.

And to my children, Sam and Emma,
You have been there with patience and support.
Your contributions to the world of education are significant.
Your feedback and guidance are invaluable.
Thank you for all of the hard work and love throughout.
May you and your children and your children's children live with
inspiration, purpose, and passion.

# Contents

**Foreword-By Ashley Burt**     ix
    *Forward (a good direction to go)* ······················ ix

**Preface**     xi
    *My Journey*·············································· xii

**Introduction—A New Paradigm**     1
    *The Tale of Two Gardens* ······························ 4
    *We could measure student achievement through a different lens.*······················ 18
    *A Philosophy Is Born* ································· 20

---

**SECTION ONE—Thought-Provoking Issues**     25

**Chapter 1—We Need a New Reform Effort**     27
    *A Brief History: How Did We Get Here?* ············ 27
    *What is Happening Currently?*······················ 30
    *Test Validity and Reliability* ·························· 37
    *A New Reform Effort*································· 42

**Chapter 2—Finland: We Can Learn from Successful Programs**     65

## Chapter 3—Sameness  77
*Incongruence: Creativity Versus Sameness* · · · · · · · · · · · · · · · · · · 85
*Sameness Affects Teachers as Well* · · · · · · · · · · · · · · · · · · · · · · · · 87
*A Sense of Individuality and Integrity* · · · · · · · · · · · · · · · · · · · · · · · 90

## Chapter 4—Horses and Carts  93
*To Require Proficiency Is Counterproductive* · · · · · · · · · · · · · · · · 95

## Chapter 5—Ever Seen a Toddler Waste Time?  103
*Lessons from Amelia* · · · · · · · · · · · · · · · · · · · · · · · · · · · · · · · · · · · · 105

## Chapter 6—Bullies  111
*The Most Important Piece of the Puzzle* · · · · · · · · · · · · · · · · · · · · 113
*Behavior and Personalities We Must Be Careful to Not Label as Bullying* · · · · · · · · · · · · · · · · · · · · · · · · · · · · · · · · · · · · 120
*Peer Judgment of Personality Traits* · · · · · · · · · · · · · · · · · · · · · · · 124

## Chapter 7—Time and Processing Capacity  131
*Engagement Versus Boredom* · · · · · · · · · · · · · · · · · · · · · · · · · · · · 133
*Aha Moments, Exploration, and Self-Discovery* · · · · · · · · · · · · · · 141
*Imagination and Creative Fulfillment* · · · · · · · · · · · · · · · · · · · · · · 145
*New Experiences* · · · · · · · · · · · · · · · · · · · · · · · · · · · · · · · · · · · · · · · 146
*Collaboration, Socialization, and Friendship* · · · · · · · · · · · · · · · · 147

## Chapter 8—A Different View of Parent Involvement and Homework  153
*Observing the Spectrum of Parent Involvement* · · · · · · · · · · · · · 156
*A Different Approach to Optimal Parent Involvement* · · · · · · · · 158
*The Homework Discussion* · · · · · · · · · · · · · · · · · · · · · · · · · · · · · · · 163
*Parent/Teacher Conferences* · · · · · · · · · · · · · · · · · · · · · · · · · · · · · 164

## Chapter 9—Essential Skills — 167

The Ability to Make Decisions and Make Valuable Choices · · · 169

The Ability to Effectively Interact, Collaborate, and Communicate · · · · · · · · · · · · · · · · · · · · · · · · · · · · · · · · · · · 174

The Ability to Think Creatively, Critically, Innovatively, and Efficiently · · · · · · · · · · · · · · · · · · · · · · · · · · · · · · · · · · · · · · · · 177

The Ability to Lead and Effectively Learn from Other Leaders · ·178

The Ability to Engage, Experience Awareness, and Learn · · · · 180

The Ability to Discover and Develop a Good Work Ethic and Be Self-Directed · · · · · · · · · · · · · · · · · · · · · · · · · · · · · · · · · · · 182

The Ability to Manage Time · · · · · · · · · · · · · · · · · · · · · · · · · · · 186

The Ability to Present Effectively and Produce High-Quality Products · · · · · · · · · · · · · · · · · · · · · · · · · · · · · · · · · · · · · · · · · · 187

The Ability to Effectively Resource Information and Expertise · 191

The Ability to Develop and Foster Authentic Relationships and Friendships · · · · · · · · · · · · · · · · · · · · · · · · · · · · · · · · · · · · 193

The Ability to Have a Good Time and Think Positively! · · · · · · · 194

# SECTION TWO—Orsch Philosophy — 197

# Capable, Thriving, Engaged Learners — 200

# The Foundation: A Healthy School Culture — 207

The First Element of a Secure Foundation: A Healthy Social Community · · · · · · · · · · · · · · · · · · · · · · · · · · · · · · · · · · · · · · · 209

The Second Element of a Secure Foundation: An Environment in which Individuality Is Not Only Honored, but Is Celebrated and Encouraged by Teachers and Peers · · · · · · · · · · · · · · · · · · 212

*The Third Element of a Secure Foundation: A Place in which Nurturing Adults Offer Appropriate Guidance, Programming, and Advocacy* · · · · · · · · · · · · · · · · · · · · · · · · · · · · · · · · · · · · 216

## The First Pillar: Independence, Flexibility, and Freedom    231
*Boundaries = Freedom* · · · · · · · · · · · · · · · · · · · · · · · · · · · · · · · · · · 233

*Academic Independence, Flexibility, and Freedom* · · · · · · · · · · 237

*Logistical Independence, Flexibility, and Freedom* · · · · · · · · · · 239

*Social Freedom* · · · · · · · · · · · · · · · · · · · · · · · · · · · · · · · · · · · · · · · 243

## The Second Pillar: Creativity    245
*Fine Arts* · · · · · · · · · · · · · · · · · · · · · · · · · · · · · · · · · · · · · · · · · · · · 248

*A Creative Environment* · · · · · · · · · · · · · · · · · · · · · · · · · · · · · · · 250

## The Third Pillar: Variety in Innovative Approaches to Knowledge and Experience.    265
*Variety in Programming* · · · · · · · · · · · · · · · · · · · · · · · · · · · · · · · 271

*Variety in Skill Level* · · · · · · · · · · · · · · · · · · · · · · · · · · · · · · · · · · · 277

## Conclusion—In My Dreams    285

## Philosophy from a Parent's Perspective—Parent Essays    293

## Acknowledgments    319

## Bibliography    327

## Notes    333

# Foreword-By Ashley Burt

### *Forward (a good direction to go)*

Educational reform is a phrase that gets uttered on a regular basis, but one that seems to yield little in the way of results. As such, it has become an oxymoron to me. We simply aren't living up to our potential for improvement. The irony is that most of the components required for real change are in place today. Much research has been done; we really do understand how children learn best. Best practices have been identified, yielding incredible results, and yet the educational system mirrors our government, gridlocked and resistant to meaningful change. We focus on blame; we become provincial and territorial. *Our obsession with measuring progress has eclipsed our real mission of creating thinkers.* Deeply rooted traditions exist on how best to organize schools, measure progress, and teach children. Ingrained biases combined with arguments from tradition stifle new paradigms. We must break down these barriers.

Orsch is a school that is first and foremost a lab. The experimentation that takes place on a daily basis has shown us very clearly that real change is possible. Real change is,

## ORSCH...CUTTING THE EDGE IN EDUCATION

however, intimidating. Real change requires us to let go of preconceived ideas, to take risks, to expose ourselves to criticism. It requires that we make a leap.

But, wait, this is America! We carve our own path. We stand up for what we believe. We take calculated risks to improve our world. We are innovators. We are leaders—except in education.

For years, I watched my wife, Jackie Burt, come home from educational conferences with new ideas, best practices, confirmed—*tested*—progressive teaching techniques. She would come home with them, get excited, but then find limited opportunities to implement them within the existing structure. The desire to have a place to use these best practices was one strong motivator for opening the doors of Orsch. What if we could really use all these great ideas? *What if...*

*What if?* Many years later, we now know "what if"—we have seen the results, we know the children, we are witnessing their potential. Low-cost, high-yield ideas and structures have made the difference. Now we want to show the world that it is possible. The end result is a combination of best practices, careful implementation, and restructuring the basic premise of who directs the education of a child (the child does). Read the pages that follow. Dwell in the possibilities... change the world of education.

## *Preface*

I would like to start by stating clearly that I fully support public education. Public education is the foundation on which our educated society was built; it is to be commended for all it has given throughout history. This book does not hope to work against the establishment of public education, nor does it aim to criticize public education as an entity. However, throughout this book, you will find many references to the way things have traditionally been done and how we can improve upon those elements. The comparisons I make are an effort to bring to light a new approach that may help traditional practices become more innovative.

The United States is home to thousands of great public schools, successful charter schools, private schools, and innovative programs. Thank you to all of the administrators and board members who facilitate such progress; your vision and your efforts make a substantial difference.

I wish to recognize all of the dedicated teachers who entered the teaching profession to make a difference in the lives of students. Teachers are wonderful, creative, and compassionate beings. They give of themselves and gain reward from a glimmer in the eye of a student. They do not stop thinking about their approach to children or their purpose in the classroom—continually striving for improvement and for a connection with students. The students and families of compassionate, creative teachers will forever benefit from their efforts.

It is my hope that teachers and administrators will connect with this book in thoughtful contemplation of how their profession might be improved upon. I celebrate, honor, and thank every teacher and administrator who has hoped for a more creative, innovative approach to educating students, and I empathize with every teacher who has wished for more autonomy. This effort is for you as well as for the students and families you serve.

It is also my hope that parents will read about the possibilities that exist for students and will begin to take part in the movement toward broad-scope improvement.

## *My Journey*

I love words. I love phrases. I love how they combine and tumble together to make meaning. I remember the day I decided I wanted to be an author. I was in fifth grade. I was asked to write an essay titled, "What Is on My Mind?" Other students struggled; I loved every minute of it. I wrote that essay while attending a small one-room schoolhouse near Afsin, Turkey. I was eleven. I had no idea that so many

## PREFACE

elements of that time would foreshadow my life. Writing. Teaching. One-room schoolhouses. Creativity. Lack of a scope and sequence in my education because I changed schools at least every year or two. Lots of life experience. The value of freedom. Following passion. The freedom I felt while writing that essay has stuck with me for thirty-plus years. I had free rein to explore, record, and ultimately produce my own thoughts. I remember the thrill I felt writing those words. I was inspired.

Maybe it was something my mom instilled in me. Maybe I sensed it all along, but I knew I would follow my heart and pursue my passions. Maybe all those grown-ups who continually asked me what I wanted to be when I grew up convinced me that I really could be anything I wanted to be. I wanted to be a teacher, and I would continue to transfer my thoughts onto paper.

I became a teacher. I adore children and everything they offer the world. I am fascinated by their potential and have enjoyed nurturing children my entire life. I appreciate children for their integrity, their creativity, and the joy, love, and hope they exude. And I want them to feel the power of following their passions, discovering their potential, and building upon their innate talents.

During my teaching career, I saw unutilized potential in students and in programming. I chose to open a school to see if I could improve upon each of those elements. I set out with $2,500 from savings to buy some computers, paper, pencils, markers, staplers, tape, and a few books. I negotiated with a few brave curriculum companies for some bargains and samples—enough to get by. I opened Orsch with twenty-two students in 2009. Their tuition would pay rent, insurance, and keep us afloat.

I had just embarked on the hardest years of my life. My family stood by me. Emma and Sam, now fifteen and sixteen, were incredibly supportive throughout and loved attending Orsch.

My husband's support is indescribable—he has been there to contemplate programming, fix computers, hang shelves, hold me and encourage me while I wept, exhausted and unsure that I could keep going, and ultimately to read, help structure, and edit every word of this book.

The results of the program were magical. The gratitude and positive feedback from students and families kept Orsch going. And now we exist as a thriving school with a team of teachers—every one of us loves what we're doing and our students love school. In addition, Orsch operates with a budget that is well below public school budgets. The results of this lab have exceeded my expectations.

I invite you to join us in the journey to inspire our students while exploring viable methods to offer them relevant, essential life skills and to offer teachers a more autonomous approach to their jobs. If you would like to learn more about Orsch, visit our website at www.orsch.net. In this book,

## PREFACE

enjoy reading all we've learned about children, educational possibilities, and how America could take steps toward meaningful educational evolution.

# Introduction—A New Paradigm

> *Our best hope for the future is to develop a new paradigm of human capacity to meet a new era of human existence. We need to evolve a new appreciation of the importance of nurturing human talent along with an understanding of how talent expresses itself differently in every individual. We need to create environments—in our schools, in our workplaces, and in our public offices—where every person is inspired to grow creatively.*
>
> —Sir Ken Robinson, *The Element*

Ella is a child. She is a vibrant and spunky child. She speaks her mind and fills her days with important thought. She questions the world around her with the inquisitive nature that every child naturally possesses. Ella is a thinker. However, she does not appreciate classically delivered academic material. Where a conversation should take place, a lecture turns her inward. When a math worksheet stares at her blankly, she yearns to add color and glitter. She is perfectly capable of learning the concepts handed to her, but she is disappointed that the delivery is not more fitting, more interesting, or more relevant to her place and time in the learning process. She will tell you exactly how she would like to learn if she is given the chance. She will gravitate toward appropriate levels and engaging concepts. She despises an idle mind, as most of us do. As a learner, Ella is among the most proficient.

Ella's life changed one school year. She was placed in a classroom that did not appreciate her ability to learn and grow at her own pace. She was criticized for the things she didn't yet know. She was labeled and identified as someone who needed remediation. Ella is one of the smartest children I've ever met. One need only have a conversation with Ella to recognize her depth, cognitive skill, and inquisitive nature. However, a conversation is not an acceptable assessment tool, apparently. And, unfortunately, individualization of educational material must take place publicly, in a world of sameness, embarrassing instead of helping. This school year, Ella had to fight for her confidence. Ella was forced to learn the way everyone learned each day. She defied it at first. She faced loneliness and ridicule. Several months later, she now plays the game; she has succumbed to the sameness in which she is immersed every day. And she is doing fine. Just fine. She is surviving.

Previously, Ella's approach to learning and development was on its own course, supported by nurturing adults and endless resources. Cruising along nicely, she was

## INTRODUCTION—A NEW PARADIGM

engaged in the world around her at a level few get to experience. She loves science most. She can engage in a scientific discussion for hours. She loves writing—words flow beautifully and creatively, though they lack correct spelling. She enjoys mathematical concepts when they really click.

She prefers to work with tangible items when learning math. Algorithms are not clear to her until she has had the opportunity to experientially absorb the concept. Ella's approach to mathematics takes more time than the student next to her, who prefers an algorithmic approach. She is also a proficient observer. She observes social situations and interactions between classmates, often commenting insightfully about her observations. She tests predictions and engages in social connections of all kinds. Ella is in a mode of constant contemplation. She may be a budding sociologist, or biologist, or actress.

Ella is the poster child for someone who will thrive in an individualized, flexible, creative educational environment. Ella is the poster child for children.

Her story is a common one. She will be just fine, learning, testing, going through her education, going through the motions. She will learn the standards, Common Core and otherwise. She will become a point of data. She will live for after-school activities and weekends. She will fight to belong during the school week, but she will not give in to peer pressure, as she is too strong. She will grow and graduate. She will pursue a path, a career. But what if potential, passion, and innate talent lie beneath the surface for a lifetime? What if sameness convinces this talented individual that she must continue following suit, fighting to fit in, and going through the motions? Have we not stifled greatness by allowing an individual to survive rather than thrive? And then, consider the millions who are merely surviving. And then, consider that millions and millions could be thriving.

The flowers are wilting.

Humans are not fit for the environment in which we immerse them during years of formal education. Sameness is incongruent with our natural tendencies, our innate abilities, and our true potential. American children are wilting.

The longer we wait, the longer we continue anti-nurturing our youth, the worse our problems will get. The following story sheds light on the extreme sides of educational progress as well as the lack thereof. It is a metaphor meant to make us think about educational evolution and the results of a less than nurturing environment.

## *The Tale of Two Gardens*

Once upon a time, there was a vast garden full of seeds of many kinds. Within every seed lay the building blocks of possibility—passion, innate talent, skill, desire, unique

## INTRODUCTION—A NEW PARADIGM

nature, and great potential. The seeds required great care, as the future lies within them.

The gardeners of this important garden were well trained. They were trained in research and in best practices, up-to-date methods and strategies. They were well versed in the seeds they would encounter and in the stages of development, from seedling to a mature budding flower. They were instructed in the individual nature of every type of plant and agreed to care for each plant's unique needs. They were dedicated gardeners, ready and willing to take on the rewarding challenges of nurturing such a valuable garden.

As the gardeners gained their certificates and licenses and headed out into the workforce, they were wide-eyed and hopeful. They could barely hold back their excitement. They felt well prepared and eager to put their knowledge and their skills to work.

The gardeners were both hired by the Powers That Be and began their very important work. They watered their seeds day in and day out. They watered with *love*. They watered with *acceptance*. They watered with *hope* and *trust*, *confidence* and *creativity*, as that was what they knew they should do.

The seeds were given the very best. The gardeners continued on, happy and fulfilled. The seeds began to emerge. All was well.

## ORSCH...CUTTING THE EDGE IN EDUCATION

The Powers That Be then offered new watering cans to his gardeners. The watering cans contained *methods* and *tools*. The gardeners happily watered with these, and the seedlings responded positively. All was well.

The seedlings continued to grow, little by little emerging from the soil. All was well.

But as the days passed, the Powers That Be began to measure the seedlings. He felt he had to make sure the flowers were receiving the right ingredients and that they were growing to the best of their abilities. So he measured and measured and measured. He felt the gardeners must be accountable for the growth of their seedlings; therefore, measurements were necessary. And funding for watering cans and nutrients necessary for flowers to grow—these were tied to measurements. So the measuring and the measuring continued. Day after day, the seedlings were measured. The gardeners were then given new watering cans meant to assist in the measuring. The Powers That Be presented cans filled with what he was told were "grow-faster ingredients" called *standards*, *Common Core*, and *additional accountability*. The loyal gardeners continued watering and measuring as they were instructed to do.

But as he measured again and again, growth began to slow. The Powers That Be was not satisfied. He measured and measured and forced the gardeners to begin watering more diligently with these "grow-faster ingredients."

## INTRODUCTION—A NEW PARADIGM

The gardeners began to lose hope, began to lose passion, but were loyal to the Powers That Be and trusted that the Powers That Be was offering the best of ingredients to their precious seedlings.

But because measurement after measurement did not present desired results, the Powers That Be reached for yet another set of grow-faster ingredients to fill his gardeners' cans—*Pacing Guides, mandates,* and *assessments.* The gardeners looked at each other questioningly, as something was beginning to feel very wrong. The gardeners began wondering if they still liked gardening, or if they really were cut out for a different profession.

More measuring, more grow-faster ingredients (*rigidity, sameness, rules, old ideas, restrictions, leveled instruction, remediation, comparisons, more structure, pressure, lack of creativity, less art*).

And then one day, long into the measuring and the watering with rigid ingredients, the gardeners began to remember their own training from way back when—training that included watering with much different ingredients. Together, they began discussing the tools they had been taught to use. *Differentiation, individualization,* and *diversity*—all of which were the opposite of the *sameness* and *standards* that the Powers That Be had insisted they use. They remembered that healthy flowers need *experience, projects,* and *cooperative learning.* Flowers were to be watered with *patience* and *encouragement* and *praise* and *guidance*, not *pressure*, *rigidity*, and *comparisons*. Flowers needed *hands-on experiences* to flourish and cultivate their innate skills. Relieved to know that they had been traveling the wrong course, they presented these ideas to the Powers That Be, certain that he would agree and would change his course as well.

Unfortunately, the Powers That Be was not at all receptive to the gardeners' pleas to change course. He had spent massive amounts of money on his measuring, and he was unwilling to see past it. He knew that his flowers were not growing fast enough and tossed around terms such as *Gardening Reform*. But, his idea of reform was more of the same, while expecting different results. But many, many followed him blindly. Many, many did not question him, for he was—after all—the Powers That Be.

From that day forth, the gardeners no longer worked in the same garden. The Powers That Be built a fence to separate them, as one gardener was willing to continue a standardized course, but the other was not.

Two gardens—worlds apart. One garden named *What Is* and the other garden named *What Could Be*. One garden watered with sameness and measurements. The other with the best of ingredients, recognizing each flower is unique; each flower grows at his or her own rate and has much to offer the world if given a nurturing, enriching environment.

## INTRODUCTION—A NEW PARADIGM

The garden named *What Could Be* began to thrive instantly. The minute the gardener began watering with new cans full of *creativity, freedom, diversity, independence, collaboration, projects,* and *experiences,* the flowers began to flourish. Feeling safe in their soil, which was full of nurturing ingredients and community, the seedlings began to develop vibrant petals and leaves. One leaf was the color of peace, one the color of passion. One petal the color of kindness, another the color of fulfillment. Confidence, skill, talent, and laughter began to emerge. Growth of satisfaction, work ethic, independent thinking, and security popped up from the soil. Passion to grow higher and to progress began to grow. Suddenly, petals of hope, perspective, love, integrity, creativity, and companionship were budding all over the garden.

The gardener of the garden named *What Could Be* began to measure as well, as he knew that the sight of a flourishing garden alone would not be enough to convince the world. His measuring sticks were much different than the old, expensive measuring sticks that contained benchmarks and age-based skill requirements of preconceived levels. His measuring sticks contained marks such as *loves learning, engaged, happy, passionate, talented, independent, confident, progressing, resourceful, collaborative, innovative, curious, solves problems, participates, responsible, respectful.* He measured often to make sure that his flowers met these important aspects of their growth. Most of the time, simply working with his flowers and being a part of their daily growth was measurement enough. Knowing that no flower fit a perfect mold, each measurement had to be individualized and personal. And generally, the flowers themselves spoke up about how their growth felt. The flowers themselves helped the gardener know best what each needed.

The garden named *What Is* slowly began to grow leaves as well, but they were not vibrant. The flowers struggled to become what they should have been. They produced petals of various dull colors, such as doubt and fear. Often a leaf of boredom sprouted out, and occasionally rebellion and bullies grew forth. Most of the flowers were frustrated. Low self-esteem was obvious as the flowers developed, producing mean and judgmental leaves. Some of the flowers were violent, some despondent, some full of anxiety. Some remained terribly self-conscious throughout their lifetime because their true nature was never nurtured. Negativity surrounded the garden of *What Is*. Many flowers became lonely or lost their sense of self. Many never found a passionate course to follow, as they were never encouraged or allowed to seek such elements.

Of course, the garden of *What Is* did produce some stronger flowers in the midst of the struggles. These flowers were at the top of the measuring sticks. They carried names such as *Survivor, Grew Just Fine Watered by a Standardized Can, Fit the Mold, Obedient, Creatively Nurtured Evenings and Weekends, Inspired Despite a World of Sameness*. Luckily, they did not question the Powers That Be and grew at an acceptable pace within his garden. One will always wonder,

## INTRODUCTION—A NEW PARADIGM

though, would even their petals have been bigger, brighter, and more filled with passion had they been watered with more nourishing cans?

Ella is a survivor. She is creatively nurtured evenings and weekends. She will grow forth, as will many. But the garden of *What Is* simply is not an optimal environment for her growth.

For many decades, our very important gardens have been suppressed and have cultivated sameness, when other nutrients stand by well studied and eager to participate. When will we take notice? In which garden should America's students reside—*What Could Be* or *What Is*?

The reality of *What Is*...

It is my belief that schools, administrators, and teachers have the best of intentions. Each exists to educate and serve students. Administrators and teachers, in general, enter the profession to give of themselves and nurture youth. I contend that the reality of *What Is* is not a result of ill intent, nor is it a result of negligence or lack of effort. Year after year, day after day, the world of education attempts to improve, reform, perfect its practices, increase accountability, and unfortunately tighten its reins, all in an attempt to improve its dire situation. But more of the same, essentially redoubling efforts, will simply not bring about the change that is necessary.

## ORSCH...CUTTING THE EDGE IN EDUCATION

The reality of *What Is* is a place where sameness reigns. *What Is* is a place where individuality is not celebrated, individual passion is not fostered, and individual pacing and/or learning styles are not honored. *What Is*—a place where community is lacking and whether or not you "fit in" makes or breaks your existence. It is a place where many students lose sight of their true nature in order to please or to become what others ask of them. It is a place where true passion and innate talent get very little attention. It is a place of too much boredom, unnecessary information, and irrelevant assessments. It is a place of gross amounts of wasted time. It is too often a stifling place, a dulling place, a frustrating place.

In an attempt to score higher, tighten down, force accountability, compete with the world on standardized tests, and claim that our educational system is among the best, the American educational system has gone backward. It has digressed rather than progressed.

The reality of *What Could Be*...

Change is possible, even easy. To change our educational system from *What Is* into *What Could Be*, we need only begin.

It's three thirty, but students don't want to go home. They are still collaborating, constructing, inventing, asking questions, investigating. They exist in a school environment

## INTRODUCTION—A NEW PARADIGM

where they are so fulfilled that they don't want that feeling to end at three thirty. They spend most days buzzing with excitement for life, learning, and community. They spend most of their hours engaged in meaningful activity. They are decision makers. They are thinkers. They are in touch with who they are and the world around them. There is no time for boredom—there is too much to accomplish. There is no need to follow, as new ideas are more rewarding. And new ideas are the norm—creativity and innovation are celebrated. In this school, individuality is honored. In this school, students have the freedom to be their best—to pursue their own interests. Students have the freedom to make decisions about their learning and about appropriate levels or methods that will engage them. They can present knowledge and understanding in ways that make sense to them and move to the next level when they're ready. Students in this school are thriving, because their educational environment answers to their needs and does its best to nurture the potential and capacities of its students.

*Such an environment should be what we demand of public education.*

In his world-famous book, *The Element*, author Sir Ken Robinson argues that we must begin to nurture individual talents and passions. In the introduction to his book, he states, "I believe passionately that we are all born with tremendous natural capacities, and that we lose touch with many of them as we spend more time in the world. Ironically, one of the main reasons this happens is education."[1]

Orsch's mission is to *lead by example toward positive educational change*. Orsch set out to break the mold, to do things very differently to see if it would work. Since its conception, our charge has been to develop paradigms that can work on a large scale to bring real reform to our educational system, reform that enhances the natural capacities of its students and helps them reach their potential while enjoying an innate passion for learning. Orsch is a school. Orsch is a lab—a working, breathing, vibrant lab. We experiment with methods and structures. We test different approaches to teaching and learning. We have the freedom to arrange our students any way we think will benefit them. We have the freedom to be creative in our teaching methods and in the experience we offer students. It is because of this freedom that we have come upon so many important discoveries about an educational environment that works. Orsch exists to find, refine, and demonstrate a better way to educate our children.

Public education's purpose is to serve the youth of our country. Its purpose is to educate. Its purpose is to prepare tomorrow's leaders, inventors, scientists, writers, entrepreneurs, performers. Unfortunately, many pages of documents and articles reflect disappointment with the performance of our students. The system is obviously broken. It is my hope that we will not continue to idly stand

## INTRODUCTION—A NEW PARADIGM

by but will unite in an important mission to utilize what we know and demand the best from our public dollars.

Educational research is brimming with successful methods that our schools are not using, and more are to be discovered. Innovative programs and creative approaches to teaching are leading the way to a "new era of human existence." It is time "we create environments—in our schools...where every person is inspired to grow creatively" (Robinson, 2009), and it is time we create environments where our children receive the best in programming. The best in programming utilizes structures, systems, and current paradigms that help students gain positive outcomes. Let us use and then build upon the wealth of information and knowledge we have about learning and best educational practices. Consider: if *known* strategies are not in place, we stifle the development of new ideas; we therefore do not improve upon known strategies. The evolution of educational strategies stalls, and we remain stagnant for another fifty years.

In his book *The Global Achievement Gap*, Tony Wagner brings to light the disparity between student performance in even our nation's best schools and the skills that students will need into the future. Wagner argues, "The problem, simply stated, is that the future of our economy, the strength of our democracy, and perhaps even the health of the planet's ecosystems depend on educating future generations in ways very different from how many of us were schooled"[2]

## ORSCH...CUTTING THE EDGE IN EDUCATION

To conquer real reform, we must directly question some of our current structures and systems: Where do they hope to take our students? Is it all working? Could we implement better strategy? Next, we must speak up—demand better—refuse mediocrity and mundane days for our students. We must ask ourselves: Is it test scores we are after, or is it capable students? Finally, we must begin introducing effective methods of engagement, productivity, and collaboration. Included in this book are thought-provoking issues and viable strategies that stand to improve educational environments. These strategies don't require more dollars. They are neither radical nor difficult to implement. They require only faith in students and teachers. These strategies are a route to student-centered, individualized, and differentiated approaches. These strategies will help our students become effective learners who enjoy the process of learning, are able to cultivate their individual talents, and thrive within authentic community.

*We cannot solve our problems with the same thinking we used when we created them.*

—Albert Einstein

Education evolves too slowly. In what other profession do we fail to use current, research-based practices? Effective methods have been around for decades, yet they are not sufficiently used in our educational system. Can you

## INTRODUCTION—A NEW PARADIGM

imagine the field of medicine inventing a successful treatment for stroke victims but refusing to use it and instead continuing to use methods developed over fifty years ago? Or sending the patient through unnecessary testing episodes at a critical time instead of administering treatment we know will make the difference? Our students are losing valuable time. Approaches that will engage and prepare our students for tomorrow can and should be utilized. Above all else, we have the potential, the knowledge, and the expertise to offer a powerful education to our students, rather than offering them mediocrity.

Innovative thinking is an essential step to reform and progress. Every important invention or revelation that has moved humanity forward has relied on thinking outside of mainstream, acceptable paradigms. Innovative thinking is not as hard as it seems. I often wonder why it is so difficult for some people to stretch their thinking. Is it because they never developed the skill necessary to do so? Is it because sameness prevented them from believing it was okay to think creatively, bravely, and outside of the box?

Entrenched thinking limits us. We must be comfortable inventing new systems to educate children, just as we are with innovative thinking in medicine, technology, and many other areas crucial for human advancement. We must be comfortable questioning the methods we currently have in place. We must be comfortable embarking on new strategies. We must be brave and inventive, or we will remain stuck and continue to stagnate rather than progress.

Fortunately, creative and innovative educational paradigms, schools, and programs are cropping up all over the country. However, millions of students still do not have access to such programs. It is time to reinvent mainstream education on a grand scale.

## *We could measure student achievement through a different lens.*

If we step back and ask what we really want for our students, a parent's list might look something like this:

1. My child is learning—he comes home with interesting knowledge every day.

2. My child loves learning.

3. My child is excited about school and happy to go to school.

4. My child continues to improve in all areas of his education.

5. My child is engaged.

6. My child enjoys a sense of individuality.

7. My child enjoys a sense of security and emotional stability.

## INTRODUCTION—A NEW PARADIGM

8. My child is confident in his thinking and in his abilities.

9. My child can respectfully collaborate and communicate with others.

10. My child is resourceful.

11. My child is curious about the world around him.

12. My child is creative and innovative.

13. My child has good work habits and a solid work ethic; he is self-driven.

14. My child can think critically, solve problems, and reason.

15. My child cares about product presentation and quality.

16. My child can focus on a task at hand.

17. My child participates in discussions and class activities.

18. My child is responsible and dependable.

19. My child is pursuing his talents and his own passions.

20. My child is exposed to many perspectives.

21. My child can respectfully speak his mind in school and respects the opinions of others.

22. My child can generally make appropriate decisions and chooses wisely.

A school environment that offers such to its students is possible. Mainstream public education itself can offer such an environment. These essential elements of a child's development and school experience are measurable, but the lens is not a standardized lens. We cannot afford to continue the loss of valuable time and create generations of students who do not experience these elements in their school environment. If the potential to create such an environment exists, we must move toward that potential—this is educational reform.

Our obsession with *high standards of accountability* and the resulting standardized testing climate have stifled our search for innovative approaches. Ironically, innovative approaches themselves are the conduit that will produce authentic high standards of achievement.

## *A Philosophy Is Born*

An educational philosophy has been developed as a result of our lab. Our objective is *capable, thriving learners*—engaged and invigorated, capable of reaching their

## INTRODUCTION—A NEW PARADIGM

potential and benefiting from the best of themselves, ultimately sharing their innate talents, individuality, and well-rounded perspective with a world community. This objective is at the top—a roof, a pinnacle. At the bottom is a foundation of security—security offered by nurturing adults and a safe and social community. Above the foundation are three essential pillars. The first pillar: independence, flexibility, and freedom. The second pillar: creativity. The third pillar: variety in innovative approaches to knowledge and experience.

This is a philosophy ultimately taught to us by the students themselves. Students thrive given these essential elements in their education, and when these elements are available, students reach for more. When allowed to learn in an environment that not only allows for these elements but encourages them, students take ownership; they are happy, love to learn, and are proficient thinkers.

When I set out to create Orsch, I was working from the premise that children genuinely love learning. They love working together. I knew they yearned to be creative. I hypothesized that I could create an environment in which there were no wasted moments, but I did not predict how significant these studies would turn out to be, nor did I realize—at that time—some of the key components that ultimately make up our philosophy. I did not know children could work so naturally and productively together and would become a thriving community. I did not realize that children would be such effective choice makers and that the route to successful, student-centered learning is through their ability to make valuable and appropriate decisions. I did not realize that academic choices would thrill them so much. I knew students loved learning, but I didn't know they would love learning about *everything*. As long as a topic is presented appropriately and students have the flexibility to explore and delve into it, they want to learn about it. I didn't realize that engagement could exist in almost every lesson. And I knew that students loved to be creative and to add their own flair to products, but I didn't realize that creative ability exists in each and every child. I didn't realize that creativity would be so motivating and inspiring and that it exists well beyond color, art, and performances. Our students have shown us that creativity is an innate way of thinking about the world.

Our students have taught us how to teach them. Because we have listened to them and responded to their needs, we have come up with a solid educational philosophy that enhances our ability to reach every learner. Our philosophy encompasses a well-rounded approach to a child's education. We hope to share this philosophy with today's educational community and would love to see schools, students, and communities benefit from some of Orsch's findings. Our philosophy has served us well, and we have our students to thank for showing us the way.

Specific students, parents, and teachers written about in this book are authentic people; however, the names of

## INTRODUCTION—A NEW PARADIGM

students and parents have been changed. It is also worth mentioning that I have chosen to use the pronouns *he* and *she*, and *him* and *her* in a natural tone throughout this book. I may use either pronoun in a given instance as to avoid the distraction of *he/she* or *he or she* each time I refer to a hypothetical character.

This book is laid out in two sections. Section One includes a culmination of the thought-provoking issues that have become apparent in our experimentation. Section Two defines and explains our philosophy. Section Two is not written to suggest that Orsch philosophy is the be-all, end-all, nor is it written to convince you to open a school or turn your school into one like ours. It is written simply to shed light on new ways of thinking about education, student capacities, and student needs.

Our hope is that parents, schools, and communities will begin taking steps to develop public educational institutions in which every student is inspired and encouraged to develop his or her own natural capacities and where groups of students truly collaborate, invent, and move forward. Fifty years from now, will we be battling the same ineffective methods, or will we have finally embarked upon a new era of education? Will we have a proficient and productive educational system that serves the potential in each child? I believe we can.

# Section One—Thought-Provoking Issues

# Chapter 1—We Need a New Reform Effort

### A Brief History: How Did We Get Here?

The current educational climate in which we operate has a history we must keep in mind. For many years, successful educational strategies and research-based practices have tried to make their way into mainstream education. Why have they not succeeded? Teachers are required to obtain continuing education credits to renew their licenses—they are sent to conferences where current paradigms are presented. Teachers attend meetings to learn about current best practices and individualization. Many brilliant books about student engagement and differentiating in the classroom are purchased each school year. Teachers return from conferences invigorated, ready to offer the best of what they know to their students, but ultimately, these magnificent insights and books, along with the continuing education credits, tend to sit around on shelves, unutilized, collecting dust.

In 1965, President Lyndon B. Johnson signed our nation's first Elementary and Secondary Educational Act (ESEA). Its intent was to bring equality to low-income educational entities by offering funding to schools in need. Within this act, which started with noble intent and solid strategy, a national curriculum is strictly forbidden in order to uphold the value of local control for states and school districts. ESEA has been reauthorized and has undergone several revisions since 1965. The act began to call for high standards and accountability. In an attempt to allocate funds only to students in need (those eligible for services based on socioeconomic data and academic achievement), ESEA's Title I revisions have required strict rules and regulations, emphasizing uniformity in funds distribution.

Along with stricter regulations, schools receiving funds faced potential punitive actions if not in compliance. The results of these changes include pull-out programs, targeted approaches, and systems that made inclusion more difficult. In order to prove that funds were being utilized appropriately, students faced separation and homogeneous grouping based on achievement. Although other improvements and acts, such as the ECIA (Education Consolidation and Improvement Act, 1981) and the IASA (Improving America's Schools Act, 1993) were attempted, none made a significant dent in the established monies tied to "high standards and accountabilities." And then No Child Left Behind (NCLB) made it much worse.

Meanwhile, back in research circles, innovative programs continue to discover effective differentiation, student-centered approaches, experiential education, project-based learning, hands-on strategies, multiage practices, heterogeneous grouping…engaged students.

## CHAPTER 1—WE NEED A NEW REFORM EFFORT

NCLB required more accountability from teachers and students, yearly standardized tests, and annual report cards noting student achievement and demographics, which were published for the public. NCLB mandated punitive actions if schools did not meet Adequate Yearly Progress (AYP) and corrective action if an approved assessment system was not in place. Schools were required to submit a plan for *restructuring* if they failed to make AYP and, therefore, were identified as "needing improvement."

Although, in theory, our nation has upheld the value of local control, federal funding has inadvertently transformed schools into places driven by "high standards and accountability," a.k.a. test scores, a.k.a. federal control.

We have long known that standardized testing is detrimental to real learning. In 1989, Lauren B. Resnick and Daniel P. Resnick presented a paper to the Invitational Conference of the Educational Testing Service titled "Tests as Standards of Achievement in Schools." The paper, which was commissioned by the Office of Educational Research and Improvement (ED) in Washington DC, argues for a *thinking-oriented* curriculum and performance-based assessments. Resnick and Resnick presented substantial research supporting the notion that standardized tests are "inimical to a thinking curriculum." The abstract from the paper states:

> A new vision of education—a thinking oriented curriculum (TC) for all students—is considered, in which education focuses on higher order abilities,

problem solving and thinking, and the ability to go beyond the routine and exercise personal judgment...performance assessments can be essential tools for raising authentic educational achievement.[3]

Included in the study are suggestions for alternative assessments, such as portfolios and open-ended products. Unfortunately, however, it is almost as if this study and others like it didn't exist. It seems it was completely ignored in policy and in mainstream thought. Instead, our educational system stuck to standardized testing. *What Is.*

If education is meant to enhance knowledge and experience, why are we focused on measuring knowledge instead of utilizing what we know about how people gain knowledge? Extensive research exists about how we best learn. Assessments that focus on memorized information or algorithms disregard such research and grossly underestimate human potential.

## *What is Happening Currently?*

In what is known as the ESEA Flexibility Package, our current administration focuses on state and local reform efforts. A state can request flexibility through waivers of specific provisions of NCLB, including no longer having to set targets that require all students to be proficient by 2014. In his Race to the Top initiative, President Obama speaks of a twenty-first-century education that fosters critical thinking, problem

## CHAPTER 1—WE NEED A NEW REFORM EFFORT

solving, and the innovative use of knowledge.[4] In March of 2009, President Obama and Secretary of Education Arne Duncan showed a desire to take authentic reform seriously, including a statement published on March 10th in which the president states, "he will push to end the use of ineffective off-the-shelf tests, and promote the development of new, state-of-the-art data and assessment systems that provide timely and useful information about the learning and progress of individual students."[5] It sounds very hopeful. I look forward to seeing the push to end the use of ineffective off-the-shelf tests.

However, instead of actually delving into *state-of-the-art assessments* and *education that fosters critical thinking*, the National Governors Association and the Council of Chief State School Officers are immersed in adopting national Common Core Standards that are slated to align with Common Core assessments. More of the same. The United States continues to utilize unreliable methods to drive instruction and standardized tests to measure progress. Unfortunately, we continue to tie funding to such assessments, and national standards are eerily close to a national curriculum.

The idea of a national curriculum stirs up uneasy feelings in many innovative thinkers. "Closing the Door on Innovation—A Critical Response to the Shanker Institute Manifesto and the US Department of Education's Initiative to Develop a National Curriculum and National Assessment Based on National Standards" states:

> We, the undersigned, representing viewpoints from across the political and educational spectrum, oppose the call for a nationalized curriculum in the *Albert Shanker Institute Manifesto—A Call for Common Content.* We also oppose the ongoing effort by the U.S. Department of Education to have two federally funded testing consortia develop national curriculum guidelines, national curriculum models, national instructional materials, and national assessments using Common Core's national standards as a basis for these efforts.[6]

The United States' obsession with measurement is holding us back. *What Could Be?* Reform won't work with more of the same. Even the most current reform efforts in the United States continue to advocate for measurements of student achievement and teacher pay based on stringent testing standards. Following is the Center for Educational Reform's official position relating to the retention of teachers:

> …we believe in the implementation of strong, data-driven, performance-based accountability systems that ensure teachers are rewarded, retained and advanced based on how they perform in adding value to the students who [sic] they teach, measured predominantly by student achievement, along with skills and responsibilities. There must be consequences for teachers who are not successful in

## CHAPTER 1—WE NEED A NEW REFORM EFFORT

> educating students, no matter how noble or caring they may be...[7]

Ouch! Furthermore, below is CER's official position relating to standardized tests:

> High standards are essential in ensuring that every student is prepared for and able to move on to each grade, and that tests, developed at the state level and correlated directly to the standards, are critical to gauge progress. We believe that every parent in America and every teacher to whom parents entrust their children deserve to have high, measurable standards against which to gauge the progress of the enterprise for which they share responsibility. We believe in accountability as a consequence of performance measured against stated measures of proficiency. Any school that consistently fails its students, no matter where those schools are or the demographics of its children, should be closed.[8]

CER advocates for tests directly correlated to the standards and claims they are critical to gauging progress. They condone consequences for teachers "no matter how noble or caring they may be," and they suggest closing schools as a viable solution. I doubt that any teacher feels that standardized state tests measure progress in students, and I know many noble and caring teachers who wish they could offer the best of themselves but are not able to do so in this climate.

*Current reform efforts are not reform.* Education, as an industry, is literally ignoring research that could lead to authentic reform.

If standards were renamed "guidelines," then they would be highly useful to teachers and would be welcome suggestions for instruction. However, the assumption that every single nine-year-old in America is ready to "[m]ultiply side lengths to find areas of rectangles with whole-number side lengths in the context of solving real-world and mathematical problems, and represent whole-number products as rectangular areas in mathematical reasoning"[9] eliminates a teacher's ability to individualize for each student. Instead of allowing a child to learn at his own pace, she must attempt to force this concept during a student's third-grade year. Furthermore, consider the child who has been conceptualizing surface area since he was four.

A teacher is faced with hundreds of such content standards each year. Her students will be tested on these standards; she will then be labeled as a teacher who was able to get standardized performance out of her students or one who could not. Instead of the engaging month-long unit on financial literacy that she dreamed of, she frets about plowing through the content standards. She is fretting because she had fallen a week or two behind when her students needed extra time to learn how to "[f]luently add and subtract within

## CHAPTER 1—WE NEED A NEW REFORM EFFORT

1000 using strategies and algorithms based on place value, properties of operations, and/or the relationship between addition and subtraction."[10] She has a varied class. Some students grasp the standards perfectly. Some aren't ready. Some are well beyond them. She desperately wished during the subtraction unit that she could offer her students more flexibility. She spends the rest of her year fighting time, battling her sense of what children need from her.

I can appreciate the logic inherent in establishing Common Core State Standards as stated on the front page of the corestandards.org website: "The standards clearly communicate what is expected of students at each grade level." I can also understand the logic in their FAQ answer to the question: *Why is the Common Core State Standards Initiative important?*

> High standards that are consistent across states provide teachers, parents, and students with a set of clear expectations that are aligned to the expectations in college and careers. The standards promote equity by ensuring all students, no matter where they live, are well prepared with the skills and knowledge necessary to collaborate and compete with their peers in the United States and abroad.

I can appreciate the logic, as it seems quite logical. But I know too much about children, their learning environments, their potential, their innate abilities, and their unique learning styles to buy into the possibility that Common Core Standards will work. And I know too much about the power of engagement and the need for flexibility in an educational environment to think that *high standards of excellence* will produce desired results.

Standards—the idea that a uniform set of criteria will establish acceptable outcomes for all. I can think of a few places where I am very grateful for standards. Standards are extremely valuable in the realm of carpentry. I trust that building code will keep me safe. I trust that the guidelines and inspections necessary to wire my house will serve me. Standards in food safety are equally comforting. I am grateful that the FDA has issued strict rules to restaurants requiring employees to wash their hands and handle food appropriately. I am grateful for traffic safety standards, as I can trust that when the light is green, it is my turn to go forth. However, anyone who has worked with children would likely agree that placing standards on human behavior, intellect, and potential makes very little sense.

It is widely established that tests, test prep, and rigid approaches in the classroom kill engagement; we've known this for decades. True student achievement should be measured by a much more meaningful yardstick containing elements such as engagement, love for learning, ability to collaborate, product-based assessments, and innovative and critical thinking, just to name a few. A one-size-fits-all approach doesn't work in even a single classroom. How can we fathom that it will work for an entire nation? It simply may not be possible to find true engagement and build tomorrow's thinkers while our classrooms are intently focused

CHAPTER 1—WE NEED A NEW REFORM EFFORT

on test scores, while teachers are faced with the pressure to obtain them, while our students are bored and scored.

## *Test Validity and Reliability*

In addition to concerns about killing engagement, we must begin to consider more diligently the *validity* and *reliability* of standardized tests in an educational environment.

For decades, the emphasis placed on test scores has captured our nation's attention. Reform efforts have a common end goal: test scores and data. Very important, life-changing decisions are based on the data derived from test scores: a child's learning plan, a teacher's tenure, a school's reputation, an administrator's trust, school programs, funding. Data drives detrimental decisions, such as the elimination of art and music programming, field trips, and the like. If such important decisions depend on "big data," as Idna Schaenen writes about in her article, "Driving Miss Data—or Is Big Data Driving Schools?"[11] we must begin to consider the *validity* and *reliability* of standardized tests in an educational environment.

Of course an extensive amount of research goes into test creation. I have no doubt that the Educational Testing Service (ETS), the world's largest testing and assessment organization and the source of almost every widely used standardized test,[12] creates tests with adequate consideration of scientific validity in mind. To earn the esteemed label of *valid*, a test must pass several highly researched standards as outlined in the Standards for Educational and Psychological Testing (1999) by the American Educational Research Association (AERA).[13] The process includes gathering evidence to provide "a sound scientific basis" for interpreting test scores. Tests hit our students' desks having enjoyed an extensive history of research and analysis. From this perspective, the tests we give our children are trusted, highly developed, high-quality materials. However, even tests of the highest quality fall short of accounting for the most significant variable: students.

As educators, parents, and administrators, even if we trust that a test is built to adequately measure what it is designed to measure—the contents of a child's school year—and even if we put our faith in the validity of such an assessment, we have still not considered the most significant and invalidating variable. For a scientific study to yield valid results, it must include reliable controls.

Standardized tests, by definition, are meant to offer a *standard* by which they are administered and scored. The consistency with which they are delivered to students is designed to eliminate extraneous variables, thus leading to a more effectively controlled study. Across a district, tests are administered on a certain day or week. Students are given a determined amount of time to complete tests. Classrooms and hallways are quiet zones meant to offer highly focused climates. Students are asked to eat well and sleep well prior to test day, and many schools offer a healthy snack before

## CHAPTER 1—WE NEED A NEW REFORM EFFORT

test booklets are cracked open. Standardized tests are to be standardly delivered. In theory, this eliminates unwanted variables. We are clearly aware of and concerned about controlling variables.

Some of the more glaring variables that students may bring to the table are also taken into consideration. Results of standardized tests often include recognition of population variables such as English Language Learners (ELL) and students eligible for free and reduced lunch (i.e., a socioeconomic element). Such recognition suggests that testing companies, governing bodies, and school officials agree that certain populations of students will alter test results. Why do we stop at these glaring variables, ignore potentially more significant invalidating variables, and call it good?

Although many children perform to the best of their ability and head into test days highly focused and ready for the charge, many others do not; this is the most significant extraneous variable facing and arguably invalidating standardized tests. Emotional, physical, and motivational factors can directly alter a child's ability to show what he or she knows on a standardized test and should be considered variables for which we do not have adequate controls in place.

Emotional factors are potentially the most significant variables entering into test day for students. While one student has had a lovely morning with parents and siblings around the breakfast table discussing the day's upcoming schedule, another child has experienced an irritable, overtired mother who raises her voice, shouting morning routine demands, allowing doubt and fear to linger. And while one child is properly dressed, feeling confident, another child cannot focus on anything beyond his high-water pants that were pointed out by someone on the playground.

Fear of failure and lack of confidence are issues for some children. Test anxiety is a very real and detrimental emotional factor on test day. Feeling the need to rush through test questions in an effort to not finish last can affect a test taker. Self-doubt or inflated confidence can both be detrimental to answering questions correctly. A bad mood can affect performance. The boredom many children experience in a testing environment can completely zap motivation and desire to perform well. And simply the unfamiliar situation that test days bring to an otherwise vibrant classroom setting can impact student performance.

Physical factors can play a significant role as well and are intertwined with emotional and motivational factors. One child is adequately fed and rested, while another feels the rumbles of a hungry tummy. Distractions, such as a noise outside or a fellow student wiggling, can be significant barriers to focus. Fatigue and lack of nutrition can change a child's ability to do well and can eliminate motivation.

All too common is the conversation in which a student admits to creating a pattern of bubbles on the answer sheet of a multiple-choice test. Variables such as these are significant and happen on a regular basis. Older students are

## CHAPTER 1—WE NEED A NEW REFORM EFFORT

regularly annoyed at having to spend the better part of a week in a testing environment. Many such students find very little value performing at their best and display passive and/or active rebellion during testing. If students know that a test does not directly affect their school-year grades, as is the case for many annual standardized tests, they have little to no buy-in. Lack of motivation in students directly affects test validity and reliability.

Testing advocates will likely disagree, turning a blind eye to the reality of such invalidating variables, but surely history will eventually reveal the folly with which our culture has revered high-stakes testing. If we could effectively eliminate emotional, physical, and motivational factors out of groups of students, then we might be more able to trust the validity of standardized tests. And we would be able to make important decisions with confidence. But we cannot. We cannot eliminate these significant factors. So, at the very least, we should give less credit to test results and data.

In addition, mainstream education and the testing industry have convinced *parents* that test scores are a viable means of measuring the success of a school or teacher. By and large, parents think a school is "good" or "bad" or a specific teacher is "good" or "bad" based on test scores. To ignore the thousands of more important factors, such as a child's well-being, engagement, social/emotional development, or essential life skills in favor of data is a short-sighted approach to sizing up a given school or teacher.

We must begin to question these practices with the doubt they deserve and turn to more valid forms of measurement and decision making for the students we serve. We should utilize current research about what will best serve students and communicate about student needs on an individual student-by-student basis. We should take a more human approach to educational reform that recognizes human nature, human tendencies, and human capacity.

Furthermore, we have much more valuable assessment options. All teachers are trained in performance-based products and assignments. They use classroom and formative assessments day in and day out. They help students through the learning process and gather feedback about student progress on a minute-by-minute basis. Trusting a teacher's ability to filter for variables such as hunger, mood, and frustration and to make instructional decisions on an individual basis over a large sample of time, such as a school year, will yield more accurate and pertinent assessment results.

## *A New Reform Effort*

*For those averse to change and the associated risks, consider the known risks of continuing down our current path.*

If we continue on this path, we will be much worse off. Past reform efforts have failed, and current efforts are failing as well. Rigid standards have not worked. Incentives have not worked. High-stakes testing has only served to derail

## CHAPTER 1—WE NEED A NEW REFORM EFFORT

productive efforts to serve students. Real reform needs to start with students, parents, families, communities, and caring schools.

Imagine a struggling public school chooses to forgo its test-prep and data-acquisition approach in favor of student-centered learning. Imagine that the administrators call a staff meeting at the beginning of the school year. At the staff meeting, they ceremoniously close their notebooks full of data and encourage their teachers to do the same. "You are not to open these pages until the end of the year," they say. "This year, we want you to go back to your classrooms and find what works. Inspire your students. Engage them in thought-provoking activity. Look beyond the classroom walls and textbooks on your shelves. Use traditional materials as needed—they contain valuable information and lots of innovative teaching ideas—but don't forget to look beyond. Recognize the thousands of resources at your fingertips and that one size does not fit all. Look to technology and current events. Look to our community. Get involved. Inspire your students to learn, to grow, to collaborate with each other. Allow them to delve into some of their own interests. Get them hooked on real literature. Make sure they are experiencing their math with full engagement and understanding—it is possible, exciting, and fun. Involve them in purposeful writing, because their thoughts are valuable. Play games with their spelling words; they will remember them better. Let them be creative. Listen to your students this year—ask them what they think about the world, their school, their lessons, and their activities. Allow them to take part in their educational choices, and don't be afraid to adjust their lessons and assignments as needed. Make every moment valuable. Don't place the same expectations upon each of them—they are not all the same. But each has brilliance to offer; look for that. Help them build upon their talents and passions. Recognize that confidence is a powerful tool and leads to more confidence and increased skill. Individualize to their needs. Guide them socially—childhood is a tricky time. Use judgment on every decision. Look to your colleagues, and share ideas. Then in March, we will still let them take the state test. We will see what happens. But we will know that their school year was not a waste of time."

The teachers look at each other and begin to smile. Already their heads are full of ideas. Wheels are turning. They sit up straighter. They leave the meeting energized, ready to delve into planning the best year yet.

Then imagine the parents' view of this school year. Students begin running through the door after school exhilarated from their day. They are excited about the project on which they have been spending time and have made a few new friends—friends they didn't really have the chance to know last year because there was less time for collaborative projects and purposeful interaction. Their children begin talking about school, what they've learned, and what they want to learn next. They begin creating things at home, because they now know the value of creativity in their lives. They need lots

## CHAPTER 1—WE NEED A NEW REFORM EFFORT

of paper and tape and inevitably end up with hot-glue-gun wounds. But they are happy, and the television and the Xbox get little attention. Their children can't wait to get to school on Monday. They have discovered that they love learning, and they are empowered to reach higher. Their social lives are less troublesome than last year. Their minds are not idle, nor do they experience frustration each day, so they don't feel the need to pressure or attack each other. Suddenly, their childhood and their potential are in full swing.

Imagine the teachers' zeal for teaching this school year. Teachers are allowed to be creative and make a real difference. They get to enjoy this year's students for the people they are. They get to share their favorite lessons and books and have meaningful conversation with their students and with each other. They have significantly fewer discipline problems, as students are not bored or frustrated. One teacher has the energy to take on a science fair; one wants to organize a school-wide spelling bee. Another is ready to fundraise for a class trip in the spring. They collaborate effectively and share ideas. They are ever inspired and ready to try the next innovative approach. And they don't miss their binders full of data, nor do they miss spending valuable class time on torturous weekly reading assessments. This year, as March approaches, they don't feel anxious. They don't fear that their employment hinges on pending data. They are able to engage this year—in teaching, in learning how to offer more to their students, and in collaboration with each other. They become better teachers, gaining the trust of their students and families, and ultimately, their community.

Tests can wait until their time—tests are for March—student engagement can happen in September, October, November, December, January, February, March (except for those few testy days), April, May, and even throughout the summer. And it is likely those testy days will yield results higher than ever before—if Finland is any indication, and I believe it is.

The conversation about school improvement and educational reform often centers on test scores, budgets, standards of high achievement, accountability, and mandates. Mainstream conversation rarely speaks of student, family, teacher, and administrator needs. In a new reform effort, realistically, what is it that students need? What do teachers need? What do administrators and families and communities need from their local public schools? The conversation must begin to suggest what each needs and what each can *do* to begin to bring about change.

Following is a glimpse into some of these needs. As you think about and engage in conversation about educational progress, consider the needs of each player. Consider children's day-to-day school lives. Consider their teachers. Consider what each really needs and what part you can play in this important endeavor. These needs can be met.

CHAPTER 1—WE NEED A NEW REFORM EFFORT

## *What Do Students Need?*

Let us begin with what students need. An industry that exists to serve *students* should focus plans for improvement purposefully on students themselves. Too many students are bored. Too many students are left questioning themselves and their abilities. Many students lose interest in school by the time they are teenagers. And socially, millions of students struggle every year. However, children love to learn, and they are genuinely social beings. We must begin to more diligently focus our attention on their needs as young humans if we are to create the most optimal environment for their development.

Students need *student-centered individualization.* Currently in education, *individualization* is aimed at finding a way to help an individual reach a baseline or standard, or at serving an individual beyond the baseline or standard. In contrast, *student-centered individualization* is the concept of using the best knowledge, tools, skill, strategy, and team accessible to help an individual reach his or her personal best and achieve personal aspirations. Helping an individual reach his personal best includes adequate attention given to innate abilities and talents, as well as to personal interests. It includes providing a community and support system that recognizes and attends to the needs of the whole child. It requires trust in students to make decisions that will help them realize their best selves, and it requires flexibility in the classroom. Student-centered individualization encompasses consideration of home life and family structure as a component of one's educational course. Student-centered individualization is possible given a willing environment.

Students of all ages need positive interactions and immense amounts of encouragement. They need love and support. They thrive within an authentic community where they feel they can be themselves and interact naturally without fear. Their educational experience needs to offer large doses of interactive opportunities for social and emotional development. They need specific and appropriate guidance with social dilemmas. Students benefit greatly from adult input in real-life, everyday issues. Even in the midst of life's inevitable consequences, they need to know they are supported by their community and that adults and peers are looking out for their best interests. They will then trust and seek the best in themselves.

Students need to learn authentic life lessons and essential skills, such as how to make valuable choices, how to think critically, and how to collaborate with others. They benefit from thought-provoking discussions and topics. Students must be given opportunities to immerse themselves in interest-based learning, explore passions, and develop talents. They also need to satisfy their desire for creativity. They need experiences that build upon their own sense of satisfaction, well-being, and sense of direction if they are to be well-rounded individuals with the confidence and skills they need to be successful adults.

Students need to know that adults trust their thinking. At any stage, a child has developed his own best paradigm for thought and decision making. If this thinking is halted, questioned, or discouraged at every turn, the child will develop a lack of trust in his own thinking, leading to diminished confidence and potentially adherence to others' thinking. In addition, the more each child is aware of different learning styles and varied readiness for concepts, the more freedom he will have to feel confident despite a lack of understanding within a given moment. The child will trust that the concept will eventually be understood and that teachers will support him as necessary. He will see himself as an individual—trustworthy and capable despite a particular moment's confusion.

Student-centered individualization is essential in reaching every student, and it is possible. Students need developmentally appropriate environments and developmentally appropriate delivery of material. They learn best from authentic experience and hands-on methods. Students are genuinely excited to learn new concepts, especially if the material carries direct meaning to them. They are natural investigators and experiment with their natural world regularly. Their school environment must answer to that tendency—to do otherwise is to inadvertently squash students' natural curiosity and quest for knowledge.

## *What Can Students Do?*

Too often, students are the topic of discussion without being involved in the discussion. Students are potentially the most valuable asset we have in the discussion about educational improvement. Even very young children will offer their insights and their preferences if their input is sought. Students are eager to communicate their needs both socially and academically; they love to offer feedback and yearn to direct their own learning. They are proficient, creative thinkers who can usually come up with a better system. Classrooms that set up a culture in which students are heard and where student opinions are valued are more harmonious and productive environments.

Students, you can begin to speak up. Talk to your parents or guardians and teachers about school—begin to get involved in improving your own education. Let the adults in your life know what you feel is working and/or lacking in your day-to-day school life. Do you feel that your needs are being met? Do you feel like you are immersed in a thought-provoking environment that satisfies your desire to learn and grow as a thinker? Are you in a secure place each day that allows you to focus on academics, or are you unable to engage in learning because of boredom or social issues? Talk to adults about your concerns and about new ideas you have for your education. Help them see that you are a valuable member of your own educational team. Engage in the conversation and the current progress in educational reform. Pay attention to model schools that may help improve your own school. Learn from motivated students who make change happen in their communities.

CHAPTER 1—WE NEED A NEW REFORM EFFORT

Parents, please engage your children in this discussion. Instead of asking, "What did you learn today?" ask, "What did you think about today?" Encourage your children to participate in the development of their education and to communicate their needs, hopes, and ideas. They will participate if they feel their input matters. They will be more aware, and their educational lives will begin to improve.

## What Do Teachers Need?

First and foremost, teachers need autonomy and flexibility. The current test- and data-driven climate offers teachers very little autonomy or flexibility. Teachers cannot perform or relate to students at an optimal level if they have no ability to format their lessons or make decisions based on their own expertise.

Teachers can use standards as a guide rather than as restrictive, unbending requirements that are often detrimental to authentic learning in a diverse classroom. Standards can be seen and used as ladders of skills. When one skill is reached, a teacher can help a student set his sights on the next rung. Teachers have access to endless resources; to limit them to a set curriculum is to require them to miss out on a wealth of opportunity for engaging activities and lessons. Teachers must be afforded the freedom to use judgment in assignments, expectations, and timing instead of trying to adhere to inflexible approaches and mandates that do not serve every student.

Mandated methods remove the ability to differentiate for students' needs. To succeed in true differentiation, they must also allow students the flexibility and freedom to choose levels and approaches that best fit them. Teachers must be allowed and encouraged to inspire and ignite their students in the process of learning and in the pursuit of their talents, passions, and abilities, and they need to have the capacity to use a variety of assessment tools and products to assess student progress. Autonomy and flexibility are essential elements of a thriving classroom.

Teachers are creative and passionate beings who need continued inspiration and professional development opportunities. Inspiration can come from continuing education, new resources, current idea generators, and, most important, collaboration with colleagues. The ideas generated within a purposeful group of teachers can ignite new systems and new paradigms—continued improvement. The sharing of ideas is an essential part of the creative process that enhances one's environment and fulfills both students and teachers.

Teachers who have lost the ability to collaborate and seek creative inspiration due to restrictive environments have lost the most precious piece of their chosen profession. Teachers must be encouraged to collaborate in the spirit of progress and innovation so that they can better meet the

## CHAPTER 1—WE NEED A NEW REFORM EFFORT

needs of their students and continue to improve their own approaches and teaching methods.

In order to be the best they can be and offer the best to their students, teachers must find joy in their profession and in their students. They need to be allowed to loosen up—to take kids outside on a sunny day for lessons or reading time, to celebrate joy and fun, to capitalize on unplanned *teachable moments*—the positive experiences will help build good relationships, optimism, and joyful feelings that lead to productivity.

Teachers must allow creativity to prosper in all aspects of the classroom. Creativity brings joy and fulfillment to both teachers and students. Creativity offers continued improvement in classroom systems and strategies. Creative thinking leads to more productive critical thinking and deep questioning. Restrictive environments are not conducive to creativity in the least. Creativity requires flexibility and time to develop but is an essential need in an educational environment.

Finally, teachers need support, continued feedback, and trust. Supportive administrators offer real-time feedback and guidance in school objectives and in problems that arise. Supportive parents create good relationships that lead to open communication and the realization of mutual goals between home and school. A school that encourages and utilizes input and feedback from its parents and the students themselves will have students' best interests at the heart of development and decisions. And well-trained teachers should be trusted by administrators, colleagues, parents, and students. Competent, compassionate teachers do their best to serve their students, especially when given the autonomy they deserve. *Trust* in the professionals serving our students cannot be underestimated as we move forward into a new era of educational development.

## *What Can Teachers Do?*

To assist in the reform they need, teachers can present to their administrators their need for flexibility and autonomy. They can present research that supports differentiation, individualization, experiential learning, project-based learning, and collaboration among students and convince their administrators that these practices are not possible without flexibility and autonomy. Instead of sitting back feeling they have no voice, they can convince their employers that they are in the teaching profession to serve students; serving students requires a human touch, an intuitive approach, and compassionate relationships. Teachers are on the front line. They are the ones who know best what their students need. They cannot be effective unless they are given the correct tools. Therefore, teachers can stand up against rigid mandates and procedures that they know will not help their students develop. Teachers can collaborate and unite in an effort to acquire more autonomy. Teachers can open up good communication with families so that they know what their families want most for their students, and they

## CHAPTER 1—WE NEED A NEW REFORM EFFORT

can communicate this to their administrators. They can request support, and they can request a sincere trust in their skills and professionalism.

## *What Do Parents Need?*

As expressed in Chapter 8, "A Different View of Parent Involvement and Homework," parents come in all shapes and sizes. Parents and families come in as many varieties as students. Within a given classroom, one family may be supplementing their children's academics at home, using flash cards and structured school-like lessons, while another family's parents work two full-time jobs and are absent most evenings. One family permits junk food and television while another enrolls the children in activity from three thirty through dinnertime. Each family is unique. Each family has its own view of a successful and fitting education, and when it comes to school-life, each family has its own needs for time, parameters, and effort level.

But as varied as each family is, one thing remains consistent. Parents and guardians want to know their children are in good hands. Parents want to trust that when their children step on the bus or walk into school, their children's experiences will be valuable. In addition, most parents value happy, fulfilled children. They want their children to be confident and self-directed. They want their children to be their best, to think, and to love learning. They want their children to perform well and to be awarded good opportunities into the future. So when a school environment does its best to care for each individual, it truly puts its children in good hands and offers parents what they want most.

Accommodating each family's needs is possible. A school that is brave enough to step out of *sameness* recognizes that it can vary assignments, instruction, and requirements for individual families. For example, a family who has no time to fit in homework will struggle and battle to get assignments finished. Another family enjoys spending the evening on homework. What if each family's needs were served by its school? What if parents could choose whether they accept homework or decide the volume of homework that fits into their lives for optimal balance? What if families could help craft educational goals for their children?

*Individualizing for each is easier than trying to make them all the same.*

Students benefiting from such accommodations recognize that their teachers and their parents are looking out for them, and adjusting their education based on family preference, personal aptitudes, needs, and goals. Students respond positively to appropriate academic individualization and personalization, even within a group or a classroom, if sameness is not the underlying culture.

Children are aware that they are each individuals; they celebrate this aspect of themselves when allowed to flourish as individuals. Students thrive outside of a world of *same*

## CHAPTER 1—WE NEED A NEW REFORM EFFORT

because it is their unique personalities and abilities that are the most satisfying and motivating, leading to genuine well-being. As we transition into a new era of human existence and recognize the value of personalized accommodations in education, we will come to realize the harmony and progress it offers. Thoughts of fairness, status quo, and comparisons begin to dissolve in favor of specifically meeting the needs of *each* student and *each* family.

## *What Can Parents Do?*

Parents generally know if their children are happily learning or struggling. Parents can converse with their children about what school offers them, about how school feels, and what their children feel they are or aren't getting out of school. Parents need to recognize that open communication with their children and with other parents is a valuable means of assessing their child's well-being. Parents also need to step out of the assessment cycle that they have been convinced is an appropriate means of measuring student success. Student success should instead be measured by some or all of the items listed in the introduction of this book under, "We could measure student achievement through a different lens."

Again, parents come in all shapes and sizes. Not all parents will want to dive in to effect change, and many parents are completely satisfied with their child's education. However, parents who feel dissatisfaction with their school or their specific situation should know they ultimately have a voice. Parents can also converse with each other, proactively present a united front, and insist on a more individualized approach for their children and for their family life.

Sometimes, parents aren't aware that they can make changes within their child's school. There are many avenues set up for parent involvement at a policy-making level. School board meetings, PTA, site accountability committees, and other organized groups are options. Parents can find out about their school's policy for parent input—what avenues are available and what avenues need to be developed. If they are prevented from offering their input for change, parents should seek to develop better policy.

The most significant change can be made with ongoing productive communication. If a school's culture is communicative and individualized, teachers and administrators will welcome feedback. They will have their sights set on serving children's and families' needs. They will respond to feedback and make timely decisions—such a culture is possible in every school.

*Individualizing for each is easier and more meaningful than trying to make them all the same.*

## What Do Administrators Need?

In the world of education—if it were a business—the *product* is a high-quality experience for students, and the

## CHAPTER 1—WE NEED A NEW REFORM EFFORT

*customers* are the students and parents. The service is provided by teachers, who are overseen by administrators. School administrators are the leaders of a very important realm in our society. They wear many hats. Their job descriptions range from behavioral management to balancing budgets and everything in between.

Today's school administrators are bogged down with policy and paperwork. They are among the most restricted by mandates. They must submit scores and evaluations to state boards. They are immersed in restrictions surrounding funds and operations. In the midst of these mandates and formalities, they seemingly have very little freedom. However, the setup of the American educational system ultimately places them in a position of authority. They are hired by elected school board members to lead and to make important decisions. They are directly in charge of a school's operations and culture. To be the best they can be—just like the students and teachers they look after— they need to be given the freedom and autonomy necessary to be their best. Administrators need to be trusted to serve students and their teachers.

First, to be trusted, administrators need immense amounts of feedback to serve the specific community of learners for whom they are responsible. The most effective administrators seek and listen to input from staff, families, and students to continually improve their school environments. They think creatively and flexibly about systems, structures, schedules, student and teacher needs, and then they implement improvements to the best of their abilities. If parents, students, and teachers feel their input is valued and their needs are considered, and if they feel that their voices can effect necessary change, they develop trust in the authority above them. They feel free to be their best and free to implement improvements. Administrators willing to accept feedback and consider the specific needs of their communities earn respect, loyalty, and trust while building an environment in which each is motivated to offer his best.

Administrators need qualified educators and staff to offer the service with which they have been charged. They can help create and sustain high-quality educators by developing good relationships with their teachers so that they can effectively guide them. Mutual trust and support are essential. Administrators can evaluate teachers with a more personable approach, offering support, feedback, training, and flexibility. Teachers who work for unbending or hard-line administrators develop a negative view of their bosses, which leads to many detrimental aspects of a school climate.

To develop high-quality, invested educators, administration can offer opportunities for team collaboration and team strategic planning. The more a school works as a team in the best interest of its students, the more effective it will be. Collaboration brings solutions to problems, prevention of problems, strategy, and structure that works for each member of the team. Progress, productivity, and harmony are the results.

## CHAPTER 1—WE NEED A NEW REFORM EFFORT

Administrators can help create high-quality educators by offering professional development opportunities and continuing education. They should also allow their teachers to use materials and flexibility that supports their personal teaching style, approaches, and unit planning. There are many valuable resources beyond curriculum sets that can help differentiate and supplement—many of them easily accessible and free on the Internet.

*Autonomy*—a crucial theme in the realm of "what each needs"—the best schools are run by administrators who offer their teachers autonomy and trust that they will reach their students at a level that tests cannot measure.

Finally, administrators need current, more relevant professional development. They are not in the classroom to the extent that their teachers are; therefore, they are expected and required to make decisions based on data. Data seems a reliable place from which to base significant decisions, but, as argued earlier, the potential lack of validity in our data should leave us questioning its value. Because we must find a way to step out of the data-driven climate in which our schools operate, administrators need professional development that is not intently focused on data. If they are not already well versed, they need to learn about effective forms of engagement and turn their focus to best practices that benefit students, rather than data acquisition that has no direct effect on student progress.

*What Could Be*? For the time being, until mandates are replaced with more effective and useful forms of guidance, administrators can submit their required paperwork with integrity while they run their schools with autonomy. Their teachers will support them. Administrators can recognize that the high-stakes testing approach has not improved educational environments; they can focus their efforts beyond tests—take a stand. Make a difference. Their students and their students' parents will appreciate all they are doing, because their children are obviously in good hands. Their results will come in the form of reputation and content school communities. They will be respected as leaders who are willing to do what they know is best for students.

To tackle real reform, we must focus our attention on engagement and student needs instead of achievement based on data. We must begin to trust our educators and allow them the autonomy to do what they entered their profession to do—teach, inspire, make a difference. And along the way, we can use the best we have to measure success—portfolios, products, presentations, outcomes, and student engagement are all methods we can trust to assess student understanding and growth. And the best measurement of all: does a child love learning? Does he love school? Is he invigorated about new knowledge, passionate about ideas?

We do not need more hours or days in school. We will never fix our nation's educational crisis with money, class size, or

## CHAPTER 1—WE NEED A NEW REFORM EFFORT

mandates. The only way out of this rut is to transition into a new age in education, at the heart of which we see students as competent, creative, and independent humans able to accomplish infinitely more than our traditional barriers have allowed.

The health and future of public education lies in its ability to effectively serve its students. Parents, grandparents, teachers, and communities—you can begin to request that your schools focus on their students, not data. You can inquire, suggest, and demand better for your children. You can begin to imagine *What Could Be*.

*You are the customer.*

## Chapter 2—Finland: We Can Learn from Successful Programs

*Someday, I hope, we will recognize the failure of the behaviorist approach now in vogue; someday we will see that our current "reforms" are appropriate for the industrial era of the early 20th century, not for the needs of the 21st century. When that day arrives, we will understand the deep wisdom of Finland, with its love for children and its respect for educators, and we will be grateful that there is a successful alternative to our own failed model.*

—Diane Ravitch[14]

In 2008, I embarked on a targeted mission to discover a better way to educate children by building an educational lab. I knew it was possible; I knew that with creative approaches and innovative thinking we could establish systems and strategies that work for deeper learning and offer development of essential skills. As the culmination of this book became a reality, I knew I had to learn all I could about Finnish schools. What makes the Finnish educational system so successful? How did they get here? What is Orsch doing that is similar? And how can we learn from their journey to further our mission of broad-range educational improvement? The Finnish educational system is truly a beacon to us; we can learn from them if we are open to new possibilities, and I am encouraged to discover the many similarities Orsch shares with Finnish schools.

If you have a heightened interest in the history, policies, and data associated with Finnish schools and the desire to learn from them, please consider Pasi Sahlberg's brilliant and informative book *Finnish Lessons—What Can the World Learn from Educational Change in Finland?* Sahlberg is the Director General for the National Center for International Mobility and Cooperation in Finland. The book offers a wealth of information on this topic and is a fascinating read.

Sahlberg states:

> Finland has a unique educational system because it has progressed from mediocrity to being a model contemporary educational system and "strong performer" over the past 3 decades. Finland is special also because it has been able to create an educational system where students learn well and where equitable education has translated into small variation in student performance between schools in different parts of the country at the same time. This internationally rare status has been achieved using

## CHAPTER 2—FINLAND: WE CAN LEARN FROM SUCCESSFUL PROGRAMS

reasonable financial resources and less effort than other nations have expended on reform efforts.[15]

One of the key factors that motivated me to open Orsch was that I knew we were not utilizing up to a half-century's worth of solid educational research in methodology and pedagogy: differentiation, individualization, student-centered learning, theory of multiple intelligences, constructivist learning environments,[16] experiential and project-based learning, cooperative learning, instruction meant to heighten critical thinking and problem solving, self-directed learning, whole-brain-based learning, and many more. In the United States, we have been sitting on innovative practices that work for children (ironically, many of which were formulated and researched here in our country) for up to fifty years, but we do not effectively utilize them. I have often said that Orsch did not invent these methods; we just created a place where we could use them.

Finnish educational reform began in the 1970s. In 1972, the National Curriculum for the Comprehensive School included the important elements of alternative instructional methods, differentiation, and heterogeneous grouping. The Finns not only paid attention to innovative and current ideas, including advancements in neuroscientific research and learning constructivist theories, they took action. It was "a time that challenged conventional beliefs, searched for innovation, and increased trust in schools and their abilities to find the best ways to raise the quality of student learning," writes Sahlberg[17]. By the late 1970s and early 1980s, the Finns began to see that teacher-centered, top-down approaches were ineffective in the nation's mission to create critical- and independent-thinking citizens.

At a time when the United States was consumed with high standards, accountability, stricter regulations, and punitive actions for nonperforming schools, Finland was utilizing cutting-edge strategy. Throughout the 1990s, and specifically with Finland's National Curriculum Reform of 1994, Finnish principals, teachers, and schools were encouraged to collaborate and network with each other and with their communities to establish active learning environments and enhance the quality of learning—an initiative known as the Aquarium Project.[18] The Aquarium Project is credited with improvement in school development, local innovations, research, and increased school autonomy. Furthermore, they value local control and self-regulation in their schools, at the same time they intentionally collaborate for the advancement of ideas and methods.

The PISA[19] (Program for International Student Assessment) results that would astonish the world came out in 2000, 2003, 2006, and 2009. The results placed Finland as a top performer in math, reading, and science[20] in each of these years. A nation that does not implement standardized testing, barely gives its students homework, and doesn't start official schooling until the age of seven has surpassed the world in achievement scores. The United States has much to learn from them.

CHAPTER 2—FINLAND: WE CAN LEARN FROM SUCCESSFUL PROGRAMS

As Sahlberg points out, "Finland's approach reflects a particular winning strategy: System-wide excellence in education is possible by doing things differently than others."[21]

## *Similarities*

Throughout my research, I have been comforted to learn that there are many similarities between Orsch's and Finland's approach to education. The similarities that stand out above all are, first, our autonomy, and, secondly, trust received from families. When Orsch teachers need to make a decision, change a portion of the schedule, or collaborate on the direction a class should take, we all get together with chart paper and markers and put our heads together.

We have full autonomy for our program. We have full autonomy to determine the best approach for the well-being of a student, of a group of students, a class, or our school as a whole. We exist in a constant mind-set of improvement for our systems and our methods. We use feedback from parents—every bit of it. The more minds we have on a problem, the better the solution.

Academically, we utilize all the best in traditional approaches—of which there are many—and we utilize all the most current innovative approaches, but we also give ourselves plenty of room to invent new methods. And it is because of this dynamic approach that we have earned significant trust from our families.

From what I have seen and read about Finnish schools, they benefit from a very similar structure. Their structure includes full autonomy. Randi Weingarten, president of the American Federation of Teachers, visited schools in Finland and created a wonderful six-minute video about her experience.[22] Finnish schools, according to Weingarten, have the right conversations about students: "All the things we say that are important for instruction for kids…the conversation is always about, 'How can we work together to help children?' People are engaged in problem solving, not in winning arguments." She also speaks of the real relationships and respect between teachers and administrators.

Teachers and principals want to offer the best to their students. Educational professionals don't enter the profession of teaching with the expectation of having no autonomy in their approaches. I would boldly guess that in today's climate, *teachers would take increased autonomy over increased salary*. And to be part of a team that collaborates in the best interest of students—I can claim from experience that there is not a better existence for a teacher or an administrator.

I imagine teacher meetings in Finland, and in every child-centered school, are just like Orsch teacher meetings. We discuss specific students, their strengths, their weaknesses, their behaviors, and their needs, and we are free to individualize the curriculum for each student's success. We discuss

## CHAPTER 2—FINLAND: WE CAN LEARN FROM SUCCESSFUL PROGRAMS

our plans and our lessons. We discuss methods that worked and methods that didn't and funny things that happened in between. We ask each other how we're doing—does anyone need backup? Then we make specific plans, doing our best to prioritize. We make plans that encompass a broad range of views and careful consideration. We have much to consider and much to accomplish. In contrast, meetings that are filled with formalities and paperwork create situations in which it takes weeks, months, or years to make changes in programming or systems, resulting in direct deficits to students.

We can certainly learn from Finland. Among the many lessons they offer us, Finnish education models a nationwide respect and exceptional training for educators. It models a successful approach to innovative educational practices, utilizing cutting-edge methods, autonomy, and collaboration. The Finnish educational system authentically looks out for children; their priority is creating student-centered environments where deep learning takes place. In Finland, students do not take standardized tests; there is a general sense of trust in its schools, its students, its educators, and its communities.

*I am often asked, 'How do you know, in Finland, that your students are learning in school?' I always say, 'Ask the teachers; they know.'*

—Dr. Pasi Sahlberg[23]

## Consider Reform: Innovation, Autonomy, Collaboration versus. Accountability

In her informative video, Randi Weingarten also speaks of Finland's true child-centered approaches and the obvious benefits of experiential learning in classrooms. Such ideas have been valid approaches to learning since the 1970s.[24]

I remember sitting in a class, in a tidy row, in 1991 when I was in the depths of my own teacher education program. My professor, Dr. Newton, was teaching us about experiential learning and how effective it was shown to be in current research. I was thrilled to be learning about current research. I could barely wait to begin implementing these amazing new ideas. Dr. Newton told us that as teachers we should plan to get kids up and moving, collaborating, discussing, interacting, experiencing, doing. I was so excited to become a teacher.

As I diligently took my notes that day, as I always did, I slowly lifted my head to glance at fellow students. Were we all really just writing this down? Were we all *really* just obediently writing down cutting-edge methodology while we sat in silent rows of old ideas? As I finished my notes, I finally bravely looked around the room. Nobody seemed to have the same thought as near as I could tell. I committed to recognizing such ironies from that day forth.

We must ask ourselves, have we avoided cutting-edge strategies in teaching and learning in favor of standards

## CHAPTER 2—FINLAND: WE CAN LEARN FROM SUCCESSFUL PROGRAMS

and *sameness* in the United States? If we can genuinely and courageously ask this question, the honest answer is that we would be much better off if student achievement and test scores were not our goal. The United States continues to strive for measurable outcomes and *accountability*—one of the "wrong drivers," according to Michael Fullan in his 2011 seminar paper, "Choosing the Wrong Drivers for Whole System Reform." If we continue to measure success with test scores and craft every move in an effort to obtain standardized student achievement, we will never really progress. We won't really teach the whole child; we will not help students reach their potential, nor will we *"develop a new paradigm of human capacity to meet a new era of human existence"* (Robinson 2009, xiii).

If we aim to establish flourishing school communities with capable, engaged, thriving learners instead of test scores, and if we allow teachers more autonomy instead of imposing rigid mandates, we will be a long way toward a successful educational system. Someday, maybe our engaged, capable high-school students will be top performers on the PISA exam, but that's not what motivates me…or Finnish educators.

Parents in Finland trust that their students are in good hands. Administrators in Finland trust that their teachers are looking out for students and that they are establishing effective learning environments. And Finland's National Board of Education trusts that each school is providing for its students. As she contemplates the contrast between the United States' approach and Finland's, Diane Ravitch, author of *The Death and Life of the Great American School System: How Testing and Choice Are Undermining Education* (2010) states:

> Teachers and principals repeatedly told me that the secret of Finnish success is trust. Parents trust teachers because they are professionals. Teachers trust one another and collaborate to solve mutual problems because they are professionals. Teachers and principals trust one another because all the principals have been teachers and have deep experience. When I asked about teacher attrition, I was told that teachers seldom leave teaching; it's a great job, and they are highly respected.

Compare this sentiment to current US sentiment. Do we trust our teachers to teach? No, we place strict mandates upon them and test their students' performance. Do we trust our districts to make good decisions? No. We tie funding to data and outcomes, forcing them to put student scores above all else. Do we trust each other in our educational communities? Do we collaborate and innovate in the best interest of our students? Sadly, no, we don't.

Does Finland have any lessons for us? Yes, they do. However, there will always be critics. According to Michael Fullan, in his book *All Systems Go—The Changes Imperative for Whole System Reform*, "Finland is too small to serve as a model for whole-system reform in North America." Pasi

## CHAPTER 2—FINLAND: WE CAN LEARN FROM SUCCESSFUL PROGRAMS

Sahlberg also expresses concern about reliance on the Finnish model, believing that Finland's society is potentially too homogeneous to reflect ours. I contend that neither of these issues is relevant. If we wish to improve learning in our schools, we can absolutely learn from the positive procedures and outcomes of successful programs, regardless of their populations.

Orsch will have many critics as well. But I know that what we do is valuable. I know that our students are first and foremost on our minds in every decision we make. I know that what we're doing is working and that our strategies stand to facilitate real change. We have a successful program—in this country, with an academically diverse population—operating on a shoestring budget. Our families trust that we make good decisions for their children. Positive educational change is possible on a grand scale with no added costs or resources, and the potential benefits are *immeasurable*. Criticism, I am ready and willing to ponder—feedback is an essential part of the equation. But I am also confident that Orsch, like the Finnish educational system, can stand up to scrutiny and that our student success can speak volumes about the power of innovation, autonomy, collaboration, and trust.

The bottom line is that students are human. They develop and learn at different rates. They have different backgrounds and come from varied familial situations. They have different interests, talents, and desires. The push to educate them uniformly will never be an effective route. They require an individualized and engaging education.

They need vastly more than a Common Core or standards-based curriculum, and America's *noble and caring* teachers are capable of providing for them and are eager to do so. We have no good reason to refuse the lessons we could learn from Finland.

## *Chapter 3—Sameness*

Snowflakes—every single one of them different from another. You have likely pondered this concept for a lifetime. Not one single snowflake like another...all those mountains of snow...worldwide...winter after winter? As a child, you studied them, examined them on your mitten. As thoughtful humans, we find this concept perplexing and fascinating.

*We give snowflakes more credit for their individuality than we give students.*

Sameness is far-reaching. Sameness is tricky. It has appeal. It has ramifications. Sameness is very destructive. Sameness is a concept that humans must challenge for progress to take place. It is a concept we must continue to explore and ponder.

Prior to elementary school, students generally enjoy a life of natural development. Young children are permitted to learn by playing, interacting, and exploring. They require a creative and flexible setting. As their educators, parents, and advocates, we respond. We speak of attention spans and understand that preschoolers have a threshold for direct instruction. We know that each child may be at a different phase in his or her development, and we allow that development to flow naturally.

Likewise, prior to elementary school, individuality is honored. Preschoolers are celebrated for the unique things they say and do. Adults appreciate their innocent and fresh view of the world. People laugh when they say something cute or clever. Preschoolers get to enjoy a few years of completely unfettered development as individuals. They learn who they are. They explore their own preferences—fire trucks, baby dolls, blocks, dress-up clothes, coloring pages. Individuality is developing—preference of activity is allowed and helps shape personality, confidence, critical thinking, and independence.

I know a preschooler with unfettered individuality, as do most of us. Nicholas is adorable! He loves mailmen and UPS drivers. He delivers packages all day long to his preschool buddies. He pretends to take orders on the phone and wears "scanning" mittens or gloves every day to fulfill his role. Nicholas's fantasy game entertains all. We often laugh, talk about him, and celebrate his funny deliveryman nature. Of course he overhears all of this and must be wondering what the big deal is. He pays no mind to it, though, because to him it's just *him*. He will explore this phase until he tires of it. He will move into the next phase after that. But he will soon be five and will be off to kindergarten. I'm quite sure he won't be allowed to wear gloves (or a cape if that is his latest phase) all day. Teachers will find these behaviors distracting, and other children will begin to tease. Nicholas

## CHAPTER 3—SAMENESS

will enter sameness. Nicholas will have fond memories of his preschool years, as most children do. He will not realize that he has entered a new realm. Young children do not question this transition, as they trust the adults in their lives to guide them.

In our culture, the concept of sameness is introduced at the beginning of elementary school. When they enter elementary school, students of the *same* age are grouped in a classroom. Students of the same age are subjected to the *same* lessons, the *same* time frames, the *same* limitations, and the *same* expectations.

Academically, anyone not reaching such expectations is targeted. In mainstream education, we call this Response to Intervention (rti4success.com). We must *intervene*. We must respond, now. Because a student is not meeting a specific level of proficiency, it is believed that he needs intervention. Intervention specialists attempt to boost students who have yet to meet requirements. We focus resources on making sure this student meets our grade-level standards of sameness. Students *excelling* beyond this chosen level of proficiency are targeted as well; special programs attempt to serve those who can think and perform beyond the expectations we have set in place. But we continue to pour resources into a flawed structure. We spend energy and capital in the attempt to bring all students to an arbitrary mark set by the flawed concept that each human develops at the same rate and should be capable of the same benchmarks.

## ORSCH...CUTTING THE EDGE IN EDUCATION

*Instead of enhancing individuals, we spend countless dollars and days cultivating sameness.*

Imagine a classroom full of twenty children. Imagine that the children are learning how to "regroup" or "carry" with multidigit addition. The teacher gives the lesson, and then assigns page fourteen, problems one to twenty-five to all the students. In the reality of *What Is*, each child must complete twenty-five problems. It is fair to assign the same amount to each student in a classroom. Or is it fair? In the reality of *What Could Be*, several students may only need to practice with ten problems and will be eager to move to a new challenge. Some may not understand and will need to use hands-on tools to grasp the concept. Some are simply not ready and could be happily building simpler skills in line with the concept, allowed to mature at their own pace. But in the garden of *What Is*, they are suddenly "not as good," "need remediation," compared to each other, fearful and doubtful of their skills and intelligence. This one moment in the garden of *What Is* stands to create lifelong issues in some children. But in the garden of *What Could Be*, children are well aware that they are not each the same and that they each have talents and skills different from the person next to them. They trust that they will understand when the time is right and trust their own thinking, because it is just that—their own thinking—allowed to progress naturally.

Mainstream education must begin to think about, and question, the age-old practice of grouping and assessing students based on grade levels. Because Orsch is a school

## CHAPTER 3—SAMENESS

without grade levels, we have the fortunate advantage of experiencing life without them. The absence of age-based grade levels offers many advantages. Students are able to enjoy a world where their knowledge, skills, and competency are not subjected to comparisons of their same-aged peers; they are not subjected to the inevitable pressures, self-doubt, or inflated successes present in such comparisons. They spend time developing skills with very little regard to others, leaving freedom for deep learning and individually paced development. Students are more able to celebrate the acquisition of skills and knowledge; the reward is personal and tangible, and it is not dependent on a scale of comparisons. Students move to the next level in any given concept or class when they're ready. They move to the next level without feeling ashamed or superior to others. Such a structure offers a school culture enhanced camaraderie and more moments of authentic learning.

The idea that every student is expected to reach the same academic level during the same academic year will most likely seem ridiculous in the future, if we begin to question it now. Furthermore, a student who is not reading at grade level in third grade likely has very intelligent interests outside of his self-perceived "boring" reading assignments. If parents, teachers, and society in general were to let go of grade-level expectations, our students would be much better off. Many students would surpass expectations in math, while moving slowly toward them in language arts. Some would take their time through concrete mathematical topics, while writing poetry that would rival the world's best.

Some students would soar above their age-based peers in all subject areas, and some would happily take their time. Regardless, each student would find value in learning and progressing at his own individual pace where learning and knowledge carry meaning, all the while enjoying a community that respects the inevitable differences in each other.

Obviously students don't like to feel behind or less capable than their age-based peers, and comparisons can cause long-term issues. But, students at the top end of the spectrum struggle in a world of comparisons and sameness as well.

Ginny is a lovely eleven year old girl. She is tall and mature for her age. She is a very accomplished student. She began reading before kindergarten and hasn't stopped her academic rigor since. Today I asked her what her favorite part of school is. Without hesitation, she answered, "I like that I can work with people in my skill level, because I am eleven, and, you know...I can work with people who are older because...I'm..." She stopped short of boasting, as she is quite sweet and humble. It is clear that she values the opportunity to work with students who are more mature and academically savvy. It is also clear that she doesn't want to stand out as someone who is above her age-based peers. She doesn't want recognition for her intelligence and abilities; she just wants to enjoy them without fanfare or isolation.

While the ramifications of sameness within the realm of academics are destructive, the biggest tragedy of sameness is the social ramifications. Too many children are afraid to

## CHAPTER 3—SAMENESS

stand out. Many children would prefer to sit in the wings and not be noticed by their peers. Children of all ages desire social acceptance. In an environment that fosters sameness, the expression of individuality is a risk to children who fear that stepping out of established norms will invite criticism. Such children suppress their desire to express themselves, and they unknowingly begin to lose their sense of individuality.

Academic and social ramifications are inescapably intertwined. Ironically, posters line the walls of classrooms touting individuality and acceptance. "We are all special." "We are all unique." As a culture, we are attempting to respond to a very deep and very real problem by hanging posters—Band-Aids to treat a fractured bone. Our educational structure models a lack of acceptance; it models a lack of individuality both academically and socially, and then we *tell* children that they are special, unique. We *tell* them to be kind and accepting. We *tell* them that they can each reach their potential and that everyone can succeed. However, children learn what they live, not what they're *told*.

I know another child, Max. He is quite a funny person. He makes his parents laugh heartily at home. He has a genuine, pleasant sense of humor. He loves silly voices and witty comments, and his interjections are well timed. When he entered kindergarten, he was under the impression that the world valued his humor. However, kindergarten asked him to stay quiet, not disrupt the class, and to be a good boy. He is a good boy, so he complied. He expressed his humorous side at home. Quiet Max went to school each day. Occasionally, in first and second grade, Max said something funny and witty during class time. His teachers were fairly tolerant, as his humor was intelligent. However, his classmates were not accepting at all. Max received only negative feedback from his peers, leading him to question himself, leading to confusion. By the time third grade came around, he was no longer Max but was a stifled rendition of himself. When funny comments surfaced, he held them back. He became scared to stand out. He questioned himself daily. Max's story is a common one. What if his peers had valued a world where things were not all the same, where expectations were that kids might be innovative and…funny?

Many children enter into our educational system with a sense of individuality that is slowly crushed and degraded year after year. Obviously, this is not the case for every child, as we still have many creative and independent kids soaring through our system, and trendsetters exist; however, the argument is made for those who do not fare well, for the millions of students who suppress their unique nature so as to not face ridicule. And I would venture to guess that even those who do fare well have suppressed much of themselves to succeed within a culture of sameness.

Sameness is to blame for so many of our troubles. It is to blame for lack of progress and lack of tolerance. Sameness limits creativity. Sameness limits potential. Sameness leaves students with a lack of contentment and a lack of fulfillment. Sameness is boring and sameness is to blame for bullying.

CHAPTER 3—SAMENESS

Tolerance comes from valuing and accepting the perspective of another, and tolerance is less prevalent in an environment of sameness. Sameness can also create animosity. Sameness often creates unhealthy competition. Sameness confuses us because we know better.

## *Incongruence: Creativity Versus Sameness*

It has long been my opinion that we are significantly confusing our youth in this country. Individuality is honored in some of our most progressive realms. More now than ever before, we have a society made up of creative individuals. Industry and popular culture condone creativity and celebrate individuality; the evidence is all around us. Marketing campaigns that grab our attention are atypical and artistic, humorous and intelligent—engaging. Currently our society very much values an unconventional approach—something that makes us think. The arts, music, fashion, literature, engineering, pop culture, technology—all of these elements of a modern culture constantly move forward, requiring unconventional ideas.

Individuality is honored in cutting-edge industries and progressive companies. Individuality is an essential step to innovation and creative thinking. Tomorrow's industries and companies do not want graduates who are the products of sameness. They want graduates who will stand out in innovative thought and self-initiated passion. Similarly, parents value their children's unique personalities and hope that they will keep their individuality throughout their lives. The youth of today do not begin as innate followers. The youth of today begin their lives feeling they can be and do anything, that they are special and unique.

Although parents, culture, and true advocates of children encourage them to be themselves, pursue their interests, take chances, and be brave leaders, traditional classroom settings work directly against this grain. Our current educational system does not mirror society. We have moved beyond the era of being fed information, into an era where our intelligence is honored and we are to infer, contemplate, and evaluate our surroundings. Yet, for most of the hours in their day, American students do not receive the same message.

American students are pressured to perform to standards. They are fed rules and procedures, algorithms and facts. In addition, American students are stuck in hierarchical settings in which they must socialize and operate. The lives of American students in a typical educational setting do not mirror the best of what our progressive society could offer them; therefore, they are not reaching their individual potential.

A setting of traditional approaches makes sense within a society where individuality is not celebrated. Sameness, rigid instruction, and group mentality make sense in a society that values those ideals. The United States of America is not such a society. We continue to send confusing and disheartening messages to our young by requiring that they submit to our rigidity and old ideas while their culture suggests otherwise. Our children live within this incongruence, and it frustrates and confuses them.

This incongruence is part of the disgust and despondency students display when they don't like their school environments. They don't feel honored or respected as individuals, and they know they should. They then lose respect for their educational environment and for the adults in their lives who do not value their individuality. This incongruence leads to an uphill battle that interferes with teacher-student relationships, trust, general productivity, and ultimately a student's sense of self-worth and potential.

*Our society rewards creativity and unconventionality; our educational system rewards sameness.*

## Sameness Affects Teachers as Well

Teachers are extremely creative beings. Most teachers enter into the profession because they are passionate about reaching children, and they know somewhere deep within that the best way to reach children is through creativity and innovative approaches. Each teacher hopes to instill a passion for learning in his or her students. Wide-eyed, newly licensed teachers are full of ideas about engagement and programming. New teachers are eager to step foot in their first classroom to begin a lifetime of inspiring children.

## ORSCH...CUTTING THE EDGE IN EDUCATION

But their curriculum, meant to keep everyone on the same page, mandates what and how they teach. Pacing guides and data-driven approaches can so easily rip away a teacher's inspiration and passion for teaching.

Rose was an excited new teacher. She could not wait to have her first class. All summer, she planned and schemed, attended workshops, collected materials. She dreamed of engaging her students. She pictured their adoring faces wanting more, more, more. She spent hours detailing her classroom, anticipating the first day of school—her heart gleaming.

As the year progressed, Rose's critical-thinking books were left to collect dust on the shelves. Her creative ideas were tough to reach. Her students were despondent—not seemingly engaged at all. She wondered why it wasn't working the way it did in her dreams. Having little experience and diminishing zeal, her joy for teaching began to waver. She worked many hours, stressing often to meet deadlines and squeeze in curriculum requirements. She became less interested in the fun ideas of engagement and changing the lives of students; she became more interested in pleasing administration. She reached for good test scores. Rose was a good teacher whose students tested well because she made sure to prepare them. She became a solid addition to the district.

Rose's professional environment eliminated the original magic with which she entered the world of teaching. Being

## CHAPTER 3—SAMENESS

the best teacher one can be requires a bit of freedom, lots of room to be creative, and huge doses of individuality. Forcing teachers to follow the curriculum to a T diminishes zeal and a teacher's natural ability to offer genuine growth to her students. A teacher who has become numb to a creative, exciting classroom in favor of solid test scores is offering her students minimal authentic development. However, in today's climate, such a teacher is deemed "a good teacher" because her students' scores meet the mark.

Consider, on the other hand, Elizabeth, another bright-eyed, excited new teacher with a much different fate. Elizabeth began her career in a school that honored her natural abilities and creative ideas, allowing her to choose her own techniques to plan engaging lessons. Elizabeth wanted to be great—she wanted the best for her students and sought self-improvement. She loved connecting with students and offering the perfect lesson. She accepted feedback from her students and tailored her plans accordingly, always trying to truly reach them. Outside of school, she saw new lessons everywhere she looked. She thought about each of her students, their aptitudes and interests. She carried a notebook around so as to not miss an innovative idea that was sure to surface. She rapidly became a talented, sensitive, nurturing teacher who was trusted by her students and admired by her peers.

Every classroom and every school in America should be differentiating for its students and offering them authentic individualized programming. The problem is that our system, which is built of and built for sameness, does not facilitate the use of such approaches. Because differentiated approaches to learning and teaching require individualization in programming, sameness makes them impossible to implement. Because individualization requires flexibility, sameness is its enemy. Because sameness is unbending, it completely eliminates the possibility for true differentiation—a concept that is inarguable in educational circles.

Many of today's schools are inadvertently eliminating a key facet. If we want our teachers to offer the best of themselves and the best in educational practices, we must provide them with the correct environment in which to establish it. An environment of sameness is not such an environment.

## *A Sense of Individuality and Integrity*

If we are to expect and nurture the best from our students, it is important that each child feels a strong sense of self. Without a healthy sense of self, children tend to mimic and become what they see in others. With a solid grasp of one's own individuality comes a genuine confidence and belief in one's skills and personality. Confidence leads to success. Success leads to more confidence, increased talent, skill, understanding of the world, and countless positive attributes, including integrity. A strong sense of self also offers students room to accept and celebrate others as the genuine individuals they are. Acceptance leads to compassion, forgiveness, and collaboration skills—social harmony.

## CHAPTER 3—SAMENESS

When a program or school specifically fosters the individuality of its students, the results are significant and evident. Students who experience a genuine sense of individuality in their school setting begin to discover what they really love, who they are, which skills they possess, which skills they want to acquire, and what they want to learn. These students are also confident in their own thinking. They have the freedom to think for themselves because each child's individuality is embraced and celebrated among classmates and teachers. Individuality blossoms in each student. Confidence and integrity increases as each student experiences daily success in various realms and is allowed to be himself. Individuality becomes a trend as students begin to see others' creativity, ingenuity, and willingness to attempt the unconventional. And failure is seen as an avenue to keep trying—students are not afraid to try, because they've experienced their classmates surviving failure with a smile.

When individuality is honored and celebrated, a group of people becomes a vibrant, fun, exciting world, and productivity abounds. Innovation is ordinary, and a celebratory feeling for life, learning, and interaction drives the group forward. Consider how far we could be in fifty years if children worldwide felt like this every day. What new inventions, what medical progress could be made if, at an early age, a sense of limitless ability was instilled in every child? And what if each of us worked passionately within the field we loved most? What if each of us, as individuals, believed in who we are—our own talents, our strengths, our ability to learn and acquire skills that serve our interests? *What Could Be?*

An authentic sense of individuality is almost impossible to foster in a setting that cultivates sameness. Therefore, we must challenge such settings and begin to implement strategy that directly enhances individuality. Students who attend programs that enhance individuality will more likely grow to be happy adults who pursue passions, have the skills necessary to seek personal satisfaction, and make valuable contributions to our changing society.

Sameness infiltrates almost every aspect of our students' lives within our conventional educational structure. The concept of sameness will resurface in many of the following chapters. It is a concept that surfaces in many of life's chapters as well.

Specific structures and strategies can be implemented in our classrooms to combat sameness—to help students reach their individual potentials. We can offer children specific structures to enhance and honor individuality. If we begin using some of these methods while continuing to look for more, we will instantly see more vibrant students. We will see fewer decisions based on affiliation. We will see more confidence, more joy, and more prosperity in the minds of our youth. And we will see less bullying; we will see a better sense of acceptance and tolerance between students.

## Chapter 4—Horses and Carts

*For decades we have been trying to push a cart with the nose of a horse.*

### The Horse

The horse is strength, freedom, individuality, and desire to run unfettered—to take an idea and explore it to its logical end, to self-direct, to be free to empower your own discovery, and, as such, your own education. The horse wants to run, and it can pull a sizable cart while doing so.

### The Cart

The cart is full of the basics we need: computational fluency, reading skills, order of operations, definitions of literary elements so that we may speak intelligently about these ideas—all of the standards.

Yes, the standards are in the *cart*. All those important, testable, measurable aspects of education are not the horse—they are the cart. Mainstream education puts them first—it has been doing so for decades. That approach may have met with more success when creativity and innovation were not such significant aspects of our culture. But now we have a lot of disgruntled horses with sore noses, many of whom would rather just stop pushing the cart forward. Many have given up, because they are tired and see no point. The horses who are still moving forward, those obedient and unquestioning horses strong enough to push on, are moving at a standardized pace that we set for them. They could be moving much faster, could be flying—pulling their testables and measurables in the cart behind them, using them as needed. The high performing students who land in *gifted* programs have successfully pushed their carts fast enough that they get to fly, despite the order of things, but even they could have gone much further with more purpose, had they been allowed.

The inability to fly feels stifling to young humans. They have zeal for learning and spirit for life when they enter school, and then, slowly, their zeal is stamped out. They know no better. They don't question the system until they are much older but already tired of pushing their cart without realizing it should be pulled. Despondency is the result. We have millions of brilliant and creative minds who are just playing along, going through the standards, not knowing that they are capable of much more.

The concept that each of our students must fit into a desired outcome or reach a designated level at a specific point in time is terribly flawed. Instead of serving their purpose, standards and benchmarks have become an entity we serve at all costs. Our educational system pours resources into the students who fall below these benchmarks; it creates special programs for those who rise above them. Mainstream education is so intently focused on these outcomes that it too often ignores the well-known and solid educational practices of experiential learning, hands-on approaches, differentiation, individualization, and student-centered strategies—all proven best practices. You will not meet a knowledgeable teacher in this country who disagrees that current best practices are the best ways to reach and teach children. However, our traditional educational culture of standard-based sameness is not conducive to their success, nor is it convenient to implement them within our current rigid paradigms. On the other hand, innovative, flexible, creative programs have beautiful horses flying toward uncharted destinations and new territories. Intrinsic motivation is all one needs to pack the cart full of important information.

## *To Require Proficiency Is Counterproductive*

In an attempt to standardize, leave no child behind, and reach rigid benchmarks, traditional public education introduces detrimental elements into a child's school life. Because schools and districts are under immense pressure to show that their students are proficient, the typical American classroom requires proficiency from each child at a specific date in his development. Kindergartners are pressured to read sight words. Third graders' math facts are

## ORSCH...CUTTING THE EDGE IN EDUCATION

tested with a timer. Students are subjected to uninteresting reading passages in an effort to increase fluency scores.

Among other risks, attempts to require proficiency can easily lead to a student's lack of confidence, lack of desire to learn, lack of interest in subject matter, and diminished thinking skills—in short, rigid requirements can crush aptitude and zeal.

Consider Annie. Annie is a precious little kindergartner. She loves to wear dresses over jeans and insists on wearing her pink cowboy boots every day. She has her own sense of style. She entered kindergarten self-assured—confident in her personality and in the love in which she was raised. She loves books. She loves to be read to and immerses herself in the aesthetic delight of the pictures. The text makes no sense to her. It seems a strange language, mixed up and confusing. She understands that grown-ups know how to derive meaning from those funny-looking symbols, but she has no interest in figuring them out. At home, she pores through books, absorbed in the story told picture by picture. At home, her parents read to her; it is her favorite moment of the day, fostering complete joy. Kindergarten starts out well enough—everyone is happy, songs are sung to begin the day, coloring feels good, show-and-tell is fun, recess is a whole new world of friends and laughter. But then the pressure starts. Flash cards full of arbitrary letters are presented to her, but she does not understand them. She feels frustration from her teachers. She is trying but cannot understand how all of this goes together. She cannot always remember

## CHAPTER 4—HORSES AND CARTS

the sound a letter makes. She doesn't always recognize the combination of the letters that are supposed to represent a word. When she opens a book, she is no longer allowed to absorb herself in the pictures but must point to clusters of unfamiliar symbols. She begins to feel differently about books. She is sad about it. They are no longer joyful, but are a reminder that she is not good at this sort of thing. She sees her peers grasp these concepts but feels frozen in fear that she will answer incorrectly, so she guesses—her fears are confirmed. She begins to lose confidence. Her peers begin to lose respect for her as they see their teacher grow frustrated. They begin to see her as dumb, and she can feel this. Later in the school year, she is whisked off to another classroom for reading, where an intervention specialist again attempts to hammer sight words in with no context. It should work this time, because the student/teacher ratio is smaller—the district has spent money on an interventionist to solve this problem.

Annie does eventually learn to read but no longer loves books. She does not develop an understanding of stories as they had originally presented themselves to her. Even though her preschool years had prepared her well, in kindergarten, she is not nurtured to develop a strong connection with a book's characters. Books are a requirement. Books are no longer a peaceful, pleasant story to her but are now something she gets through to satisfy teachers. By second grade, students begin commenting on her cowboy boots—they adhere to sameness as they have been inadvertently taught to do. Annie is forever changed. A child who came into her school career a budding, creative lover of literature is now unknowingly going through the motions, questioning her intelligence, lacking confidence. But Annie doesn't know any better. She is too young to question the grown-ups. She doesn't lament her lack of self...yet. She is relieved that she can finally read, even though she is in special classes and even though it is hard—at least she has passed the test. That is what her education wants of Annie—at least she has passed the test. She has a safe pair of sneakers now too.

If Annie had been allowed to learn to read within her own aptitude, without fear, perhaps with a more creative approach—if she had been allowed to develop within a supportive environment, she would not only be a proficient reader, but she would have retained a love for literature and, most important, herself. But traditional education is not patient enough; it too is fearful of not meeting its own benchmarks.

Hans came to Orsch after a year of high-pressure kindergarten. He still fears those letter combinations meant to represent a word, but he is making progress. He has been in our program for just over a year now. He finally shows an interest in books. He finally doesn't shout out, "I hate reading." He now participates in letter bingo and word games. Because no one is forcing him out of his confidence zone, he is beginning to see that written words and letters are potentially a fun thing to know. He will learn to read; there is no doubt. And he won't have any fear or hatred toward literature when he gets there.

## CHAPTER 4—HORSES AND CARTS

Harold is a strong-willed, very smart kid. He came to our school because he feared timed math facts tests. His fear was crippling. His disdain for this element of his day was flooding over into other aspects of his learning. He can calculate just fine, but he cannot do it under the pressure of a timer. His school would not bend; they would not accommodate or consider that he might be able to learn higher-level math, despite the fact that he can't seem to get a hundred facts correct within two minutes. Their benchmark is set. Therefore, Harold must need remediation, homework, meetings with parents. I cannot understand this logic. One conversation with Harold reveals that he is too scared to think in this situation. He knows his facts but cannot present his knowledge in the manner that is required by the school. Would the real world require this presentation of his skills? Is this method of presentation really a skill he needs to become successful?

Such situations illustrate that traditional education is concerned with benchmarks over what will actually teach a child, concerned with scores over finding out what will enhance a child's educational experience.

To *force* proficiency is a fallacy and is counterproductive to authentic education. Introducing doubt and frustration into the mind of a kindergartner will undoubtedly hinder confidence. She will then lose belief in her ability to learn other skills and gain knowledge. Furthermore, when a specific proficiency is required, students can easily lose their desire to learn as well as lose interest in a given subject matter.

Although learning is naturally enjoyable, it becomes mundane and uninteresting when it is forced; deep learning requires that content carries *meaning* to the learner (Sousa, 2006). Thinking skills develop in young minds through exploration and experience, which takes patience—*each learner requiring a different time line*. Pushing kids beyond an absorbable level or pace does nothing to benefit them.

Isaac is a vibrant student; you will read about him again in coming chapters. When I met him four years ago, his biggest challenge was his academic confidence. Beautifully nurtured at home, he had a deep belief in himself, but that did not shine through during math class. After a math lesson he would head into assignments uncertain but afraid to speak up. He would nod his head as if he understood the concepts, but he was frozen in fear, knowing that he didn't actually understand. For months, he pretended to know the concepts in the attempt to please his teacher, afraid to be wrong.

Instead of remediation, he received patience. Instead of pressure, he received understanding.

Four years later, he is one of our top-performing math students, and mathematics is among his favorite activities during the school day. In retrospect, we believe he is currently proficient—even above grade level—because he was allowed to mature mathematically along his own time line. Instead of convincing himself that he would never have the capacity to adequately learn math, he was offered the

## CHAPTER 4—HORSES AND CARTS

patience to mature. It would not surprise me if he chose a career in math. But I know that a standardized approach for those four years would have crushed his aptitude and would have convinced him that math was "not his thing." He never would have fallen in love with mathematical concepts. He would have avoided math beyond requirements.

And remember Ella, our survivor? She used to love math when it fit her. But after being uprooted and replanted, she is now forced to race through math concepts, barely hanging on, and claims to "hate math."

Which student is more likely to pursue a career in higher-level mathematics? Ella or Isaac? Isaac is pulling his cart. Ella is pushing hers. Is it possible that our rigid approach is the reason that our country's numbers of higher-level math and science students are diminishing?

Forcing proficiency is not only a fallacy but may actually be to blame for crushed aptitude as well. Sore noses. Horses pushing carts.

If we truly want proficiency, we must be willing to allow it; we cannot force it. We must be willing to be creative in our approaches and assessments. We must be willing to trust that children are capable, able to be proficient within their own time line and within their own style. Rigid requirements are largely to blame for lack of proficiency.

# Chapter 5—Ever Seen a Toddler Waste Time?

A toddler is constantly bumbling around from engaging activity to engaging activity, often choosing activity over food or sleep, sometimes getting herself into trouble. A toddler is frustrated when she is bored. She will demand interaction. She is not in the mood to waste her moments—ever. She soaks up every new, stimulating lesson and indulges in learned skills. She is in charge of her learning—doing, watching, interacting, touching, testing limits. Of course, the adults in her life must keep her safe, but within safe parameters, she is in charge of her own engaging lessons in life.

We entrust toddlers, preschoolers, even babies with their own learning. We offer experience. We guide them toward constructive playthings. We encourage and arrange interactive play. We find toys to keep them occupied. They are in a constant state of learning. They seek new experiences innately. They have an obvious inner desire to learn.

*At what point in a child's life do we stop trusting self-guided learning?*

## ORSCH...CUTTING THE EDGE IN EDUCATION

Unlike toddlers, we've all seen plenty of elementary, middle, and high school students drag their feet, procrastinate, and waste time in school. They procrastinate at home as well. It has become cliché—mainstream school-aged children are typically not excited to do homework or boring school assignments. Can you blame them?

The day they enter school, mainstream education stops trusting students to seek knowledge and experience on their own. We become fully in charge of their learning. Because every child—every snowflake—must reach mastery by a certain age, adults have decided they know best. Teachers and administrators are in charge of *what* and *how* a child learns. Our educational system leaves very little room for self-guided learning, causing students to exhibit a lack of engagement and a general lack of excitement for learning. But a school-aged child behaves no differently than an exuberant toddler if allowed to seek experience and knowledge on his own.

School-aged children who are free to make choices about their learning are fully and intently engaged at all points during the learning process—as long as they're actually learning—just like the toddler. Whether the activity or lesson is hands-on, lecture-based, independently sought, or any number of other opportunities for learning, appropriate learning and appropriate skills mastery is innately engaging. Engaged students commonly beg for more practice relevant to topics they have just mastered, such as long division, subject-verb agreement, and

### CHAPTER 5—EVER SEEN A TODDLER WASTE TIME?

multiple-digit multiplication. We have found that students even enjoy lecture-based lessons when timing and presentation is applicable. Learning and mastery that are just right and self-chosen are invigorating. When a child has just grasped a new concept, a practice sheet is actually *fun*. If, on the other hand, a practice sheet or homework is busywork or not appropriately leveled, a child will suffer from motivational issues.

## *Lessons from Amelia...*

Not so long ago, I watched a three-year-old dance on stage. Amelia watched her instructor intently. She was purposeful and engaged. Her attention did not waver; she executed her dance moves with perfection. Her fellow dancers were not as engaged; their actions were more in line with typical three-year-old behaviors.

Amelia's parents trust her judgment. Amelia commonly comes into Orsch with her own agenda. She is not yet a student but joins her sisters at drop-off and pickup. She often decides she will be staying for a bit. Luckily, her mom has the luxury to support this desire. Amelia knows where the crayons are; she knows how to extract clean white paper from the copy machine. She knows which kids are in which classes and where to find the books she likes. Amelia is in a constant state of reaching for more. She loves learning. Amelia exhibits no shortage of attention span. She loves doing and growing, and she loves experience.

## ORSCH...CUTTING THE EDGE IN EDUCATION

Amelia is allowed to fully engage during almost every moment of her day, because her parents realize the value of exploratory, self-guided learning.

She *chose* to dance that well. Amelia is completely in charge of her actions. When I observe her, I can almost see the synapses and cognitive functioning pop out of her little piggy-tailed head like confetti. The level of concentration apparent on Amelia's face during her dance recital was not a new level of concentration for her. She is quite familiar with that level of concentration, experiencing it the majority of her day—day after day. She loves dance; it is clear. Dance and coloring are two places where Amelia finds engaging brain activity and immersion. She is fully engaged; she is developing cognitive ability. I cannot fathom a more important use of a three-year-old's time than to bop around the world as little Amelia. She will be one powerful thinker if she is allowed to continue on this course.

But they don't stay three years old for long.

Cognitive capacity grows as the child grows. Coloring pages and imaginative play don't satisfy forever. A competent self-guided learner will seek new knowledge. *If the learning environment offers limitless options for learning (just as the real world does), the self-directed learner will never stop reaching for higher heights.* Learning does not become boring. Our research shows that every human child genuinely loves learning. Children despise boredom—they want to be actively engaged all day long and even after bedtime.

## CHAPTER 5—EVER SEEN A TODDLER WASTE TIME?

A child-centered classroom is a vibrant place where cognitive activity and productivity are in full swing. Where a toddler enjoys fitting blocks through similarly shaped holes, a fifth-grader enjoys calculating the area of a complex polygon—as long as the level is appropriate, as long as he feels it fits him. Our research also shows that given options, students will choose a slightly challenging level.

Children are capable beings. Our culture and specifically our traditional educational system do not give children nearly enough credit for their abilities or capabilities. Our culture is intent upon labeling, measuring, and categorizing the abilities of its youth. However, we often mistakenly measure children and create expectations of children through adult eyes. Unless you are on the cutting edge of brain research in developmental psychology or are a parent like Amelia's, you are probably guilty of underestimating the minds of children.

A three-year-old cannot balance his father's checkbook, but he is engaged in many important thoughts. He is collecting data and memorizing patterns (Gladwell, 2005). He is observing and experiencing life through all five senses, sometimes all at once. He is studying behaviors in others, gathering information on all sorts of stimuli and interactions. He is (whether grown-ups are willing to admit it or not) making important decisions and becoming a self-sufficient being.

Imagine youth. Each of us was there. Energy. Imagination. The world a big and wonderful place. Learning taking place everywhere. New tastes. New sights. New friendships. New games. Skill development—daily.

The next time you get the chance, spend a few minutes observing a very young child watching something. He is in the arms of someone he trusts, using minimal muscle power to hold his torso and head in place. He is content. His eyes dart back, forth, up, around, blinking only when necessary. If you watch carefully, you will see intent processing, a little mind soaking in everything he has the capacity to grasp, wondering about the parts he doesn't grasp. He is in the moment; there are no outside pressures, no plans to make, no concerns, no reason to leave the moment. And nobody crafted this moment for him; no one placed expectations, standards, or outcomes upon his ability to gain knowledge from this experience. Another interesting chance for observation is to specifically watch a child playing alone. If unencumbered, play has a dynamic flow and intense focus. Children often talk to themselves or have imaginary conversations—creating entire scenes within their imaginations. Focus is usually intense in this situation as well.

Current brain research is brimming with pertinent information about what will engage a child and how student interest plays a significant role in motivation, content relevance, and understanding (Sousa/Tomlinson, 2011). Orsch has discovered that student interest is heightened in almost every subject matter when the child is given the ability to make choices about his own learning.

## CHAPTER 5—EVER SEEN A TODDLER WASTE TIME?

To easily offer students opportunities to make choices about their learning, teachers can plan their lessons with student variation in mind—multiple intelligences, differing abilities, different levels of readiness, different interest levels. Further, instead of a teacher preassessing and categorizing each and every student—his preference in how he will best learn at that particular time of day, his readiness level, and his prior knowledge—a teacher can simply *offer* multiple approaches and choices. It is the student's job to choose how best to grasp a concept. It is the student's job to choose his level and his avenue for learning. Students are *eager* to learn in this setting, no matter the content.

By contrast, a child who exists in an educational environment that he finds uninteresting or inappropriately leveled will disengage, feel bored, and exhibit despondency. He will resist practicing concepts and building upon skills. He will not show a zeal for learning new material, nor will he actively participate in his own learning. *Once a child's passion for learning is crushed, he doesn't know he must find it.* It is a reality and a travesty that millions of American students feel this way every day. It should be education's mission to nurture each child's passion for learning.

Toddlers do not waste time, nor do ten-year-olds, if their environment is stimulating. Students are innately engaged in life and learning, given an environment that facilitates their natural tendencies for such. They are sponges for experience and knowledge. If allowed to make choices and engage in self-initiated learning, they make great strides forward and display exuberance for new knowledge. Students will engage and experience authentic interest in almost any subject matter if they are afforded elements of independence and varied options. We see the reality of student-initiated learning every day in our environment. Students make appropriate choices about their own learning, which makes a truly student-centered environment a tangible goal and a potential reality in our educational system.

## Chapter 6—Bullies

School-aged bullying has gained recognition as a national problem. Let us define the word *bully*. Google's definition:

> 1. (noun)—A person who uses strength or power to harm or intimidate those who are weaker. 2. (verb)—use superior strength or influence to intimidate (someone), typically to force him or her to do what one wants.

Stopbullying.gov's definition:

> Bullying is unwanted, aggressive behavior among school aged children that involves a real or perceived power imbalance. The behavior is repeated, or has the potential to be repeated, over time. Both kids who are bullied and who bully others may have serious, lasting problems.

In order to be considered bullying, the behavior must be aggressive and include:

1. An Imbalance of Power: Kids who bully use their power—such as physical strength, access

> to embarrassing information, or popularity—to control or harm others. Power imbalances can change over time and in different situations, even if they involve the same people.

And

> 2. Repetition: Bullying behaviors happen more than once or have the potential to happen more than once.

Bullying is a serious issue for school-aged children, and the trends seem to be worsening. Currently, it is estimated that 77 percent of all students have been verbally bullied at school and that one in four students are bullied on a regular basis. In addition, cyberbullying offers a very easy avenue for bullies and is becoming a rampant problem. It is estimated that about 2.7 million American students are bullied each year and about 2.1 million students are bullies themselves (www.bullyingstatistics.org).

Obviously, the majority of schools attempt to create safe, bully-free environments for their students. Antibullying campaigns include suggestions of policies and rules and the enforcement of those rules. Campaigns also include education for parents and students about the definition of a bully and how to manage incidents. Efforts to combat bullying suggest that students stand up to each other and support one another when they witness bullying. Schools have created informant systems so that peers feel safe reporting

## CHAPTER 6—BULLIES

incidents. Schools offer appropriate adult supervision and post antibullying posters. All these tactics are valiant efforts to stop and prevent bullying, but our attempts to eliminate bullying with campaigns and posters are largely failing. Bully behavior is still on the rise.

### *The Most Important Piece of the Puzzle*

I believe every school has the potential to strategically eliminate bullies, using a different approach and a new focus. We have tested this hypothesis at Orsch and have seen wonderful and significant results. First, if a school has a true sense of community and a nurturing environment, the school will set up an optimal culture for positive peer interaction. Effective strategies used to develop such an environment are explained in Section Two within "The Foundation: A Healthy School Culture." But within a healthy school culture, there is an even more important piece of this puzzle that we simply must address if we are to effectively eliminate bullying. The most significant piece of the bully puzzle and the most powerful and effective facilitator of harmony among student groups is an *authentic and content sense of self in each child*.

Children who are content with their true sense of self do not feel the need to criticize or make fun of one another. They do not feel the need to hurt one another. They feel confident. They trust who they are and trust in their own talents. They feel no need to control or harm others. They value each other's differences as much as they value their own differences. Children who are content with themselves do not need to garner attention or false support from their peers. When each student is content with himself, no imbalance of power exists. And a true sense of self is a prerequisite to a true sense of belonging.

An eighth-grade student was asked, before enrolling in Orsch, what percentage of his day was affected negatively by social interactions. His answer was 100 percent—an answer I've observed to be the case for most students. Students are significantly affected by their peers. Students are more affected than we realize. It is well established in psychology circles and mental health research that the desire to belong and experience acceptance from others are significant and innate human needs. The need for love and belonging is evident in infancy and in early childhood; the need for acceptance in society and social groups is evident as a child grows. The desire to belong and fit in can be an overpowering emotion, and the desire for friendship is equally as deep. These desires are more significant to children than a desire to learn math; therefore, in a school setting, these emotions dominate a child's inner being. Children will reach for acceptance and belonging first and foremost.

A solid sense of belonging and acceptance begins within a child's inner self. This sense is generally established in a child's family life and in playgroups during his early years. For example, Nicholas, our preschool deliveryman, enjoys the adoration and acceptance of others. His personality is

## CHAPTER 6—BULLIES

celebrated, and his behaviors are encouraged. Nicholas has no reason to question himself. He experiences feelings of self-expression and fulfillment with no risk of social backlash. In most of his moments, he is full of good emotions, and his basic human needs are met. Because Nicholas receives positive feedback, he is free to accept himself, and he is free to believe he is a valuable person. He likes the person he is. At its deepest level, his sense of belonging comes from within. His sense of self is solid and he accepts his own personality with confidence. All my experience with children has shown me that the most powerful and basic sense of belonging and acceptance is first the authentic acceptance of oneself.

Unfortunately, even a solid acceptance of oneself is placed at risk in many school settings. Because the desire for acceptance and belonging is such a powerful force, children often seek such feelings at great costs. If a school environment promotes sameness, then individuality is at risk. If individuality is at risk, an authentic sense of self and a child's inner acceptance and belonging is at risk as well. If a child doubts his own personality, his skills, his talents, his thoughts, and his behaviors, he loses some of his own acceptance of himself. If he continues to question himself, he will experience fewer and fewer feelings of personal acceptance and belonging. He will then seek extrinsic sources for acceptability. To find social belonging he will need to conform or find a niche within a fabricated world of other children who have also aborted their true sense of self to become what their social climate asks of them.

By contrast, if a group of children is made up of people who *each* enjoy the innate personality and character that satisfies so deeply within, the group becomes a vibrant, thriving social setting that promotes belonging and acceptance within each individual. When individual personalities are celebrated, the room becomes full of confident, fulfilled individuals who have no need to seek extrinsic acceptance and belonging because those needs are met within. They are ready to reach for higher human needs and begin to experience self-actualization.

As the climate becomes one of genuine acceptance, children become open to and accepting of others' perspectives, new ideas, and unique qualities. They work together in harmony. They enjoy the variety of personalities, talents, skills, and thoughts within their social network. They each feel confident. They each like who they are. They build upon the positive attributes of each other, and they have absolutely no need, no desire, no reason to bully each other.

An authentic acceptance of oneself is developed by many factors—among them: a happy home life, peer acceptance, nurturing adults in a school setting, and a purposeful existence. Unfortunately, not all children have a happy home life, and it is not within the scope of a school's mission to tackle this piece. Peer acceptance is the next significant factor that can be facilitated with many strategic tactics in a school setting. Nurturing adults are a key piece of the foundation for self-acceptance; they have the power to build a child up or tear him down. Finally, a child who

## CHAPTER 6—BULLIES

has a *purposeful existence* will feel deeply satisfied within. Interesting thoughts, new ways of thinking, new information, projects, goals, passions, new skills, quality conversation, puzzles, and problems to solve are among the millions of purposeful moments that very much fulfill students. When students are immersed in purposeful moments, they have neither the desire, nor the time, to attack others.

I interviewed several children about the issue of bullying. The answers I received, interestingly, mirror what one would expect from adults. It is possible that these conversations have happened at home and the children in my interviews were well primed for these answers, but it is also evident that many children have very clear views of why people treat each other poorly.

Following are direct quotes I received from children ages eleven to fifteen. The question: Why do people bully?

"They are scared."

"They are insecure."

"To bring someone down."

"The need for power."

"To impress someone."

"They are selfish."

"They want to have the identity of *tough guy*."

"They want to demand respect."

"The need for companionship."

"They feel yucky inside."

"Their family life isn't good."

"They want attention."

"They are trying to blend in."

"For entertainment."

"They are bored."

"To be a ringleader."

"They really want to be like you but don't know how to express it."

All of these answers reflect a child's understanding of the basic human need for belonging, acceptance, and purpose. If you examine each of the above answers and any others you feel would be relevant to the question "Why do people bully?" you will find that a positive, solid sense of self and inner acceptance of oneself would almost completely prevent the need for bullyish behavior. Encouraging a true

## CHAPTER 6—BULLIES

sense of belonging and true sense of self are the first authentic antidotes to bullying.

It is easy to conclude that a child who has a true sense of self is more confident, more content, and ultimately more likeable to his or her peers. Orsch has enjoyed countless positive peer interactions that would have been opportunities for insults, hurt feelings, or mean behavior in a world where individuality is less acceptable. Many of our students who would have questioned themselves in an environment of sameness, instead, proudly stand out and garner respect from others.

A school's culture has everything to do with the prevention and/or cultivation of tendencies to bully. A culture that honors individuality will see endless positive results. This school year we were blessed with a new seventh-grade student who had been expelled from the community school. He struggled at first; he showed off; he made an attempt to gather a clique. He metaphorically pushed a few people around. He said mean things to one or two easy victims. But, his peers stood up to him. His peers did not allow him to speak poorly of others, show aggressive posturing, or leave someone out. It is simply not cool to be mean to others in our environment. Over the course of a couple of months, he has transformed. He is becoming his true self. He is enjoyable, funny, and kind. Last week, out of the blue, he came to school in a Tigger costume. His creativity and individuality was respected. High-fives flooded the hallways. Students laughed and joked. And the next day we had another silly costume show up, a flying squirrel. It warms my heart to know that a child who previously had to take on the persona of "tough guy" was now showing up in school dressed in a Tigger costume. This is his true self. Loving. Silly. Creative. Sweet.

## *Behavior and Personalities We Must Be Careful to Not Label as Bullying*

A solid sense of self can be nurtured and appropriately guided, as long as a child is not misunderstood or labeled.

Occasionally students will forget to respect each other or will display innocent, normal rivalry. Parents and schools must be diligent in recognizing the difference between *bullying* and behaviors that are just part of a child's personality, mood, or developmental stage. Personality traits and unwanted behavior can easily be mistaken for bullying. Teachers and administrators who are not tolerant of personality traits can cause more trouble if they mistakenly label behavior as bullying. Furthermore, parents are protective of their children and often jump to the conclusion that their child has been bullied in situations of normal childhood interaction.

A school is a community made up of a variety of personalities. The more we understand, accept, and nurture innate personalities in children, the more positive their development will be.

## CHAPTER 6—BULLIES

The nature/nurture argument is worth mentioning. Innate personality traits exist, and children learn what they live. We will not try to delineate personality traits, behavior, or moods as either *nature* or *nurture*, but will assume that nature (the biological traits with which a child is born) and nurture (the environment in which the child has developed) each play a role. Nature and nurture are so deeply intertwined that they are impossible to separate.

For example, a child may be naturally bossy and may have siblings he is accustomed to bossing around. The child is authoritative and pushy at school. He tells others what to do and insists that his friends sit with him at lunch. He is domineering. His friends oblige because they don't yet question authority. From the domineering child's perspective, this is the way you treat your friends. It has always produced desired results at home; his little brother does just what is demanded of him. The child does not feel *mean* inside, nor does he feel he is more powerful or better than his peers. He is just displaying his natural behavior that he has been allowed to foster from day one. If the teachers in his life see this behavior as bullying, he will be labeled, punished, and pushed toward actual bullying, because he is told he is a bully. If, instead, his teachers guide him toward more positive interactions while giving him the benefit of the doubt, he will learn that his peer relationships improve as he becomes less domineering.

Some children are naturally selfish. They have a tough time considering others' needs; they are completely consumed with their own needs. These children want to be first in line, want to receive their snack first, and they don't understand that they must share materials and resources. Self-serving children are often mistaken for bullies. They are self-important and self-centered. The behavior they display is offensive to others and misinterpreted as mean. Again, the child displaying this behavior may not feel mean inside. He is simply looking out for himself. He means no harm to others; he has never even thought of how others may feel. A nurturing adult will help guide this child toward a broader perspective, where he can appreciate the needs of others and develop skill to combat innate selfishness.

Girls, as any girl knows, tend to be naturally cliquey. Girls like to group up, and, for some strange reason, they like to leave each other out. Some girls prefer one best friend; some girls prefer a big group of tight, giggly friendships. Girls begin displaying cliquey behavior as early as preschool. Girl interaction is tricky and delicate. They hurt each other's feelings easily and are prone to misunderstandings. But these natural tendencies should not be seen as bullying behavior; they should be recognized and specifically guided.

In addition to personality traits and innate behaviors, children are prone to mood swings, developmental phases, and outbursts of raw feelings. They are in an almost constant state of physical growth and hormonal influx. Children

## CHAPTER 6—BULLIES

are often grumpy or oversensitive. They are intensely affected by lack of sleep or by hunger. Home life and family interaction can be difficult and confusing, leading to a change in mood and well-being.

The norm for children is an imbalance in feelings and emotions due to numerous biological and environmental factors. It is extremely important that a school environment constantly consider these factors as it educates its children; to ignore these factors is to ignore most of the child. Schools that resort to labeling or punishing such behaviors miss valuable opportunities for guidance, growth, and development.

A school environment has the opportunity to positively nurture innate personalities and understand fluxes in mood, or it can choose to ingrain negative labels. Students need specific and targeted guidance from the teachers and administrators in their lives. Bossy, domineering students can learn that there is a better approach. Self-centered children can be shown new perspectives. And girls can learn how to manage their innate desire to form cliques; they can learn that there is a healthier approach to their friendships. Children need immense amounts of guidance in these departments. Under appropriate guidance, these behaviors can lead to communicative, effective relationships and lifelong skills. Teachers and parents can guide students in the right direction, or they can negatively label children and actually allow these behaviors to lead to bullying situations.

## Peer Judgment of Personality Traits

Peer judgment of personality traits can lead to misunderstandings and unhealthy rivalries, relationships, and interactions. Unless a school environment specifically celebrates individual personalities and individual differences, students will tend to form opinions and create harmful interactions. Peers who judge each other and have a desire to conform miss out on valuable personalities and quality peer interactions.

Shyness is a personality trait that is commonly misunderstood. We have two amazing individuals at Orsch who are very quiet people. They speak very little. They have no desire to be boisterous or stand out. They are highly respected among their peers, and they have complete confidence in who they are. However, I taught one of them in a traditional setting before she came to Orsch. Alysa was a third-grader at the time. She is now a tall, beautiful, accomplished seventh-grader. Alysa came to my classroom for accelerated reading and math. Each day, as students would file in, she stood out among the crowd. She stood out because she chose to head directly to her seat and wait patiently for class to begin. The others came flooding through the door in conversation of one kind or another—sometimes laughing, sometimes discussing previous events on the playground. They saw themselves as the "normal" bunch—a confident, lively bunch. Alysa was the "shy" one. Alysa was a delicate little third-grader who loved learning and loved academics. But her classmates could not seem to accept her for who

## CHAPTER 6—BULLIES

she was. Routinely, her fellow students would make comments. "Alysa never talks!" "Alysa is so shy." "Alysa, why don't you say something?" It broke my heart for her. I knew she was full of amazing thoughts and important ideas, because those ideas came out in her written work. I knew she was content with herself deep inside, because she showed no signs of lacking confidence. However, as an eight-year-old, she was suddenly forced to question her own personality because the others insisted on pointing out that she was different. She began to develop an intense reputation for being "shy." Her classroom teacher mentioned her "shyness" in parent-teacher conferences as if it was something she needed to move past. It seemed that everyone around her was asking her to change so that she could fit their vision of the way a child should interact. She began to internalize her differences; throughout her third-grade year, she began to hold her head slightly lower. She attempted to fit in; she exchanged her glasses for contacts and adopted a fashionable look. But she was never any louder.

In the fall of 2009, Alysa began her life at Orsch. She was a fourth-grader at the time. She wore her contacts and her cute fashions and began the year with her head held high. It was a new opportunity to enjoy school. The climate in Orsch is one of complete acceptance. Students and teachers speak often of personalities and differences among each other. Alysa was allowed to be her observant, quiet self. Nobody criticized her for it; they accepted her for the wonderful person she is. When Alysa was asked to present in front of the class, she spoke confidently and intelligently.

## ORSCH...CUTTING THE EDGE IN EDUCATION

She is, to this day, one of the best teammates a collaborative group can have. If your group is lucky enough to include Alysa, you will have excellent leadership and group dynamics. Alysa is highly respected by her peers. She is kind and generous, loving and helpful. She has also developed her talent for music and is quite an accomplished performer.

What if she had not been able to believe in herself as a quiet, valuable person? What if her third-grade year had set the stage for more years like that? She would have questioned her innate personality more and more. She may not have been able to express herself musically, nor would she have been able to shine as a leader. Peer perception and judgment of her personality would have destroyed so many of her talents and qualities. She would not have questioned their view of her but instead would have internalized it and allowed it to shape the person she is.

Alysa moved to another city in May. Before she left, she gave the following letter to us.

> Dear Orsch,
>
> I've always loved writing letters and this seemed to be a perfect time to write one. Though this letter is for everyone in Orsch, it's especially for Jackie. Jackie, you've created not only a school, but a place for kids to truly explore their individuality and to find who they are. Before Orsch, other kids, as well as myself, considered me shy. Throughout these four years in

## CHAPTER 6—BULLIES

*Orsch, I've come to learn that I'm more than that. I'm an observer. I'm a performer. I'm ME and I'm proud of that. And I know that without you all, I couldn't have been these things. I will continue to be these things as I move on from Orsch. This isn't goodbye, because friends don't say goodbye. They simply say, "See you soon." I'll visit you all! You've helped me find myself and though I have a long road ahead of me, I'll remember each and every one of you. Though miles may lie between us, we are never far apart, for friendship doesn't count miles, it's measured by the heart.*

*Love,*

*Alysa*

*May 25, 2013*

Isaac is another very quiet person who attends our school. Similarly, he is very highly respected among his peers; in fact, he was crowned king at our last school dance. He, too, is a leader—wise, careful, thoughtful. He is well spoken and is also quite an amazing performer—musically and theatrically. He has an excellent sense of humor and often makes his classmates roll with laughter, especially when he's on stage. He is quiet most of his hours, but he is completely confident speaking and presenting when the time is right. In a traditional setting, I wonder how his peers would have treated him throughout these impressionable years. He has a delicate personality, so my guess is that his incredible talents would have been buried so as not to invite ridicule.

Consider the young boy who doesn't prefer conventional sports-oriented play on a playground that is dominated by sports-oriented play. The boy instead prefers to pretend and engage in imaginative play. His peers too easily judge his preferences and behaviors, expecting conformity rather than individuality. His peers will continue to make comments, continue to break down his confidence, and degrade his positive sense of self. The boy is then faced with the decision to uphold his own personality against the pressures from his peers or to change his preferences in an effort to fit in. All too often, children choose acceptance over self.

Sadly, the need for acceptance and belonging is more powerful than the need to serve our individual personalities and innate talents. In many students, it is more powerful than the desire to learn. But lack of acceptance can be minimized with a culture of tolerance and a culture that truly celebrates individual preferences. An environment that serves both the need for belonging and enhances individual talent is an environment that will produce the best in human potential.

*To combat bullying, we must combat sameness and conformity.* And we must nurture the true self in each individual

## CHAPTER 6—BULLIES

while offering our youth an authentic community made up of individuals. It is in environments such as this that all children have the opportunity to thrive and enjoy an education free of bully-like behavior. Many such environments exist today, but many more can be established.

## Chapter 7—Time and Processing Capacity

I have a theory about time and processing capacity. It is an interesting look at our use of time in an educational setting. Orsch's motto is *not one wasted moment*. Living up to this model and offering only valuable time to students takes effort and strategy. To adhere to this motto, it helps to consider the finite resources of time and processing capacity.

In any given moment, we have the resources of time and processing capacity at our disposal. The choices we make in each moment determine our use of such resources. The scheduling choices we make for children determine their use of time. The educational choices we make for children directly affect the processing skills they will develop. Every given choice—every given moment—contains both time and processing capacity. At every point in our waking hours, time is passing while our brains are processing. Currently you are reading. As you read these words, time is passing and you are processing the information contained within this page—hopefully. You might also be processing other thoughts. What will I make for dinner? Make sure to get Johnny to baseball practice early for pictures…How will we pay the mortgage this month? If you are an effective critical thinker, you will simultaneously read these words and compare similar ideas and thoughts to your own experience. If you are more of a convergent thinker, you might be waiting for more examples so that you can develop a conclusion to these ideas. If you are more of a divergent thinker, you might be reaching for your own examples to expand your current level of understanding. If you are a proficient creative thinker, you might be creating new paradigms that combine your own experience with the ideas on these pages. Regardless of your approach to processing information, your own processing capacity affects your ability to think. Each of us has a specific capacity for processing information, but the capacity can grow and develop or it can stagnate. Underdeveloped processing power results in underutilized capacity. Well-developed processing power will likely result in better processing capacity (i.e., thinking skills).

What develops or limits processing power? It seems the more actively engaged we are in a given task or thought, the more processing power we allocate to that task or thought. If we are only partially engaged in a task, our brains concurrently dedicate processing power to other thoughts. Any good thinker knows that the more he thinks, the more efficient his thinking becomes. The more puzzles we solve, the better skilled we become at solving them. Thinking skills can be trained and practiced.

## CHAPTER 7—TIME AND PROCESSING CAPACITY

## *Engagement Versus Boredom*

If a child is required to listen to a lesson that is uninteresting, below her level, above her level—or any number of reasons for why she would not be engaged—she will use her time otherwise. She may ponder the ceiling tiles—how do they install those? She may think about what is in her lunchbox. She may do her best to hang on to the teacher's lesson but find it impossible to actively use processing power on a topic that does not fit her needs. Teachers have very little control over a child's thoughts, but in any given moment, they also have ample opportunity to actively engage their students.

At any given moment in an educational setting, a spectrum exists. On one end of the spectrum is boredom, on the other end—engagement. A student cannot be fully engaged and bored at the same time, but she can be partially engaged while feeling slightly bored or she can be mostly bored while absorbing some meaningful information.

Let us look at an example:

The lesson—combining short words to create contractions. Consider that most young children do not initiate learning grammar on their own. Grammar rules and skills are something that adults introduce into their lives. Grammar skills are necessary tools; therefore, they are a required element in a child's education. Of course, any given classroom has a wide range of student aptitudes for learning grammar. Some children absorb rules of grammar easily. Some students struggle to grasp the concepts. Regardless of aptitude within a given classroom, the concept must be presented. In this example, our objective is *proficient contraction-makers.*

Teacher A presents examples on the board. She writes the words *is* and *not*, and then writes the word *isn't*. She offers several such examples to her students. Sara gets this concept right away. Neil, however, sees little use for the skill and has no interest in learning it. Mrs. A continues to present examples. Several of her students enjoy the concept and grasp it right away. They are actively engaged. Neil and many other students, however, struggle. They are bored with this concept. They are busy studying the ceiling tiles. When it comes time to complete the worksheet, Sara is invigorated! She is ready to strut her stuff and blaze through the worksheet. Mrs. A struggles to reteach the lesson to seven of her students who still don't understand, nor do they desire understanding. She walks around the room trying to touch base with each of the seven students who struggle. They are bored with this concept and cannot wait for recess. Meanwhile, the others are finished with their assignment, asking, "What do I do now?"

Consider the resource of time. Given the hour allotted to Mrs. A's classroom, how much more processing power could have been utilized? Had Mrs. A offered various approaches, she would have offered a much more valuable

## CHAPTER 7—TIME AND PROCESSING CAPACITY

experience to each of her students and would not have struggled to convey the concept to each of them.

Miss Erica, realizing the limited resource of time, planned a valuable approach to the concept of contractions, which offered each child in her class a beneficial use of his or her time. She briefly presented the concept using a humorous story of two words becoming one, and then she pulled up *School House Rock* on YouTube. At this point in her lesson, she observes that her students have a slightly heightened interest for this concept. Her students know that an effective activity is around the corner. They have come to enjoy everything Miss Erica hands them, because regardless of the concept, the methods with which she delivers her lessons are engaging. Students love learning new concepts, and they value *aha* moments. Each student knows that at some point within the next few minutes, he or she will grasp this concept at some level and will experience success. Each student knows that he or she will have the opportunity to explore many contractions and will be able to add art and creativity to the ideas. They are eager to understand. They are eager to develop their understanding, because they trust that Miss Erica will allow them to explore the concept from a variety of fun angles.

She presents today's options. Students may choose to draw a contraction factory in which two words enter and one comes out. Students may choose to search through a stack of books for contractions and then present a written list of contractions they find; the list can be presented creatively, in poster form, on sticky notes, or on a collage of construction paper scraps. Students also have the option of working with cards of prepared words—they can find two words that will create a proper contraction and then write them on the whiteboard. Students are welcome to work in pairs or in groups and are welcome to choose their activity. Students are given ample time to explore the concept. Every student in Miss Erica's class is actively engaged. As students become proficient at making and finding contractions, they are welcome to show what they know in a variety of ways. Miss Erica also has a classic worksheet available, as some students love classic worksheets. She will accept student posters and lists as presentation of proficiency, and she offers extensions to those who wish to go further.

During this lesson, at no time was a student bored, despondent, struggling, or wasting his or her valuable time. The concept of contractions infiltrated every student at some level. Each child was able to feel success within the lesson's objectives. Many of Miss Erica's students will need more practice with this concept; many of them have already reached proficiency. Regardless of where each student ended up at the end of the lesson, each made progress and no time was wasted.

Students in Miss Erica's class enjoy an almost constant state of engagement and use of brain power. They spend almost

## CHAPTER 7—TIME AND PROCESSING CAPACITY

every academic moment enhancing processing power in some form or another. They are energized with feelings of productivity, and each feels capable and smart, as if he or she has the power to learn anything—and they do.

We must give every child the chance to learn how to create and use contractions. To accomplish our objective, our methods must be engaging. And to engage every learner, our methods must be varied. Our approaches must offer an appealing option to every student. How many adults today would grasp rules of grammar more appropriately if they had been fully engaged in their youth?

We need to begin to see everything a child does when he or she is engaged as valuable. Even if the concept does not sink in fully, the child has attached at some level if engaged. If disengaged, a child will not only miss the concept completely but will spend cognitive capacity elsewhere during that particular moment in time. *Because learning itself is innately engaging, it is conceivable that a child could spend her or his entire school career feeling no boredom, wasting very little time.*

Cognitive neuroscience studies support active engagement in school settings. Studies show that active engagement is linked to increased motivation and achievement, productivity, a sense that learning is rewarding, competence, self-determination, persistence, satisfaction, greater attention span, increased willingness to learn, and intrinsic motivation (Sousa & Tomlinson, 2011). Boredom, on the other hand, is linked to ailments, listlessness, fatigue, depression, anxiety, loneliness, hostility, aggression, impulsivity, destructive behaviors, vanity, self-absorption, and lowered work performance (Koo, 2011).

Any parent or teacher knows the detriments and misery of boredom in a child's day. How do children themselves feel about boredom? I asked a group of children how it feels to be bored:

*"When I am bored I can't think. It makes me feel empty or like a piece of me is missing."*

—Millie Murray, age nine

*"Like a crushing sense of emptiness has infested and taken over your life."*

—Dakota Lock, age fifteen

*"When I'm bored, I feel all alone."*

—Peyton Utt, age four

## CHAPTER 7—TIME AND PROCESSING CAPACITY

*"Generally I'm hot when I'm bored and I feel a little bit sick. It feels like you've got melted rubber in you. Like saggy, droopy, blehh."*

—Sam Burt, age thirteen

*"It feels kind of irritating and it makes you feel lazy. It makes you feel unsatisfied. It shuts off your drive."*

—Emma Burt, age fifteen

*"I feel angry because I feel there is nothing to do."*

—Ruby Houghton, age ten

*"My brain is tired."*

—Garth Shanklin, age eight

*"Boredom is that state of mind when all you have left to do is clean your room."*

—Natasha Cowger, age twelve

## ORSCH...CUTTING THE EDGE IN EDUCATION

Is it possible that we actually create learning delays? If schools offer moments of despondency, disengagement, and boredom for young minds, are they partly responsible for a lack of cognitive functioning? Are some of our schools responsible for missed opportunities of active cognitive functioning? Is it possible that they create complacency?

Given the multitude of engaging options teachers can offer and the benefits therein, there is absolutely no reason that we should waste the cognitive moments of our students. Time is a resource. Processing capacity is a resource. We can use time to enhance cognitive functioning or we can use time to allow disengagement.

A school's most important mission is to educate its students. Given that students would not choose boredom and that engaging methods exist, are easy to implement, and bring harmony to classrooms, schools and teachers have no excuse for bored students. Too often schools and classrooms spend gross amounts of time trying to hammer in basic skills with no real engagement from students. Students will naturally pick up the basics—the items in the carts—because they are thinkers. They'll either know them or source them—they will not let basics stop them. *They are thinkers.*

In addition to engaging lessons and activities, there are many other valuable uses of time that public education must offer its students. The following elements utilize time and processing capacity effectively and are essential elements of a high-quality education.

## *Aha Moments, Exploration, and Self-Discovery*

When a child learns a new concept or skill he experiences an *"aha"* moment. *Aha* moments are obvious. They are accompanied by a smile, excitement, and a quest for deeper understanding or practice. For example, when a child first learns how to regroup in subtraction (a.k.a. "carry" or "borrow"), she shows excitement, making comments such as "I get it," and "Oh, that's fun—can I do another one?" The mere comprehension of a concept seems to be intrinsically motivating. The development of a new skill seems to be intrinsically motivating.

Think of a child who has just learned to dribble a soccer ball. He may spend hours on the field practicing and perfecting his new skill. A child will spend immense amounts of time drilling skills that are relevant and appropriate: cartwheels performed over and over again until they are smooth, video games, blowing bubblegum bubbles, Sudoku, puzzles, yo-yo tricks, hopscotch—you name it. Children genuinely like developing new skills. Their academic lives are no different. *Aha* moments are motivating and inspiring all on their own. Perfecting an academic skill is just as rewarding as learning to dribble a ball. We have found that as long as the academic skill presents itself as an authentic *aha*, students respond with zeal and desire practice of such skill—consider Amelia from Chapter 4.

Every *aha* moment is extremely important in a child's academic life. It communicates to her that she is capable of learning. The more moments like this, the more she believes she is a competent learner. *Aha* moments are more important than knowledge acquisition or rote memorization. We are finding that knowledge acquisition and rote memorization of necessary information comes fairly naturally in actively engaged students. Remember that excitement for learning is the horse and basic concepts are the cart. If we neglect the excitement for learning in favor of knowledge acquisition, we put the cart before the horse. When the cart comes before the horse, we often eliminate zest for learning.

Equally important to *aha* moments is time for exploration and self-discovery. As I mentioned earlier, children are natural learners who observe and reflect on their world constantly. Children investigate new textures and tastes, sights, sounds, feelings, and knowledge. They examine the way things fit together and interact with the natural world. They are natural investigators; they are naturally curious and inquisitive; they seek understanding. Children build conclusions and important revelations about their natural world when we allow them to investigate on their own. And in addition to building important conclusions and revelations, when they are given adequate time for exploration and

## CHAPTER 7—TIME AND PROCESSING CAPACITY

self-discovery, they learn that they are resourceful, capable learners who have ownership in the connections they make.

Sometimes adults need to resist the urge to teach a child every step and point out every conclusion. For example, we have an electrical circuit board kit in our school. It is wildly popular. It comes with instructions for building circuits to power lightbulbs and electronic sounds. Students gravitate toward this kit, not because of the end product, not because they are intent upon learning the ins and outs of electricity, but because they can explore and discover on their own. I don't think the instruction booklet has been cracked open, but each conducting snap, each wire, each cool trinket within the kit has had its share of building connections while teaching students how electricity works. I remember learning about electricity in fifth grade. I learned about conductors and circuit connections, but I didn't get to discover or draw conclusions on my own. I remember pictures in a textbook of kids connecting lightbulbs to the ends of wires. It looked fun. I remember wishing I could be one of the kids in the textbook. Now, I get the joy of overhearing many *aha* moments when a circuit is complete and the kit's lightbulb turns on.

Many good science kits and science instructors offer experiential and hands-on approaches to their students during units of study, but the results that come from allowing open-ended exploration and self-discovery are potentially even more valuable than specific instruction of the same material. I'm quite sure that the students who gravitate toward the circuit board kit develop an understanding about the flow of electric current. They understand exactly how a switch operates and what materials do and do not conduct electricity. When they land in an upper-level science class that delves deeper into that material, they will have an authentic basic understanding and a heightened interest.

Wooden blocks are common in preschool classrooms and even in some kindergarten classrooms. However, students as old as thirteen and fourteen still play with blocks if they are available. They test the limits of engineering and design. They build ramps and bridges and play with the physics involved. They challenge themselves and their peers to create interesting or useful designs. Recently some of our students began bringing matchbox cars—for weeks a group of boys got to school early enough to have adequate building time. Every day, the entire collection of blocks was turned into a city with highways and ramps and bridges. They crammed in as much playtime as possible each morning—building, balancing, and creating structures. Their structures were purposeful, and the skills and knowledge they concurrently developed about engineering will serve them for a lifetime.

Children who are encouraged to explore and investigate become quite resourceful and purposeful in seeking knowledge. Whether they are observing erosion in a sandbox or looking up the answer to "Why is the sky blue?" children are confident accessing and analyzing information of various types. They are eager to satisfy their innate curiosity

## CHAPTER 7—TIME AND PROCESSING CAPACITY

and feel empowered when they have the skills to find information on their own. Children should be given much more time for open-ended exploration and investigation of their natural world. In doing so, they become actively engaged and gain understanding that we couldn't hope to offer from a textbook or a teacher-led lesson.

### *Imagination and Creative Fulfillment*

Most children are very imaginative. *All* children are creative. Imagination leads to new thought and new thinking skills; it is inventive. Creativity is easily accessible in children, and if present in an educational setting, creativity flourishes in all students. Creativity is a significant piece of Orsch philosophy and an invaluable use of students' time. Time to be creative and imaginative should be offered to students, but imagination and creative fulfillment can also be interwoven into a student's day in a multitude of ways, requiring no additional time. Our observations and approach to creativity are explained in greater detail in Section Two.

Twenty years ago, imaginative play used to be a significant portion of a kindergartner's day. Imaginative play has been replaced with academics in kindergarten classrooms across America. Instead of playing dress-up and superheroes, students drill sight words. I can assure you that a young child is not fully engaged while drilling sight words. Drilling letter symbols is not naturally engaging to most young children. Children need time to indulge in imaginative play and imaginative thinking. Consider that Finland, well known for its successful educational system, does not send children to school until the age of seven. Is it possible that their system that allows students to foster imaginative play and socialization in their early years leads to broader and more effective thinking in later school-aged years?

When we consider the resources of time and processing capacity, we must consider the decisions we make for young minds. Time for imagination and creativity is naturally engaging to children; their minds are active and purposeful in these moments—an excellent use of processing capacity.

In addition to the value we have seen by offering time for imagination and creativity, Orsch has learned that these elements themselves add motivation and engagement to a student's school life in general. Students who have been allowed adequate time to think creatively seem more fulfilled and content throughout some of the inevitable mundane tasks within a school day. Is creativity a sort of fuel for the brain, a fuel for motivation? We are beginning to see its exceptional value.

## *New Experiences*

Offering new experiences to children is an extremely valuable use of time. New experiences stimulate a child's brain, build new synapses, and enlighten children to new interests

CHAPTER 7—TIME AND PROCESSING CAPACITY

and curiosities. A child who visits a fire station may be suddenly more interested in learning about fighting fires. A class field trip to a local archeology dig may ignite a budding scientist. Ooblek play (cornstarch and water) leads to discovery of non-Newtonian fluids and to a genuine experience of the natural world. The more experiences we can offer students, the more likely they will discover or develop interests and engage in deeper learning. Again, it is a valuable use of time and processing capacity.

## *Collaboration, Socialization, and Friendship*

Social time in traditional school environments is awarded little emphasis. Too often, children are asked to sit quietly and to stop interacting with each other. We miss valuable moments for social development by asking children to halt interaction. Children throughout modern history have been passing notes to each other in class. Students are social beings who desire peer interaction. And, in addition to developing essential social skills, schools can actually utilize student desire for peer interaction to facilitate engagement in the learning process. To develop the skill, obviously we must allot an adequate amount of students' time to it.

Typically, students are given time to socialize at lunch and at recess. However, students need much more time than lunch and recess to develop good interactive skills. They also need varied settings and situations to develop adequate social skills. Students often need adult guidance in social situations. School years are formative years that require lots of adult wisdom to help children maneuver through the nuances of friendships, behaviors, and attitudes they encounter daily.

Social time during a school day can come in many formats—group work, partner projects, group discussion, and time to work on choice activities without the restrictions of time, noise level, and space. Student conversation thrives when students are busy and purposeful with their hands while allowed to interact. For example, students can gather all the information and pictures necessary to create a collage about East Africa and then spend an hour cutting and pasting together. They tend to chat incessantly when their hands are busy and their brains are free. Peer interaction flows; children actively listen to each other and participate in lively conversation. Busy hands with free minds that are allowed to interact should be an element of every child's school week. Grouping opportunities should be varied and dynamic, allowing students to experience interaction with a mixture of personalities and abilities. Open-ended discussions allow students to participate in purposeful discourse, developing good discussion skills—the more students interact, the more comfortable and skilled they become. Such skills take time to develop.

Friendships and social acceptance are extremely important aspects of a child's life. As mentioned in Chapter 6, "Bullies," the desire for social acceptance is a very high priority and affects a child's well-being. Friendships take time and skill, like anything else of value in our lives. Children

## CHAPTER 7—TIME AND PROCESSING CAPACITY

who are offered guidance in this realm from a caring adult have the opportunity to learn how to manage peer interactions and friendship trouble much more effectively than children who are left to these lessons on their own.

Students need to feel they are safe within the social aspects of their lives. If teachers offer appropriate guidance and help students with strategies, children feel safe, supported, and armed with effective social skills. Taking the time to help two girls work out a playground misunderstanding instead of shoving them back into class feeling hurtful is time well spent—troubled little minds are much less able to focus and much less able to absorb learning. Students who have the support of adults in their lives for social issues quickly develop good social problem-solving skills on their own. Alli, Yolanda, and Amy are a group of wonderful little fifth-grade girls. They are energetic, lively, friendly, and fun. They are the best of friends; they are the…not so best of friends. They spent most of last school year in a phase of pure friendship bliss, but occasionally, they had some significant trouble. Knowing the support was available, they sought help from their teachers. Throughout the year, several small "friendship meetings" were called. A friendship meeting usually involves a teacher, the students who need guidance, and a few moments to hear each other out, offer apologies and hugs, ideas and strategies, and then everyone moves on—with improved skill and no sadness. Late in the school year, I found a child-made poster behind a door (accessible to students who knew it was there). It was named the *Peace Chart*. It was a tool for Alli, Yolanda, and

Amy. Each time they recognized that they needed to be more accepting or loving toward one another, they added a sticker to the chart. They came up with this on their own—no adult helped them with this system. They had become self-sufficient in solving their friendship problems. The guidance and support they were offered led to increased ability to manage on their own—a skill and a confidence that will serve them throughout their lives.

As discussed in Chapter 9, "Essential Skills," collaboration skills are among the most important skills we can offer students. *Two heads are better than one.* Several heads are better than two. And the ability to effectively interact toward a specific purpose will serve students, industry, progress, humanity, and our future. Students must be given adequate time and extensive opportunities for collaborative situations of all kinds. There is no shortage of strategies and ideas to get kids interacting. There is, however, a gross shortage of time and processing power allotted to such skills in a traditional school setting.

Time is perhaps the most finite resource we have. Once it is gone, we cannot get it back. We must use it wisely. In addition to all of the important uses of time illustrated above, students still need downtime and time for freedom of thought. They need adequate time to develop personal thoughts and to form their own opinions. They need time to read independently. They need time to absorb the outdoors

## CHAPTER 7—TIME AND PROCESSING CAPACITY

and engage in nature. They need time for exercise and eating well. They need time to accomplish projects and independent work. They need time to socialize unencumbered and time for unencumbered fun. Given all of the important uses for a child's time, how can we justify ever subjecting him or her to ineffective uses of time?

Finally, optimal use of processing power requires immense amounts of energy for students. Rest, rejuvenation, and balance are required for optimal use of school time. Students who have had a productive and engaging morning can be visibly exhausted and desperately hungry by lunch. We know that the more intensely they have focused and the more actively engaged they have been, the more they will eat for lunch and the longer they prefer to read silently on cozy beanbags.

Although students in highly effective educational programs undergo intense utilization of their time and end up exhausted and hungry, they are *content*. One of the most common pieces of feedback we receive from parents is that their home lives improve when their children enter Orsch. Students may be showing signs of cerebral fulfillment and satisfaction that last throughout the evening. They enjoy the downtime away from school. They process the day's events—most of our students are eager to tell their parents details about their day. And because we do not require homework, students return to school rejuvenated, ready to learn more, experience more, grow and thrive—ready to dedicate their moments to optimal use of time and processing power day after day.

## Chapter 8—A Different View of Parent Involvement and Homework

Parents, like children, come in all sorts of shapes, sizes, and approaches. Some parents walk their children to the school door every day. Some shove their kids out the car door without a second thought. Some are in the know about each and every detail of their child's school day, participating, engaging, and staying connected. Some trust a school to be doing what it needs to do without input or involvement. And some really don't have an interest in their child's education at all. That is OK. It is reality—we must work within it. And within that reality, an optimal parent-school relationship is attainable.

*Accommodating for each individual is easier than trying to make all of them the same.*

Parents are busy people. Parents are doing their best and ultimately *want* the best for their children, even when they don't know how to provide it. A school's job is to educate its students and care for them. A school should be looking out for each and every student and should have each student's best interest at heart. If each element of the above is doing its job effectively—a parent supporting and inviting what is best for his or her child, and the school having a child's best interest at heart—then harmony emerges.

Parent *involvement* comes in all shapes, sizes, and approaches as well. It is the school's responsibility to accommodate. A school, public or private, charter or home-based, provides a service. For a school to *expect* a service from its parents in return is unreasonable. *Accepting* parents who want to be involved is wonderful—*expecting* involvement from those who don't choose involvement naturally won't offer positive outcomes but will serve to frustrate school, child, and parent.

Research says that parent involvement is among the most significant differences leading to successful students.[25] Yes, for the fortunate children whose parents choose to be involved—yes. The movement toward increasing parent involvement is strong. Logically, one would think that if parent involvement increases student success in schools, then we must get parents involved to increase student success. However, this is a flawed argument, because so many factors are overlooked. A clear correlation exists, but if we closely examine the cause and effect side of parent involvement, we will likely determine that our efforts to force involvement will not lead to increased success in students.

Involved parents have successful students for many reasons. Parents who are involved in a classic sense have likely played a significant role in their child's development since

## CHAPTER 8—A DIFFERENT VIEW OF PARENT INVOLVEMENT AND HOMEWORK

day one, including healthy meals, positive interaction, plenty of attention, and academic support, such as reading to them from an early age. Children from such homes have an obvious advantage. If education is valued in a home, the child is primed and conditioned to care about his education. Statistics may show that increased parent involvement correlates with increased student success, but statistics cannot claim success in forcing parent involvement, nor can they claim that convincing otherwise uninvolved parents to help with homework or show up at Parent Night will lead to student success.

Schools do not stand to significantly change a child's home life or parental habits, nor should they attempt to change these elements. Public education was founded on the principle that our country would educate its youth, regardless of home life. Now we blame a child's home life and family's level of involvement for his or her poor performance? It is a school's job to nurture and educate its students, regardless of home life.

Too often, "parent involvement" takes the form of homework or home-based assignments. The children who have supportive homework environments do well with this setting. But for the many students whose parents do not naturally interact well when it comes to involvement in homework, consider:

- Does a school realistically stand to change parental homework habits in a positive manner?

- In a difficult family structure, do we expect homework to bring harmony and success? Or is such a requirement more likely to lead to added frustration and negative interactions within a family?

And if a child has no school-related support at home, should we give up on him at school, write him off, or blame the parents? This seems ridiculous, but it happens on a regular basis. A student who has little academic support at home *must* find it at school. It is the school's job to inspire, build good work habits, engage, and develop skill in its students, regardless of a parent's role.

Often a struggling student will be given homework assignments in an attempt to "catch him up." When this fails, a parent meeting is called, and parents reluctantly come to the meeting. After the meeting, a good old-fashioned scolding follows—parents who are not innately inclined to be involved are not likely to take personal responsibility for their child's lack of performance, nor do they necessarily know how. Asking for more parent involvement in such a situation is like asking the sun not to set.

## *Observing the Spectrum of Parent Involvement*

Because parents come in as many forms as students themselves, schools are exposed to a wide array of approaches to involvement.

## CHAPTER 8—A DIFFERENT VIEW OF PARENT INVOLVEMENT AND HOMEWORK

Hyper-involved parents e-mail or call a school or teacher on a regular basis. They sense or hear of the slightest issue and are, as Jim Fay, author of *Parenting with Love and Logic*, would say, "Helicopter Parents"—hovering over every situation, ready to save the day (Fay, 1990). Hyper-involved parents are often present at school watching over their child's teachers and peers. They offer a sense of mistrust in their child and in the school itself. Hyper-involved parents cause more damage than good. Their intentions are good, but their behavior is detrimental.

Parents on the other end of the spectrum have little involvement in their child's day. Uninvolved parents do not have any connection with a child's school life; they find no value in their personal involvement with school issues or day-to-day operations, nor do they desire involvement.

Most parents fall somewhere between these extreme examples. Most parents have some interest in their child's day but trust a school to provide appropriate programming. Most parents wait patiently for parent-teacher conferences to learn of their child's performance in school. They bring cupcakes occasionally and attend school performances. They ask, "How was your day?" and "What did you learn?" to which children answer, "Fine" and "Nothing." And then they carry on about their duties of homework and signing permission slips. In a traditional setting, it works…for the most part.

But it can get better. And it is the school's job to create a culture in which parents are part of the team. Even though a school has little to no control over a parent's tendencies for involvement, it is the school's job to set up an effective system for *optimal parent involvement.*

## *A Different Approach to Optimal Parent Involvement*

What does optimal parent involvement look like? Optimal involvement includes accepting a family's preferences for the level of involvement they wish to offer, and optimal involvement includes excellent avenues of communication between school and home. Orsch parents are invited to be a part of their child's education at whatever level they would like to be involved. We have some very involved parents, but not because they are forced to do homework or come to bake sales. We also have some very absent parents—parents who value their child's education immensely but trust us to teach their children without their involvement. All parental approaches can work positively toward the best outcome for their children.

Last school year, a parent sent me an e-mail that reached me instantly on my phone (I love today's effective and efficient communication). She wrote, "I'm concerned about Harold's reading." I dropped what I was doing to do a brief assessment on him, find out what books he was choosing, interview him about his reading habits, and have a conversation about it. I was able to call her back in twenty minutes with a great deal of information and insight. We found

## CHAPTER 8—A DIFFERENT VIEW OF PARENT INVOLVEMENT AND HOMEWORK

some appropriate and engaging books, and his love for reading was instantly rejuvenated. Although this may seem a "hovering" interaction at first glance, it is not. This parent observed and sensed that something wasn't optimal. She knows that access to her child's teachers is encouraged. Solutions were in place within minutes. Had she wondered and worried for several weeks or let it build and fester until conferences, Harold would have wasted valuable time. He is now engaged in just the right book series and happily reading. A teacher is generally doing his or her best to accommodate and offer an individualized approach to every student, but often it is a parent who sees a change or senses an imbalance first in the child. And finding effective solutions in good time is far more effective than allowing bad habits or problems to take hold.

I am fond of another story as well. I received an e-mail from a child's mom that explained she had had a difficult morning. The child's mom felt terrible; she had responded with a lack of patience and then sent her daughter off to school. She hoped I would relay the message to her daughter that she was sorry and that she loved her. I was able to show the e-mail to the student and let her write back, and then both mom and daughter felt much better, likely leading to a more productive day.

The traditional approach to parent communication about each individual child is to hold parent-teacher conferences twice per year. It seems ludicrous to me to wait several months to communicate a concern or touch base. Children develop and change so quickly. To miss even a week of a child's life where a solution to a problem could be put in place is detrimental to good programming.

Regardless of how many cupcakes or volunteer classroom hours a parent offers, it is his or her involvement in the child's well-being that matters most. If a parent knows that he or she can ask for input, offer input, and generally feel a part of the team, he or she will be involved at an optimal level. The child will come to appreciate the open communication as well and will learn that communication is the key to a harmonious existence in school.

Establishing a culture in which open communication is the optimal parent involvement scenario is beneficial to the school community as a whole. A successful communicative culture offers many benefits, including but not limited to:

- A teacher's confidence. If a teacher trusts that when a problem exists or a student or parent is not content, the parent will make contact, then she or he can trust that the default is "things are good." This confidence is encouraging and motivating to a teacher.

- A sense of ownership and trust from the parent. If parents know that their input is valued, they are confident to offer it. Information leads to understanding—understanding leads to all things good.

And parents feel confident that their children are getting the most out of their days.

- New ideas flow freely. Our program has gained so much insight from parents. Parents are creative as well, and they know their children better than anyone else. They often have important ideas about the direction of a program or a fun twist on an assignment. It is wonderful to implement ideas from a broad range of perspectives and backgrounds.

- Progress, progress, progress. We are a team, each of us looking to improve even the good stuff, and parents are included in the constant evolution of their child's education.

In addition to establishing a culture of communication, it is the school's job to value parents' perspectives. A school that understands that each parent is as unique as each child will gain positive insight into its students' needs. Parents should feel free to express even the smallest of observations, concerns, and preferences for their children. Parents should also feel free to leave it all up to the school if that is the approach that fits them best. Orsch has parents of both types. We have a beautiful mix of parents who are a key part of paradigm development and parents who are completely content, needing no other input or consultation. Allowing parents to be as involved as they see fit is the only route to a harmonious relationship between school and home.

## ORSCH...CUTTING THE EDGE IN EDUCATION

I have learned, however, that it takes diligent effort to convince parents that we value their input. They are accustomed to a more traditional, hands-off approach. We continue to ask for feedback and encourage open communication, and they are slowly becoming more comfortable with the idea. Concurrently, our program continues to improve and individualization for each family continues to improve.

Additionally, we have found that many very involved parents become less and less involved as they feel content with their children's environment. Less involvement in these cases does not translate to diminished student performance or less success in school. The more content their children are in school, the more a family trusts the school environment; therefore, they are less involved in day-to-day operations.

We have also found that most of our students talk incessantly about school when their parents pick them up. They are so thrilled about the day's activities or an ongoing project that they can't wait to inform their parents. Because we do not require homework, families are able to enjoy each other at home. Students run through the door invigorated, content, and happy. Parents need nothing more. They have an evening full of family time and conversation. As a parent of such an environment myself, I can attest to the fact that our home life is a joy. I have fulfilled children who tell me detail after detail about their day, and I do not need to force homework time. I can allow them to enjoy time off to rejuvenate and spend quality time with me and their dad.

## *The Homework Discussion*

Our traditional educational system sends work home with students for ten to eleven years, and then these students spend their adult lives trying to learn how *not* to bring work home with them. Some traditional educational environments allow students to waste immense amounts of time during their school day and then make up the schoolwork at home. Some educational environments feel they cannot cram in enough material during the school day; therefore, work must be done at home. And much of the time homework is nothing short of busywork that serves no meaningful purpose.

We have some students who choose to work on projects or practice skills at home; self-selected homework and home-based academics are acceptable but are never required. We do not require homework for several reasons. First, our students are engaged and actively participate in brain activity all day long. They need time to rejuvenate throughout the evening. We want fresh, ready-to-go brains during our school day. Secondly, and most importantly, children have busy lives and family time outside of school. Today's students have sports and clubs and events to attend. They get very little time with their families. To require a family to spend its precious evening time on homework asks too much.

Our families have responded very positively to Orsch's homework philosophy. They value their time at home and know that their children are receiving plenty of engaging academics during the day. Students love that they have free evenings. They are more motivated and interested in learning during the day with rested brains. Someday when another school or college requires homework of them, they will learn how to manage. They have effective time-management skills and an excellent work ethic. It will make no difference that they have missed out on learning to manage homework in the evening. They will be happier, more well-rounded individuals for not having spent the majority of their childhood evenings doing busywork.

## *Parent/Teacher Conferences*

Orsch does not offer seasonal parent/teacher conferences. It is our belief that our staff should remain open to communication every day of the year. As needed, parents schedule meetings with us to discuss concerns, current issues, questions pertaining to projects, or to just touch base about their children. In one such parent-initiated meeting last week, I realized, even though I wasn't aware of what she wanted to discuss, that I was there to tell Mrs. Bessinger how wonderful her children are. One of her children had faced a few behavioral challenges this school year. He is learning to keep his need to wrestle and play roughly in check. Each of the teachers with me at the meeting had the same input to offer. With our guidance, the challenges he

## CHAPTER 8—A DIFFERENT VIEW OF PARENT INVOLVEMENT AND HOMEWORK

faces already have solutions in place. He responds well to the guidance we offer, because it comes from a place of understanding and strategy. It struck me in that meeting, that we were telling a parent that her son had grown in maturity, was responding well, and that we believe he will continue to improve in this particular area. Our discussion continued, including aspects such as his determined approach to academics, his tendency to be a perfectionist, his insatiable quest for knowledge, his sister's positive attributes and the few things Mrs. Bessinger would like to see added to her children's academic lives.

Because these types of meetings are now so common for me, I usually don't notice how different they are from the parent/teacher conferences I used to attend for my own children's early years in our community school. These conferences were a scheduled twenty minutes long, and chock full of data. They included graphs about my children's performance compared to district and state norms. They included discussions about areas in which my children needed to improve. One of my children received perfect marks; her conferences were only ten minutes long and ended with polite "thank yous" and handshakes. My other child was less mainstream, less conventional. We had to discuss his day-dreaming nature and his desire to doodle instead of "pay attention." Inevitably, the next scheduled set of impatient parents waited in the hallways while my husband and I nodded our heads, agreeing to help our child "step it up." Uncomfortable moments at best. Where was the positive feedback? Did they know how sweet he was? Did they know he loves space ships and makes up his own knock-knock jokes? Has he shown kindness to others or a desire to use his time wisely?

In the meeting with Mrs. Bessinger, it struck me: Orsch meetings are different. Our objective is unspoken, but never waivers. We aim to communicate to parents all of the progress and all of the positive attributes their children possess. Every child is learning to be his or her best self. Every child makes mistakes. Every child has his own interests, goals, talents, and needs for improvement. Parents trust us to help guide their children positively. Any negative issues have already been directly targeted and communicated to child and parent with strategies in place. It is pure joy to attend a parent meeting in which we know the child well, see direct progress, and can offer plenty of positive and constructive feedback. What if every parent/teacher conference, every school year, focused on student successes rather than comparisons and criticisms?

A school exists to serve its student body; a school should do this to the best of its ability regardless of a child's home life. The school/home relationship can be understanding of individual family needs and it can communicate effectively with authentic, relevant discussions. And the school/home relationship can be more personable, more purposeful, and more productive for all parties involved.

## *Chapter 9—Essential Skills*

The idea of offering students twenty-first century skills has taken hold in conversations both in and out of school environments. With a bit of investigation, one can find multiple lists of twenty-first century skills that our students should be acquiring in their school settings. Generally included in these lists are elements such as critical thinking and problem solving, communication and collaboration, agility and curiosity. It seems our culture, as a whole, is alerted to the essential needs of future generations; however, in the data-driven climate of our current educational system, there is little preparation for such.

Orsch has developed a list of eleven essential skills, many of which are also on the varied lists of twenty-first century skills. Adequate development of these essential life skills should be paramount in an educational setting; schools can successfully create environments in which each is fostered. It takes only strategy to do so. These essential skills are also innate human tools—naturally accessible and easy to develop. Many twenty-first century skills are natural by-products of a dynamic and child-centered program; they do not require specific programming. For example, students are naturally agile and adaptable if their environment allows. They also have a deep sense of curiosity and imagination that flourishes in an exploratory, child-centered environment. Given the opportunity, students love to analyze information and problem-solve on their own without being told to do so. Given freedom, children have innate and genuine creativity.

Schools can develop the following essential skills through deliberate programming structures:

- The ability to make decisions and make valuable choices

- The ability to effectively interact, collaborate, and communicate

- The ability to think creatively, critically, innovatively, and efficiently

- The ability to lead and effectively learn from other leaders

- The ability to engage, experience awareness, and learn

- The ability to discover and develop a good work ethic and self-direction

- The ability to manage time

## CHAPTER 9—ESSENTIAL SKILLS

- o The ability to present effectively and produce high-quality products

- o The ability to effectively resource information and expertise

- o The ability to develop and foster authentic relationships and friendships

- o The ability to have a good time and think positively!

### *The Ability to Make Decisions and Make Valuable Choices*

The ability to make a decision or a choice is a skill. Making a decision requires the collection of data, the consideration of past experiences, and the consideration of future possibilities. It requires independence and confidence in one's own thinking—and it requires practice. Making effective decisions often requires having made some poor ones as well.

The more decisions we face, the more effectively we choose. For most of their school careers, children are told what to do, when to do it, and how it should be done. They are told how to do their assignments and when to line up. They are told how to answer and exactly what is expected. They are told when tasks should be accomplished and how to perfectly label an assignment. The typical American student does not get enough practice making decisions throughout his or her school career, especially in the early days of development. Imagine the growth and development opportunities that are absent from such a system. It is possible to expect and nurture much more from a child, therefore allowing the development of a much more skilled individual.

Schools should create an atmosphere in which students are accustomed to making decisions and absorbing the inevitable lessons. As advocates for the growth and development of children, we must be comfortable allowing them to make mistakes. We need to specifically grant students the authority to make choices throughout their day. A school environment should aim to offer as much self-choice as possible. Using the restroom, choice of seating, choice of paper or writing tool, choice of learning tools and resources, the ability to snack when hungry, drink when thirsty, the chance to converse with others, freedom of movement within the classroom, and even choice of appropriate levels of academics—these are among the hundreds of choices children are capable of making on their own.

Putting responsibilities such as these in students' hands offers many benefits. Students become efficient thinkers, able to make good decisions and valuable choices. When able to make decisions about their learning, students feel a sense of ownership in their education. Students begin to believe in and trust their own thinking. They become brave

## CHAPTER 9—ESSENTIAL SKILLS

about questioning and contemplating the world in general, which leads to better critical thinking skills. In addition, *our effectiveness in assessing, measuring, and categorizing students' abilities and needs pales in comparison to a child's ability to do this for him or herself.* A broader explanation of this strategy is found in Section Two within "The Third Pillar: Variety in Innovative Approaches to Knowledge and Experience." The earlier we can offer young humans the ability to make their own decisions, the better they will do so. Our current educational system grossly underestimates a child's ability to make decisions. Children are capable beings if we allow them to be.

When allowed to make choices and to be respected as competent decision makers, students rise to the occasion. They value freedom and responsibility; rare is the child who challenges such a benefit. Many schools outlaw "nuisance toys" (trading cards and small toys that kids trade and collect) and electronic devices. Consider the contrary: Nuisance toys can be seen as an opportunity to learn and practice responsibility, courtesy, self-management, timing, sharing. It seems illogical to knowingly take away opportunities to learn these valuable skills. Eliminating nuisance toys may be the easy way out in the short-term, but the short-term is not the objective.

Children need ample practice making more important decisions as well. One of the best and most fascinating examples of productive student decision making is in John Hunter's World Peace Game. Hunter created a game in his classroom that gets students thinking about the broader world and multiple perspectives. I encourage you to learn more at www.worldpeacegame.org. Hunter's talk on the World Peace Game was voted the Most Influential TED Talk of 2011. A film *The World Peace Game and Other 4th-Grade Accomplishments*, produced by Rosalia Films and directed by Chris Farina, is available for viewing on a public broadcasting schedule and at scheduled public screenings in major cities. Information is available on their website. In the World Peace Game, John Hunter's fourth-grade students are required to analyze multiple layers of information and deal with world conflict, perspectives, and priorities. The game requires that students make decisions that theoretically affect large populations. They must deal with natural disasters and differing political views. The children lucky enough to have attended Hunter's class will likely make a significant impact throughout their lives because they will know how to make important decisions that affect a world community. They will be among the most highly skilled decision makers, who are able to communicate and collaborate with others literally toward world peace.

The most dangerous result of an environment void of decision-making opportunities is that children who are not competent decision makers quickly adhere to the decisions and opinions of others. They then tend to grow up making decisions based on *affiliation* instead of critical thought. In order to make one's own effective decisions, a person must be skilled and confident in one's own thinking. Decisions that are based on affiliation rather than objective thought

## CHAPTER 9—ESSENTIAL SKILLS

are dangerous. Anyone who is not confident in his or her own thinking may be swayed or convinced too easily, leading to actions and thinking that are not beneficial to the individual or to a group of individuals.

We see the adverse effects of *decisions based on affiliation* every day in the world—political agendas, mass thinking, followers, peer pressure; these are all examples of the detrimental effects of individuals who are accustomed to making decisions based on affiliation to a group or set of ideals. Would we not, instead, prefer that our students become competent and confident thinkers, able to choose their own important ideals that will benefit their own lives and society with objective, critical thought? Would we not prefer that a group of people question each other's thinking so as to avoid dangerous and potentially harmful agendas? How many young lives would have been saved without the group-based decision to get in a car with a drunk driver? How many teenagers would make better choices if they had developed the skill necessary to do so?

Children simply do not have the opportunity to become effective thinkers or decision makers if an authority figure makes the majority of choices for them. Most children do not question authority. They become accustomed to being told what to do by an authority figure from the beginning of their existence. Authority figures are necessary, of course—for obvious reasons. As authority figures of young children, we keep their hands far from hot stoves, and we keep unknowing toddlers from running into the street. However, consider the infamous "terrible twos"—a toddler's first attempts to communicate to others that he is a capable, independent being. The parent who offers no leniency and remains in control of every behavior and action of a strong-minded, independent toddler faces more resistance and experiences the terrible twos more intensely. The parent who establishes a trusting relationship while honoring the toddler's abilities to make many of his or her own choices builds a communicative and healthy relationship while granting the child ample opportunity to practice decision making.

Ultimately, the more a child can choose, the better choice maker he is; the more competent and self-assured, the more he knows himself, his limits, his *element*—"the meeting point between natural aptitude and personal passion" (Robinson, 2009). He develops an intangible sense of ownership. How many of us did not feel a sense of ownership in our own lives until the first semester of college? What more could we have been? What more passion, productivity, and capability could we have experienced and offered the world, had we had the respect and freedom to make more of our own choices?

## *The Ability to Effectively Interact, Collaborate, and Communicate*

Similarly, the ability to effectively interact, collaborate, and communicate are skills for which children—humans in general—need immense amounts of practice. Communication skills are developed through consistent

## CHAPTER 9—ESSENTIAL SKILLS

interaction and feedback from real-world situations. A school setting in which student-to-student interactions are scarce misses valuable opportunities for growth and development. Again, the more practice, the better the skill.

The development of collaborative skills is a crucial piece of any good educational paradigm. Effective grouping options can be utilized to enhance collaborative skills. In the real world each of us belongs to several groups—family, work, social groups, athletic groups. Education should strive to offer students many grouping options. Groups can be teacher arranged or student chosen depending on the project or lesson's objective. School settings need to proficiently and frequently utilize grouping options, such as partnerships, small groups, whole groups, interest-based groups, skill-based groups, and multiage groups; each offers a unique benefit to students.

Multiage groups are probably the most fun grouping option utilized at Orsch. Multiage groups are smaller (five to seven students) and include students of all ages. They are *cooperative groups*[26] that get together to accomplish projects or compete as teams. They collaborate using the skills and talents of each member, even if one of the member's best skill is coloring a poster. These groups offer many benefits to students. They discover leadership. They learn how to make it through frustrating or difficult situations. They become friends with children of all ages. They distribute their duties effectively, just like they'll need to in the real world.

Peer interaction is also shown to benefit students academically. Extensive research has concluded that cooperative learning is an effective tool for students. Cooperative learning leads to increased motivation, more critical-thinking skills, better retention of information, and deeper learning.

> In extensive meta-analyses across hundreds of studies, cooperative arrangements were found superior to either competitive or individualistic structures on a variety of outcome measures, generally showing higher achievement, higher-level reasoning, more frequent generation of new ideas and solutions, and greater transfer of what is learned from one situation to another. (Barkley et al, 2005)

Furthermore, heterogeneous groups of students are shown to develop a deeper understanding and remember more than those in homogeneous groups (Wenzel, 2000).

Many cooperative learning strategies exist in today's wealth of effective educational tools, and schools are beginning to catch on to their appeal and their value. Kagan Publishing and Professional Development produces many styles and formats to enhance interaction in the classroom. Paula Rutherford's book *Instruction for All Students* contains many effective strategies. Schools of today should, without question, utilize cooperative groups in their classrooms daily.

The benefits from a program that focuses on collaborative options for students are many. Students who collaborate

CHAPTER 9—ESSENTIAL SKILLS

on a regular basis are great teammates, able to learn from each other and listen to each other. They develop the ability to objectively consider each other's perspectives. They quickly begin to realize that there are multiple avenues to solutions and that, if they work together, problems are solvable and fun. Communication skills develop rapidly in children when their environment helps facilitate their development. Creative ideas and effective solutions grow rapidly in a well-functioning collaborative group.

Keep in mind that these skills aren't measurable or testable; they are valuable—essential—but are not testable in a standardized format.

## *The Ability to Think Creatively, Critically, Innovatively, and Efficiently*

The ability to think creatively, critically, innovatively, and efficiently is also an essential skill that is given little opportunity to develop in traditional schools. These elements thrive in programs with adequate amounts of independence. At Orsch, we believe we are able to attain them specifically because of our programming structure. An environment in which students collaborate, think for themselves, solve problems, and are confident speaking their minds is an environment that facilitates these essential skills.

Students need *not* be taught how to think creatively—they do it naturally. Students naturally think critically and solve problems as well. They have an innate desire to figure things out and find answers. They have an innate ability to ask questions. They simply need a classroom environment that allows and encourages these skills. When allowed to think, speak their minds, and question naturally, children become efficient thinkers who believe in their own abilities and trust their skills—all the while developing increasingly more mature skills and greater ability. In contrast, students whose days are full of being told what to do and how to do it do not have the luxury of developing these innate skills.

## *The Ability to Lead and Effectively Learn from Other Leaders*

Leadership is a concept that is interwoven into many facets of our culture. Leadership is present in all social circles and in every human setting. Any group of people is made up of a combination of leaders and followers, each person falling somewhere on the broad spectrum of leader to follower at any given point. Leadership in thought, actions, and interactions is an essential skill that will serve children throughout their lives. Likewise, the ability to trust the leadership of others and learn from others is an essential skill.

A leader and a learner exist in each of us. In one situation, we may look to the guidance of others, and in another situation, we may take charge. The leadership qualities and abilities in children are quite fluid; they are learners and experts at the same time. For example, Evan is an excellent leader

## CHAPTER 9—ESSENTIAL SKILLS

when he works with a group of classmates in a craft setting. He knows how to effectively use the glue gun. He knows how to properly put materials away. Others look up to him in this setting. On the other hand, he is not a leader during writing; he must look to others for guidance during portion of his day. Children are natural leaders within settings in which they feel competent and they are natural followers in situations in which they are less experienced.

Children also seem to have an innate tendency to boss others around *instead* of lead when they are the experts; however, there is only one way to develop better skill. The only way to develop good leadership skill in an otherwise bossy child is to expose him or her to leadership opportunities while appropriate guidance from peers and adults is readily available.

Offering variety in group activity leads to leadership discovery and development. When students are exposed to a variety of collaborative projects and opportunities to work with others, they are able to gain insight into the behaviors of their peers. They observe what works and what doesn't. They receive instant feedback from their peers or a teacher about their methods and approaches to communicating with others. They make decisions together. They often disagree and must find a way to work through a problem.

Successful leadership methods become the winning paradigm in each child—they realize a tactic worked, so they try it again. Skill develops. As the makeup of the group changes, group dynamics change; each child has the opportunity to lead in some form or another, depending on the task at hand and the makeup of the group.

An environment that specifically fosters leadership skills will serve a child far more than an environment in which student leadership is accidental or fabricated due to a stifling setting.

## The Ability to Engage, Experience Awareness, and Learn

*Engagement is paramount*—a mantra in our school. A child who is engaged is actively learning and is gaining immeasurable benefits from his experience. In the beginning phases of planning for Orsch, it was the despondent and disinterested look on the faces of students in traditional classrooms that drove me forward. *We have taught them not to listen*, I remember thinking, *because their own minds are so much more interesting*.

In a typical classroom, instructions and lessons are often given multiple times or delivered with monotony. Students who catch on the first time are then subjected to intense boredom while re-experiencing the redundant information. Students who are accustomed to multiple ramblings of the same instructions know that they can disengage for most of a teacher's presentation and then ask questions afterward. This all-too-common approach actually *teaches* them

## CHAPTER 9—ESSENTIAL SKILLS

not to listen. Any child who thinks school is "boring" has undoubtedly been subjected to this element. New knowledge is not boring, nor are interesting instructions leading to meaningful activity.

Engagement is a habit; it is a habit that teachers are directly responsible for fostering or crushing in their students. The student who has become despondent and disengaged has not had the opportunity to develop the skill necessary to pay attention, nor does he have the desire to do so—a catch-22. In contrast, an engaged student has likely been inspired by his teachers with invigorating lessons and activities that are relevant to him and his level of learning.

Similarly, awareness is a skill and a habit. The student who is actively aware enjoys a state of alert ability to learn. All students possess the aptitude to be alert and aware. It is their environment that is to blame for fostering or crushing such aptitude.

The following is food for thought: I have conducted informal interviews with many students who have been officially diagnosed with ADD or ADHD. These students are not hard to find, as diagnosis is a problem that has become rampant in this country. Schools are quick to diagnose students who don't seem to engage properly. First, I have always found it absurd to diagnose a child for an inability to sit quietly, listen for up to six hours, and pay attention to material that is delivered without choice. I'm uncertain why so many school entities think the expectation of *sitting quietly and listening to irrelevant information is normal* and then diagnose the child with a *disorder*. My informal interviews and discussions about this issue have led me to believe that these particular students do not lack the ability to engage at all. On the contrary, it is my conclusion that these children actually have six or more thoughts going on all at one time.

Instead of prescribing a drug to these students, schools should offer strategies, such as music for independent work or something quiet with which to play while listening to a lesson. Innovative environments have found much success adding options for additional brain activity to students who seem to have trouble focusing on only one thing. More research needs to be done; however, experimentation at this level may go a long way in solving the problem without dreaded prescription drugs being given to our children. And what is the long-term plan for these children who have been drugged throughout their young years? Are they to remain on mind-dulling drugs for their adult lives, never having developed the skill to actively engage and find a way to compartmentalize six concurrent thoughts? Have we not missed out on nurturing an otherwise brilliant mind?

## The Ability to Discover and Develop a Good Work Ethic and Be Self-Directed

A good work ethic and the ability to be self-directed are essential skills. Anyone who does not mind hard work, who is

## CHAPTER 9—ESSENTIAL SKILLS

willing to go an extra mile, or who puts in the effort needed to obtain a goal has more opportunity for success. A good work ethic is intrinsically motivating. Some children pitch in and work hard all day long. These kids are eager to take on challenging tasks and meet their goals. These children are, by far, the most satisfied among classmates. They are motivated, cheerful, kind to others—fulfilled. Some children, on the other hand, prefer to do the minimum—they seem to be less exuberant about life in general.

Work ethic is something that seems to come naturally to some but is, without question, a learned skill as well. Orsch students who exhibit a seemingly innate lack of motivation are showing encouraging signs of developing good work ethic. These students may be realizing that they enjoy a bit of hard work and they don't like wasting time.

Yvette and Rachel are two such students. During year two at Orsch, they were very hard to motivate during independent work. Big project due dates would hang over their heads, and they wouldn't do a thing about it. We tried every "help motivate a kid" trick in the book, but neither of them budged. Ultimately, we're not really sure what happened to kick them in gear. Maybe it was the fact that they saw their classmates move on to more fun activities while they were stuck getting the first one finished. Maybe they were extremely tired each day and are getting a bit more rest now. *Maybe it was that they were tired of feeling lazy and despondent.* Regardless of the reason, each of them has had a change of heart. Now we can't stop them—they are two of the most motivated children we have. Each of them is always asking for more and is completely on task and caught up. I don't think they will ever go back to their unmotivated selves. The happiness is evident on their faces and in their interactions. They are deeply satisfied. Somehow, Yvette and Rachel found—in themselves—the desire to work hard.

My best guess is that good work ethic is innately rewarding and laziness brings us down. Yvette and Rachel went from one extreme to the other, but most children are somewhere in the middle of the spectrum, even vacillating on the spectrum day to day, moment to moment. Some activities, times of day, and learning situations are simply more motivating than others for each individual student.

Even though Orsch offers ample opportunity for independent choice and freedom, children are not permitted to waste time or shirk responsibility. We know the importance of work ethic and the ability to persevere under pressure. We do our best to create an environment in which students are driven intrinsically. So, when Yvette would not respond and when Rachel would not respond, we were lost. We made small strides and got them through with sticker charts, rewards, and some good one-on-one, but we were not satisfied. Rachel and Yvette were not intrinsically motivated to work independently, and we could not figure out why. We still don't know why, but they are motivated now. In a traditional environment, they would have done the minimum each year and received the assignments and homework that everyone else received. They would then be

## CHAPTER 9—ESSENTIAL SKILLS

graded on their performance—compared to the others in their classes. Report cards and teacher conferences would reveal lack of motivation and concern. Had they continued year after year receiving mediocre marks and getting away with the minimum, they would not have realized a better world was possible. But it is my guess that because Yvette and Rachel had the chance to struggle through in a real-world situation, paying authentic consequences (not feeling good about their actions and choices), they were able to make the independent choice to adopt good work ethic and drive. I am grateful that they did not have to wait until they graduated from high school or until adulthood to recognize that a good work ethic is something they want for themselves.

In the real world, adults face deadlines and stressful moments. We have to be able to perform under schedules and pressures. We must be able to overcome adversity and lack of motivation. We must be able to work hard and push ourselves, but it is best if we learn to enjoy working hard—to feel motivated inside. Children who are able to make choices about the way they spend their time learn that they prefer the joy of hard work, or at least the joy of the accomplishment that accompanies hard work, rather than feeling despondent and lazy. Some children may take a long time to learn this, but a child's only chance to learn that he will feel better choosing a good work ethic is for him to learn to choose it. If his educational environment crafts every moment for him, then he has no opportunity to learn about his own drive.

Students with little work ethic are not persuaded by grades or scores. They are not motivated by a parent's or a teacher's insistence to work harder or more efficiently. They don't care. They see no reason to try hard. And if their motivation comes entirely from extrinsic reward or from constant nudging from adults, they will be less likely to develop intrinsic motivation that will carry them through life.

## *The Ability to Manage Time*

As any adult knows, time management is an element people juggle throughout their lives. Time is a valuable asset but can easily be wasted or squandered. Students don't realize the value of time until they are able to experience it without minute-by-minute structure. Perhaps even adults would have a more realistic perception of time if we had experienced its reality more fully in childhood. Traditional educational environments that structure a student's entire day to the clock leave little room for a child to learn time-management skills. An environment that allows choice and independence will offer opportunity for students to learn the value of time.

Students are notorious for thinking they have ample time to finish an assignment or to take on a giant project. Angel took on a giant project in May. She set out to write, cast, film, and produce what she titled *Orsch Fairy Tales in Black and White*. She envisioned the successful production of seven classic fairy tales. She worked diligently. She gathered her cowriters and her costumes. She held auditions for

## CHAPTER 9—ESSENTIAL SKILLS

parts. She dreamed of sets with lights and props just right for filming. We enlisted the help of a local college student, thankfully. Angel did pull it off in one month—but she only pulled off one of the fairy tales. The other six lay dormant. Each of us watched and knew. We did not discourage her; she had so much passion—to tell her that the reality of time was against her would have flattened her. Instead, we gently steered her toward finishing one fairy tale at a time. She was pressed and stressed to accomplish the first one and worked diligently to finish before the end of school, but she did it! If we had crafted each moment for her or intervened in her vision, she would not have realized the value of time firsthand. In the end, she was content with her lesson—she even laughed about the grandeur of her original goals. And the adults in her life are thrilled at the outcome. Angel did not fail; she learned the value of time. The next time she takes on a massive project, she will have a slightly more realistic vision of time. She will have improved her time-management skills, maybe spending a bit less time creating costumes and props and more time developing the script.

### *The Ability to Present Effectively and Produce High-Quality Products*

The ability to present effectively and produce high-quality products is a skill children will need throughout their lives, whether they are submitting a scholarship application, a résumé, or a persuasive letter, or presenting a new idea to management or potential clients. Whatever their lines of work, people find themselves in need of presentation skills, yet we spend very little time on them in traditional education. Creating opportunities for presentation skills and individual product quality should be a top objective in today's schools.

Students should have ample opportunity to create high-quality products. Products are used to communicate a student's understanding of concepts and development of skill or knowledge. Products come in many formats—posters, poems, practice sheets, essays, reports, electronic communication, verbal communication—any assignment a student completes is seen as a product. A good program will require that products are done to the child's best ability. Teachers know what their students are capable of producing; they are in direct communication with students about the quality of their work. In Orsch, sloppy, incomplete, or weak products must be redone or corrected; many of our students have had to redo entire projects, because they were capable of better quality. Product quality is an important element of any school experience. If students are expected to present the best of themselves in their assignments, they build good habits, develop better work ethic, devote attention to detail, and establish the ability to create meaningful products.

Opportunities for student presentations are an essential part of any good program and should be offered as often as possible. Students who feel good about themselves and their community are eager to present to their peer group. They love creating and acting out skits. They love reciting or reading to each other. They love to show what they

## CHAPTER 9—ESSENTIAL SKILLS

have created or publicly brag about a great final product. Students especially enjoy creating electronic presentations, such as videos and slide shows. As students become more comfortable presenting, both their personal confidence and presentation quality increases. The more students present and the more high-quality presentations they see from others, the better presenters they will be. Students will greatly benefit from presentation skills and the confidence that accompanies them throughout their lives.

An added benefit to presentation-oriented environments is peer engagement and audience feedback. Students are generally intently interested in a classmate's presentation, especially when the environment has facilitated high-quality products, and especially if the presentation contains creativity and good humor. The results are self-assured students and engaged classmates who are learning from their peers. Students quickly learn that the audience prefers a confident, well-planned presentation and that a giggly, shy, embarrassed approach to a presentation gains no positive reaction from the audience. We now have very few bashful presentations; there were many in the beginning, but the bar has been raised. Students have risen to the occasion.

Students also develop talent when given the opportunity to present. Whether the talent is communicating an idea in a well-made PowerPoint, acting, singing, speaking, or playing a supporting role (to name a few), students are specifically developing their natural talents when given the opportunity to present in front of a group.

## ORSCH...CUTTING THE EDGE IN EDUCATION

Presentations create a wonderful opportunity to speak one's mind. When an entire class or student body is watching the presentation of one child, the child must own his creation and his delivery. Although this can feel risky to a child at first, he quickly comes to enjoy the individual attention and appreciation he receives. In turn, the attention and appreciation offer validation to the presenter, leading to belief in his own thinking and abilities.

*Performances* are a special type of presentation. Students love to take their skills and talents to the stage. Before I knew better, I predicted that a small percentage of our students would be drawn to performing-arts options. I was hoping for a small group of high-performing actors, poets, musicians, comedians. It turns out that about 95 percent of our students yearn for the stage. We have had many student-created original performances, including plays, musicals, talent shows, holiday shows, singing and musical instrument performances, skits, stand-up acts, and high-quality impromptu showing-off moments. In an environment that supports and nurtures an avenue for student performances, students are confident strutting their stuff and continue to create ways to get back on stage. Such confidence is evident in our students—we continue to get comments and positive feedback from our community about the level of performance-based confidence our students exude. Certainly, this confidence and skill will be a lifelong benefit.

CHAPTER 9—ESSENTIAL SKILLS

## *The Ability to Effectively Resource Information and Expertise*

Curiosity is present from the beginning of one's life. Seeking knowledge begins very early. Babies watch, listen, feel, and taste as much as they can, gathering relevant information from the day of their birth. This behavior builds the beginning of a resourceful being. This behavior continues. Every young child I have ever encountered experiences a "why" phase. "Why is the sky blue? Why do I have toes? Why does my puppy bark instead of talk? Why is ice cream cold?" Children are naturally curious. They yearn to put pieces together and build upon known information with new information and new experiences. They are very thoughtful beings and naturally question the world around them.

Resourcefulness is a skill that must be given adequate development throughout life. As children grow, their minds become complicated places, full of questions. The desire to know more can strike a child in an unexpected instant. The more capable he feels seeking answers, the more fulfilled, knowledgeable, and experienced he will be. But what if he is unable to do that for much of his day? I fear that a stifling education has the potential to erase the natural ability to be resourceful. A school day is busy with standards and Common Core, assessments, and the like. There is little time for natural curiosity and independent knowledge-seeking in a typical classroom. And what if a child feels that school is the only place to gain knowledge? Many children feel that after school is time to shut off one's brain, "veg," watch TV, or hit the skate park. A child who is not proficient at seeking information or gaining knowledge on his own will simply avoid doing so.

When my daughter wanted to include a no-handed cartwheel, a.k.a. aerial, in her competitive dance routine, I suggested that she watch YouTube videos, as that is how her brother learned all of his yo-yo skills. She was throwing an aerial three hours later. I didn't need to hire a coach or send her to a class. Definitions, how-to videos, relevant articles, current events—our students live in an era in which they have access to limitless information. Proficiency in finding relevant information on their own and knowing the ins and outs of trustworthy resources versus inaccurate information are essential twenty-first century skills we must offer our students. The more they access information on their own, the more skillful they will be.

Knowledge and experience come from many resources. Sometimes a classroom discussion goes off topic because children are naturally curious about one or two elements a teacher presents. A knowledgeable, effective teacher will allow such a discussion to take place. A rigid educational environment would instead stick to the pacing guide, unable to serve natural curiosities in its students. Asking pertinent questions is a skill that a flexible educational environment will enhance and a hyper-structured environment will squash.

### CHAPTER 9—ESSENTIAL SKILLS

If a child feels proficient seeking knowledge from a variety of resources and experiences, he will naturally do so and will become more and more resourceful throughout his life. In addition, he will likely feel a sense of ownership in self-sought knowledge. It is a school's responsibility to foster this element of a child's education, because "after school" is a different world for every student.

## *The Ability to Develop and Foster Authentic Relationships and Friendships*

A marriage counselor often says, "Good relationships take lots of work." Happily married couples would certainly agree. Good relationships require work. They require skill, and they require time. Skills that foster good relationships include communication and listening skills and the ability to be compassionate and empathetic. All of these extremely important aspects of humanity can be either stifled or enhanced in an educational setting.

In addition, healthy relationships make or break a child's ability to be his or her best. A child who is alone or does not have authentic relationships experiences large amounts of doubt and fear. For an in-depth look at these elements, as well as strategies and structures that help foster relationship skills in a school setting, see Section Two under "The Foundation: A Healthy School Culture."

## The Ability to Have a Good Time and Think Positively!

How much laughter is heard in a typical school building? How many moments of joy? Although school should be a place of productivity, hard work, experience acquisition, and learning, it is all more rewarding and more effective if it includes elements of humor, joy, and positivity. Too often, students are grumpy or mad, sad, bored, or mean. An educational environment that allows humor and specifically inserts moments of joy into students' lives will benefit immensely while, again, building a real-world essential skill and positive-thinking habits.

Humor is a skill that can be improved upon. Isn't it a relief that our children grow out of the knock-knock joke phase? As they grow, their humor becomes more intelligent, if they are allowed to develop their abilities. School is the perfect place to enjoy good humor, as there is always an audience, and it is also the perfect place to learn about appropriate timing and appropriate material. Grown-ups have ample opportunity to help guide their young comedians. A stuffy teacher who allows "no funny business" will stifle this natural tendency in her students. A teacher who recognizes that humor has a place in each of our lives will help nurture and guide this development. Any teacher or school that encourages good humor is no stranger to its benefits.

Joy can be added into the school day in so many different formats. Encouragement, smiles, positive discussions, parties, celebrations, music, and good relationships are all

## CHAPTER 9—ESSENTIAL SKILLS

aspects of a joyful environment. Joy builds people up. Joy is motivating. Joy spreads goodwill and minimizes negative feelings, which are detrimental to groups of people and to productivity in general.

Life throws hardships our way, there is no doubt. Mistakes happen, unexpected events and accidents occur, moods, limited time to do what we want, unpleasant interactions, fear, injuries, sickness—many of these are beyond our control. It is my opinion that a person who experiences very little joy in his or her life will have less armor to withstand life's hardships and that a person filled with joy and happy experiences will weather the storms more easily. Some think that the school of hard knocks is a productive place and that children should deliberately face regular hardship so that they can withstand unexpected tough times. I think that is a recipe for a very unhappy existence. In the face of adversity, a positive outlook and a joyful demeanor will take one much further than having experienced a life of inflicted hardship.

A positive outlook, or optimism, can be a natural tendency in individuals, but it can also be a learned skill, enhanced by one's environment and interactions. Negativity can become a terrible and debilitating habit in children and can be enhanced by an environment that lacks joy and humor. Thinking positively is a skill that can be practiced, modeled, encouraged, and taught. Positive people are creative, upbeat, and proficient problem solvers. Optimists also endure hardship more easily. Think of someone you know who sees the glass half-empty. Is his ability to withstand tough moments better or worse than his half-full counterpart's?

The more skilled our students are in positive thinking and in the ability to have a good time, the more well-rounded and productive they will be, and the more they will be able to withstand life's inevitable ups and downs.

In addition to the essential skill development schools should offer in their programming, it bears repeating that students are naturally agile and adaptable if given the chance. They are innately curious and imaginative—creative and innovative. Children analyze information naturally when given opportunities to think and speak for themselves. All children exhibit innate initiative within subject matter that is in line with their passions and develop initiative within other realms, as they learn that they love learning for the sake of learning and that they enjoy working hard for the sake of working hard.

As educators, we have so much to accomplish—so many purposeful, engaging activities and lessons to offer. A successful school environment must offer ample opportunity to develop essential life skills; to do otherwise is to limit the potential of our youth.

# Section Two- Orsch Philosophy

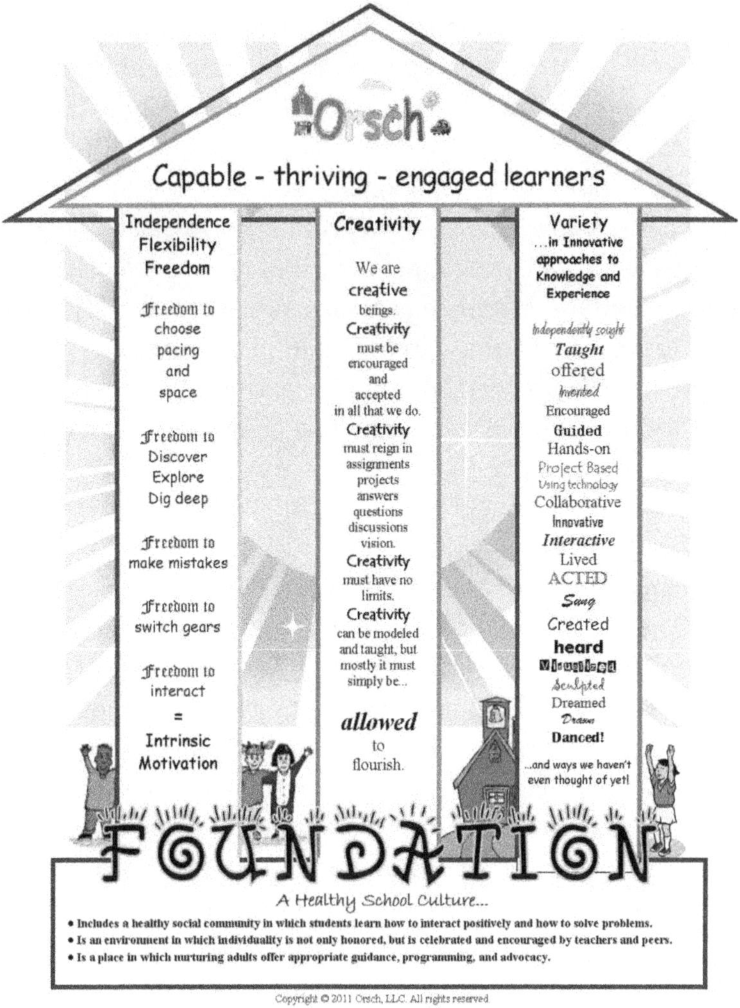

# Orsch

## Capable - thriving - engaged learners

| Independence<br>Flexibility<br>Freedom | Creativity | Variety<br>...in Innovative approaches to Knowledge and Experience |
|---|---|---|
| *Freedom to* choose pacing and space | We are creative beings. **Creativity** must be encouraged and accepted in all that we do. | *Independently sought*<br>*Taught*<br>offered<br>*Invented*<br>Encouraged |
| *Freedom to* Discover Explore Dig deep | **Creativity** must reign in assignments projects answers questions discussions vision. | **Guided**<br>Hands-on<br>Project Based<br>Using technology<br>Collaborative<br>Innovative |
| *Freedom to* make mistakes | **Creativity** must have no limits. | *Interactive*<br>Lived<br>ACTED<br>*Sung* |
| *Freedom to* switch gears | **Creativity** can be modeled and taught, but mostly it must simply be... | Created<br>**heard**<br>Visualized<br>Sculpted |
| *Freedom to* interact | ***allowed*** to flourish. | Dreamed<br>*Drawn*<br>**Danced!** |
| =<br>Intrinsic Motivation | | ...and ways we haven't even thought of yet! |

## FOUNDATION

### A Healthy School Culture...

- Includes a healthy social community in which students learn how to interact positively and how to solve problems.
- Is an environment in which individuality is not only honored, but is celebrated and encouraged by teachers and peers.
- Is a place in which nurturing adults offer appropriate guidance, programming, and advocacy.

Copyright © 2011 Orsch, LLC. All rights reserved

ORSCH...CUTTING THE EDGE IN EDUCATION

# Capable, Thriving, Engaged Learners

*It will take a shift in mind-set, but our objective in education should be to produce capable, thriving, engaged learners, rather than students who simply attain knowledge or pass tests.*

*Capable learners* are confident. They naturally think critically and creatively. They believe in themselves as intelligent beings who can problem-solve, invent, and gain knowledge. They are resourceful and use available tools. They are innovative. They adhere to their interests with fervor, wanting to know more, wanting to grow and develop their skills. *Engaged learners* dig in deep and enjoy their time within a lesson or project. They are hungry for knowledge and excited to be involved in the process of learning. *Thriving learners* encompass everything a true student should. They are curious, eager to learn, comfortable making mistakes. They question. They are comfortable sharing their knowledge. They make choices about their learning and collaborate with others. They are effective thinkers, and they thrive within an innate human desire to learn and grow—whatever the topic or skill may be. They yearn to explore and to discover. They are confident making presentations and communicating important matters. In short, they possess the *essential skills* that will serve them throughout their lifetime.

Capable, thriving, engaged learners show exuberance for life and for learning; they are purposeful and passionate. They are intrinsically motivated and show persistence. They easily connect and communicate with others. They are capable of reaching their academic potential and finding their own passions. They want to develop their own passions and talents. The goal of every educational program should be to produce capable, thriving, engaged learners. These are the students who possess essential skills, will surpass expectations, and will serve a world community that needs them into the future.

Of course, students must know the basics before they can move on to more complex elements of a topic. A top-ranked high school chemistry student must know how to read the periodic table so that he can intelligently combine elements and observe compounds, but does he need to have memorized the periodic table's structure from fifth grade? Or is he better served if he remembers that he learned it easily back in fifth grade and that it interested him back then? The fact that he was inspired, when he was young, to learn how the periodic table was structured led him to desire learning more about this topic. How many more high-level mathematics students would we have if they had been inspired by mathematical concepts at a young age, hooked by their feeling of success at whatever level that was, instead of struggling or waiting for others to meet benchmarks of sameness?

Consider, again, horses and carts. Elementary school is a time to learn that you *can* learn and that learning is valuable and beneficial and innately enjoyable. It is a time to open up to all the possibilities that one's education has to offer.

## ORSCH...CUTTING THE EDGE IN EDUCATION

As I have discussed, *aha* moments are more significant to a child's early education than facts. *I can learn...I like that learnin' feeling...*Such realizations are infinitely more important than simple memorization. The *"I get it"* feeling convinces a child that she can learn anything, leading to confidence and the desire to reach for more.

In elementary school and even into middle school, students need to know they are *capable* of learning the basics, they can learn easily, and they like learning. Herein lies the difference between focusing on mastery too early (requiring proficiency) and genuine inspiration (capable, thriving, engaged learners).

Every student can like math. The reason every student can like math is that each student has the potential to experience the *aha* feeling that is so readily accessible in mathematical concepts. If each student is permitted to learn at her own pace and is given ample flexibility to attain skills by whatever means fits her, she gains skill and knowledge; students enjoy gaining skill and knowledge. Ultimately, students enjoy a given topic or subject simply because they "get it."

In a child's education, necessary facts will be used over and over again and will naturally stick. Spelling rules, word families, math facts, and algorithms that are useful are concepts that will serve students throughout their school years as memorized, permanent knowledge. These concepts become tools—they are in the cart. These facts become part of a student's knowledge base and will serve him throughout life; however, if he has no zeal for learning, no passion for engaging concepts, he will grow weary and disengaged in his education. He will only push his cart so fast, so far, and for so long. It is the freedom to love learning and to aspire for deeper understanding that is the horse. As pointed out in Chapter 4, the horse must go first.

And when it matters, a student must write a professional letter or turn in a perfect paper. Capable students use today's tools to help them reach proficiency. They use spell check and grammar check—these are tools available at their fingertips. They no longer need to have every rule of grammar memorized by the fifth grade.

Because today's teachers are pressured to hammer in specific skills before state tests each year, they don't feel they are able to focus their energy or classroom time building engaged learners. Teachers are pressured to build test takers. Ironically, these same students would perform better if their education had been engaging, if they were capable, thriving learners. And teachers would be happier people too, more engaged in their missions.

Capable, thriving learners love to show what they know. We don't have to wonder if they are learning. They are experts at presenting their knowledge in effective and creative ways and are eager to use skill and knowledge and apply it to real-world situations. Thriving learners are the students who enter essay contests and science fairs. They have meaningful conversations with each other and with adults. They are lively and engaged in important topics. They are vibrant, productive people. The results are obvious—we can assess their performance and their understanding almost by just being around them.

## *Imagine Tomorrow*

Because at Orsch we have a school full of little scholars—children who love learning—it is hard for me to imagine each of them not continuing their quest for more knowledge, more understanding. I predict that, as they grow, these students will yearn for concepts in higher-level math and science, literature, and fine arts. Therefore, I conclude that if we were truly able to create a generation full of capable, thriving, engaged learners, instead of despondent, bored students, in just a few short years, we would not have a shortage of higher-level math and science students. We would have innovative thinkers flooding our high school hallways, ready to indulge in the higher-level education offered to them. They would have retained their zeal for learning new math skills, as new math skills have always been thrilling to learn. And science is fascinating, especially to such students—they will have retained their desire to understand, experiment with, and test the natural world. And because these thriving learners know that they can learn anything and that learning in itself is rewarding, they will seek even more knowledge and more understanding. They will find their passions and find purpose in their education.

## CAPABLE, THRIVING, ENGAGED LEARNERS

And then, hopefully, they will put their passion to work in a valuable career that satisfies and serves.

Consider an environment that met most of students' needs—as many needs as possible. *What Could Be.* If a garden has the right nutrients, it will produce better plants. If an educational setting offers its students the very best in programming and community, it will offer its students the best chance of success during their school years and beyond. If a garden faces harsh environmental elements and limited nutrition, it will produce weak plants, as well as some survivors. Consider the many children who struggle every day to find innate talent, to find the skills that make them feel valuable.

Consider the many children broken down each and every school day by bad grades, lack of engagement, lack of friends, peer pressure, fear, teacher and parental pressure. *What Could Become* of them if they were offered a more nurturing environment every day? Would they find talent? Develop more skill? Learn more easily? Would they step out of expectations and limitations and into possibility?

The following chapters detail how Orsch is able to establish an environment in which our students become capable, thriving, engaged learners. "The Foundation: A Healthy School Culture" explains the foundation in Orsch philosophy. The foundation is the most important aspect of a child's education; it is the jumping-off place from which learning and development take place. "The First Pillar:

Independence, Flexibility, and Freedom" explains how student independence is an essential element in our program. "The Second Pillar: Creativity" illustrates the importance of creativity and the benefits it can offer any educational environment. "The Third Pillar: Variety in Innovative Approaches to Knowledge and Experience" explains how we utilize variety and innovative approaches to realistically meet the needs of all learners.

## *The Foundation: A Healthy School Culture*

Among the most important discoveries we have made at Orsch is the significance of a healthy school culture. A healthy school culture—an environment in which children feel secure—is the foundation of a positive educational program. Students do not feel free to learn if their environment is fearful, stifling, or boring. A successful program will have a culture of acceptance, belonging, and fulfilled freedom in its students. The culture should also contain a vibrant love for learning, a desire to excel, and passion for new experience. The culture Orsch aims to establish is one of positive, productive feelings and natural interactions between students themselves and between students and teachers. The positive effects of a healthy school culture are fully supported in educational neuroscience (Sousa and Tomlinson, 2011).

Emotional security is an essential foundation for each student. Emotional factors directly affect a child's ability to learn. A student must feel emotionally safe and well balanced to absorb academic material at an optimal level. Confidence and a sense of security offer freedom of thought and the ability to focus on a task at hand. Our teachers understand that a secure child is able to collaborate, communicate, and problem-solve much more effectively than a child who is distracted by emotional factors.

As pointed out in the section on test validity and reliability in Chapter 1, consider the number of potential emotional factors a student might face on any given day: the effects of an unsustainable breakfast, a stressful morning with siblings or parents, trouble with friends, insecure feelings stemming from a variety of sources, growth, change in hormonal levels, heavy expectations from adults, uncertainty in general, midday hunger. Learning to operate effectively within these factors is tricky in and of itself and is a reality for all students. Therefore, a school environment that does its best to minimize negative emotional factors will offer a student significant advantages and enhanced opportunities for successful learning.

Several key strategies ensure a secure and healthy foundation at Orsch.

- A healthy social community in which students learn how to interact positively and how to solve problems.

- An environment in which individuality is not only honored, but is celebrated and encouraged by teachers and peers.

- A place in which nurturing adults offer appropriate guidance, programming, and advocacy.

THE FOUNDATION: A HEALTHY SCHOOL CULTURE

## *The First Element of a Secure Foundation: A Healthy Social Community*

Our students make up a true community where they work together, side by side; they honor and care about each other; they support each other; they question each other; they learn from each other; and they teach each other. They feel safe together. Each student feels a deep sense of individuality within this community—each person is honored for who he or she is. Through specific systems and strategies, students learn to interact positively and learn how to solve problems.

Too good to be true? How many times have you heard the phrase, "kids are mean"? Our studies have proven otherwise. Kids are not mean. Kids are kind, gentle, and loving creatures who exude good feelings and mimic kindness if they live within a culture that contains these attributes. But it takes lots of good strategy to set up a culture in which students can be their best and enjoy a community that offers them the best. Kids are "mean" when they feel frustrated, bored, or lack the opportunity to honor their own individuality. Because the Orsch community is family, we laugh at our shortcomings and celebrate funny, silly milestones in each other. When we're all honest about ourselves—our goals and our shortcomings—we can genuinely celebrate our own successes and each other's successes.

We have discovered the power in getting to know each other. In the typical American school, students are shuttled here and there, given lessons, given tasks, and rarely have the opportunity to learn about each other. Students who know each other well benefit from deeper, more meaningful interactions and community. Students who know each other value and respect each other's differences, and exhibit tolerance and appreciation for each person's unique nature. Students who know and appreciate each other build valuable relationships that are a foundation to both collaborative efforts and the freedom to think independently.

Effective strategies for genuine student interaction and community are more in-depth than the typical "get to know you" games of summer camp introductions. A true community develops when students are given ample opportunity for self-expression and peer interactions. The integration of people and differences in perspective becomes fertile ground for ideas and innovation and authentic community.

Affection is also an important part of Orsch's healthy peer community. Young children love to sit in laps and hold hands with their friends. All children love hugs—they hug each other and they hug their teachers. Affection is an innate human need and is especially necessary for young children.

Humor is glue. Orsch students value and express humor at numerous points throughout their day—with their peers and with their teachers. Thankfully, they have come to enjoy and appreciate intelligent humor. Students know that good humor is appreciated by all; they look for it, love it, and benefit greatly from sharing humor with one another and their teachers.

One of the few rules we have at Orsch is: *You may not compare yourself to others*. Students adhere to this rule surprisingly well and don't seem to mind a reminder when they forget. It seems they agree with the rule. They like learning in an environment in which they won't be compared to others, so they respect the rule and try not to break it themselves. Students are encouraged to compare their own behavior and their own progress to themselves. Did *I* improve? Did *I* grow? Did *I* learn? But, "I know more than Johnny," or "I finished in five minutes and it took Nancy ten minutes," are forbidden comments at Orsch—such comments work against a nurturing environment.

Students need adequate social guidance as they learn to effectively interact with their peers. In most typical school environments, students spend most hours in class, in direct instruction, or in targeted academic moments. They are then released onto the playground for their social and play time. They have had very little social guidance and no social training. So the playground too often becomes a *Lord of the Flies* setting where alpha children dominate and omega children cower. Followers follow. Ringleaders lead. Trouble ensues. Children need a great deal of social guidance from adults. They need help solving their social issues and their friendship troubles. They need good strategy, and they need immense amounts of practice if they are to become communicative, well-functioning citizens. Our school offers time in and out of the classroom for positive social interactions and productive adult guidance.

One result of our program that has surprised me is the level of positive group ethics present. Students encourage ethical behavior in each other. They value positive community. They encourage each other to consider the perspectives of others. If anyone is chastised by his or her peers in our school, it is the child who disrupts a class, displays disrespect for a teacher, or acts selfishly. Such behaviors are just not popular or acceptable among our student body; they happen occasionally, of course, but the behaviors don't continue for long. I can only conclude that learning time is precious to our students, and that they value their peers and their teachers, as well as embrace and take ownership over our positive, nurturing environment. As a result, group ethics are solid.

## *The Second Element of a Secure Foundation: An Environment in which Individuality Is Not Only Honored, but Is Celebrated and Encouraged by Teachers and Peers*

A culture where individuality is the norm is much more natural and appropriate for a group of people than a culture of sameness. As we examined in Chapter 3, "Sameness," and in Chapter 6, "Bullies," a school environment that enjoys a community full of individuals realizes its beneficial attributes and can easily see that the culture is one of positive

## THE FOUNDATION: A HEALTHY SCHOOL CULTURE

human interaction and harmony. Allowing individuality to prosper is easy. A school can specifically insert strategies to foster individuality in its students.

As mentioned earlier, the Orsch rule, "You may not compare yourself to others," goes a very long way toward social harmony, and students oblige surprisingly well. In contrast to comparing students is the idea of *contrasting* students. Contrasting students takes some getting used to, especially for students and teachers who have come from an environment of sameness, but the practice is immensely valuable. Contrasting students is an effective way to celebrate differences among them and to highlight individual talent or skill.

Teachers who are allowed the freedom to do so know that they should highlight how each student arrived at a solution differently, as a think tank is better than one method and sharing strategies for problem solving leads to many more solutions. These teachers know they can stand two kids up in the middle of work time to show the entire class the differences between the ways each student approaches the assignment—each is a valued approach. Differences such as these are simple for a teacher to point out and help communicate a culture of individuality. Teachers can also point to and celebrate the differences in learning styles between students. A teacher can say to his class, "Johnny prefers to read the directions on his own. Megan, LuAnn, and Joey can read them as a team. I will work with a group of students who prefers to have the directions read to them."

## ORSCH...CUTTING THE EDGE IN EDUCATION

Last school year at Orsch, students in Miss Erica's class were given an assignment to complete a time line representative of their lives. Students had parameters within which to work but were encouraged to display their time lines however they saw fit. As the time lines began to form, the differences were celebrated and the overall products became more and more unique. One time line was three-dimensional. One was full of googly-eyes. One was decorated with cycloptic farm animals. One had a built-in stand so that it could sit on a desk. One came with fridge magnets—ready to hang the day it reached home. As they were completed, the unique nature of each time line was presented to and celebrated by the class. Each time a student's product was celebrated, individuality was highlighted and appreciated. Each time, a culture of individuality was enhanced.

When teachers point out differences among students' work and differences in students' thinking, they promote independent thinking and increase student confidence. Contrasting students' skills, products, and learning styles publicly is a tool schools and classrooms can use to enhance and celebrate individual differences. In addition to celebrating differences, such practices suggest and encourage high-quality work and creative thinking.

Students feel invigorated when their efforts are highlighted and their differences are honored; they quickly become accustomed to appreciating their own differences and the differences in others. They display obvious pride and fulfillment when their individual talents are recognized, and they show obvious contentment when their individual learning styles are brought to light in the midst of a group. Just one moment of differential recognition in a student's day builds him up, gives him more confidence, and enhances his unique and true sense of self. Consider the culmination of many such moments throughout a week, a month, or a school year. Consider the culmination of these moments in not just one student but in every student over a week, a month, or a school year. And then consider this trend over multiple school years and in hundreds of schools.

Individuality is enhanced when classrooms individualize and differentiate academically, as explained in further detail throughout this section. When students feel free to suggest activities or assignments; when their academic lives and expectations are tailored to their individual needs; when assessment options are varied and appropriate to each individual; when independence, freedom, and creativity reign, each child's sense of individuality is enhanced and his peer group as a whole ceases to be hung up on comparisons to the norm, which divide rather than unite.

Individuality shows up in many places in a thriving social community. Fashion, personality, creativity, brave performance, the ability to step or think outside of the norm, spontaneity, initiative—all these elements are present in our society in general. However, they could be thriving elements of a progressive tomorrow if our young students were immersed in a culture that offered the highest potential for their development. I fear that these attributes are too often only accessible to the *popular*, well-accepted trendsetters. A culture of sameness is not very tolerant of unique personality traits outside of each population's status quo. Many brilliant and creative minds remain hidden or crushed beneath sameness, when instead they could be soaring.

A fundamental belief at our school is that the more a student realizes that she is a unique individual with her own talents, her own attributes, and even her own shortcomings, the more she appreciates her sense of self, accepts herself, and accepts the others around her. And the more a group of people realizes that each member is a unique individual, the more nurturing that group becomes; the more they benefit from and realize *What Could Be*.

## The Third Element of a Secure Foundation: A Place in which Nurturing Adults Offer Appropriate Guidance, Programming, and Advocacy

> *Nurture: 1) To care for and encourage the growth or development of. 2) Cherish (a hope, belief, or ambition)*
>
> —Google 2012

## THE FOUNDATION: A HEALTHY SCHOOL CULTURE

A nurturing teacher puts a child's well-being above a lesson plan. A nurturing teacher senses whether or not his or her lesson is getting through—Is there growth or development? A nurturing teacher believes in his or her students and their ambition. A nurturing teacher cares for his or her students in every realm.

A nurturing teacher is never authoritative. We have discovered that authoritative behavior only stands to alienate a good teacher-student relationship, leading to distrust and an unproductive hierarchy. Authoritative persons in a child's life also create an authoritative nature within the child. Children mimic the behavior they see; children who are immersed in an authoritative environment are bossy and impudent themselves. When authoritative figures enter their worlds, students challenge, rebel, or generally feel discontent. They experience anxiety, and some will feel a need to please, losing some of their confidence and sense of self. Instead of an authoritative approach, a teacher should establish good avenues of communication and mutual respect with students. Many good things come from such a relationship; students show ownership and work toward positive interactions. A student's ability to respect authority is not diminished by relationships founded upon mutual respect; rather, it is enhanced.

A nurturing teacher is never brash. A brash attitude toward a child sends all sorts of confusing messages, leading to a child's lack of confidence in the relationship and ultimately in oneself. Anything a teacher says can be said respectfully—even when a stern approach is necessary for a scolding or doling-out of consequences.

A nurturing teacher is approachable—even in her busiest moments—and recognizes that children are looking to her for guidance and love. She responds respectfully always. She listens to feedback from students. She considers their opinions, and they value and trust her for this. She is there for them when trouble happens on the playground or when their worlds are falling apart. She knows the value of a good relationship with her students and remains someone they can go to for guidance.

A nurturing teacher will be generous with positive feedback and wise with constructive criticism, realizing how motivating the former and how vulnerable the latter. A nurturing teacher is encouraging, sending students the message that they are capable. Nurturing teachers give authentic praise at appropriate times. When a student receives a compliment that is deserved and believable, the feedback may stick for a lifetime, adding to his potential and his belief in his abilities. Teachers can look for sparks of ability and small improvements to offer positive feedback. Positive feedback is powerful to children of any age and is an integral part of a healthy teacher-student relationship.

On the other hand, negative comments can be crushing and have lifelong effects. I recently met with a potential music teacher for Orsch. He can play any instrument. He is a brilliant musician who plays with some of the best in the world.

## THE FOUNDATION: A HEALTHY SCHOOL CULTURE

During his interview, he shared with me that he doesn't prefer to sing, although he does sing in some of his gigs. In the midst of sharing his philosophies and his no-nonsense approach with children, he launched into a story from his childhood. He loved music and was talented from the beginning. However, he had one teacher tell him he was not a good singer. He explained that it was crushing. He never truly believed in his ability to sing from that day forward, even though he is in fact good enough to carry a tune among the famous musicians with whom he plays locally. He focused on other instruments throughout his life and continued his passion for music but committed from that day forth to never saying a negative word to children about their abilities.

A nurturing teacher constantly looks out for the well-being of each student, of groups of students, and of the class as a whole. A nurturing teacher is in touch with his students' needs, whether he needs to stop everything to discuss a social issue or bail on a lesson that is wasting everyone's time. At the risk of altering his plans, he will make decisions that benefit students.

A nurturing teacher will help her students feel joyful. She will add silliness and will appreciate good humor. She will be accepting of creative approaches and new ways of doing things. She will offer a colorful, inviting, comfortable atmosphere.

A nurturing teacher accepts student input. He listens to students' suggestions and considers their perspectives always. He includes their opinions in his approach to their education and is sensitive to their needs. Many studies show that students who are involved in their academic programming respond with ownership in their education and are more motivated to meet academic challenges (Carroll et al., 2009; McQuillan, 2005). Our studies and experience concur with current research. In *Differentiation and the Brain*, Sousa and Tomlinson conclude that "having a voice reinforces [students'] feelings of personal control and responsibility, which are essential ingredients of a positive school climate." A nurturing teacher will specifically seek feedback from individual students and his class as a whole.

A nurturing teacher realizes that social issues are part of human nature; he will be there to guide students through tricky social situations, offering patience, coaching, and support.

And a nurturing teacher loves. She loves with hugs. She loves with smiles. She loves with praise. She offers her lap to little ones and jokes with good humor. She cares deeply—this permeates everything she does—and children love back. Children are strongly motivated by a loving relationship. They feel safe, secure, and are able to take on the world.

A nurturing teacher will create an environment in which no discipline is necessary—only discussions of mutual respect. His environment is engaging and productive—each student is content. Behavioral problems are minimal. Educational neuroscience agrees with our findings and suggests that, "when students take part in meaningful learning experiences their cerebral reward circuits are activated and distracting behaviors are avoided" (Sousa and Tomlinson, 2011).

Nurturing teachers offer their students appropriate programming and appropriate academic guidance. They use the best of differentiation strategies, taking into account their students' level of skill, aptitudes, interest levels, and engagement levels. They adapt their lessons and their programming to fit each student's needs. They use creative and engaging approaches and constantly consider valuable uses of their students' time.

Finally, a nurturing teacher will move his students forward with momentum using his own style. Some teachers are "no-nonsense," some are sweet and sugary, some are all business, some use a comedic approach, and some take a more serious approach—students will benefit from all types of teachers and will gain valuable experience from a variety of personality types, as long as they are truly nurturing to their students.

## *Appropriate Guidance, Programming, and Advocacy*

The more positive experiences we have in our lives, the more we feel good. Good feelings and positive moments help us reach our potential. At Orsch we've learned that a positive environment can be built using a multitude of strategies. In addition to positive teacher and peer interactions, the environment itself should offer positive feelings. Many schools and programs have strategies and systems for establishing positive environments. However, some schools and programs may find themselves entrenched in less flexible, suppressive environments and may not realize how simply a positive environment can be established. Following are some of the strategies and highlights we think are important in establishing a positive environment that includes appropriate guidance, programming, and advocacy.

## *A Yes Culture*

A yes culture is one in which its teachers or leaders try to say yes. It has been my experience that many adults, especially within the realm of dealing with children, respond to requests with a knee-jerk no. Children often think outside of the box and want to do things a little differently. Children are creative beings. They love to try new methods and head down new avenues, so they often ask, "Can I...?" Adults like things orderly and familiar; they aren't as up for new experiences as often as their students are. It takes some training and diligent practice to try to say yes, but a yes culture creates an environment that truly dwells in possibility. Saying "yes" to a student empowers him or her to try new things and to seek new answers. A yes culture is a fun place to work and learn, because everyone feels potential and possibility.

THE FOUNDATION: A HEALTHY SCHOOL CULTURE

## *A Cheerful Environment*

A school should be a cheerful place with smiles and positive, can-do attitudes. When children arrive in the morning, they should be greeted with smiles and should come in contact with teachers who are genuinely happy to see them. Throughout the day, teachers should offer a cheerful, smiling demeanor to students—such interactions will motivate and inspire. If there is a general feeling of exuberance within school walls, school becomes a place where both children and staff want to be. In contrast, if teachers and administration are tense or grumpy, students will feel fearful, tentative, and hesitant.

## *Morning Meeting and Multiage Grouping*

Instead of heading straight to academics, each day at Orsch begins with a multiage meeting. Students of all ages gather in a circle. Many good things come from multiage interaction to begin each day, including modeling, acceptance, differing viewpoints, new interests, and genuine friendships. Multiage grouping options are utilized often, giving all students the ability to interact and collaborate with a wide range of abilities and personalities.

Morning meetings and multiage groups offer positive outcomes due in large part to our youngest members. Tiny Club members and Pints (a.k.a. kindergartners, first- and second-graders) are Orsch's keepers of integrity. Young children speak their minds—and most of the time, they offer genuine humor and adorable comments. They keep us laughing, and they keep us centered. Their ability to display such integrity is contagious to older kids. Older kids honor their little friends and respect their viewpoints with love and acceptance. Such feelings seem to flow over into additional social interactions for older students. Older kids keep in touch with their childlike sides due to interactions with younger kids. Our older students interact with love and nurturing behavior; young children respond positively with the same love and acceptance that they have been offered.

Morning meetings can happen in any classroom, even if classes are not multiage. Any amount of gathering, listening to each other, and sharing with each other will help establish community and camaraderie in a classroom. Single-grade classrooms can also consider offering multiage meetings. Schools can combine two, three, or more grade levels.

*The Morning Meeting Book* by Roxann Kriete (2002) is an excellent resource for schools that want to implement a structured morning meeting. As Kriete explains, "The time one commits to Morning Meeting is an investment which is repaid many times over...Morning Meeting is a microcosm of the way we wish our schools to be—communities full of learning, safe and respectful and challenging for all."

THE FOUNDATION: A HEALTHY SCHOOL CULTURE

In her book, Kriete introduces greetings and games that help bring students together and promote a student sharing time as well.

## Congratulatory Systems and Awards

Congratulatory systems are immensely important in a positive educational environment, as students are highly motivated by recognition and praise. Among the systems we utilize at Orsch are awards, proficiency charts, and public celebrations. Awards are given regularly and presented publicly for exemplary work or performance. The most common awards are given for student effort, milestones reached (big or small), innovation, creativity, and product quality. Specific awards are given, such as "Essay of the Week" and "Perfect Spelling." Attitude and ethics are also awardable.

Awards have proven to be motivating and inspiring and seem to consistently raise the bar in product quality. Students are able to observe exceptional products their peers have completed. Proficiency charts are utilized often in Orsch. When a skill or concept is understood, students sign their names to a poster or chart. They are proud to add their names—leading to increased motivation and positive feelings. Public celebrations can be planned or impromptu. When a child reaches a significant milestone, we celebrate in some format. Children genuinely enjoy celebrating each other's successes. Good feelings spread, and this helps build community and positive interactions.

## Solutions

As needed, we have *Solutions* to solve problems that arise. Sometimes, Solutions is whole group. Sometimes, it is made up of smaller groups or specific class groups. Sometimes, Solutions is teacher initiated, but more often, it is student initiated. Solutions is a time for students to express any issues they may have within their school community. Issues range from "Kids are not flushing the toilets!" to "My feelings were hurt yesterday," to "I think we need to install a pencil sharpener on the south wall of the art room." Every child is heard, and as a group, we collaborate on possible solutions. We have yet to meet a problem we can't solve together. Solutions helps give students ownership in the harmony of their environment. Solutions engages students in real-life problem-solving skills, while actively modeling the idea that all problems have a solution.

## Community Projects

*Community projects* is another strategy that helps promote a positive environment. Community projects can range from helping a neighbor plant a garden or walk a dog, to significant projects such as global outreach. Students find true passion in their community projects. Community projects help get kids thinking beyond their own existence and help them think globally and take action for the good of others, leading to rewarding feelings.

## *Organizational Systems and Pleasing Aesthetics*

Organizational systems and pleasing aesthetics are utilized by most schools and classrooms. Teachers understand the value of effective organizational systems and cheery aesthetics, but they are both worth mentioning as an element of a positive environment. Good organization leads to productive feelings and efficient use of time and space. Pleasing aesthetics add joy, cheer, and inspiration. I have not seen an elementary school that lacks color or vibrant walls. However, the walls of many middle and high schools surprise me. They would do well to spice up their walls to make classrooms more inspiring and inviting. Humans do not mature out of aesthetic needs. Color, art, and inviting décor are inspirational and pleasing to every age.

## *Acoustics*

Acoustics in a school environment are crucial for positive feelings. Music can be a powerful element to add to a child's educational experience. Often, music can motivate or inspire. We allow our students to bring earphones as they wish, and teachers often play music during class time. An acoustic environment in which students are happily working seems to motivate and enhance productivity even more than silence; children are not naturally silent beings. However, some children prefer to work in silence at different points in their day—such an environment should be available to them as well. In a single classroom, a teacher can offer a myriad of acoustic options throughout the day to attempt to satisfy each child's needs.

## *Parties*

Celebratory events and student parties are important in so many ways. Some schools today have eliminated holiday parties and celebratory events in favor more academic time. The positive attributes celebrations offer far outweigh the limited lack of academic time. Parties and celebrations bring a community of students together in jovial purpose and in common experience. Students can participate in planning parties and celebrations. Parties and celebrations offer students something exciting to anticipate that is beyond their academic school life, further facilitating community and positive energy among a group. Holiday parties can be a time to dress in silly costumes and show one's most outrageous self. Dances, lock-ins, talent shows, ice cream socials—all of these are potential opportunities for positive feelings and jovial moments. Organized social

## THE FOUNDATION: A HEALTHY SCHOOL CULTURE

events offer a healthy social environment in which students are free to be themselves and enjoy the benefits of authentic community.

A healthy school culture is the most important factor in a vibrant school setting—it is the foundation. A healthy school culture leads to a group of people who are able to reach their academic potential and who are able to be the best of themselves socially as well. If children are emotionally stable and feel supported in their environment, then negative feelings and doubt do not hinder learning and growth. If teachers are vibrant and positive, they love their jobs and are highly effective in their interactions with children. Because a healthy school culture is easy to establish and can be implemented effectively with a few key strategies, we should expect such a culture for our students and our teachers.

Atop a secure foundation are three pillars. Each is attainable and is essential to achieving capable, thriving, engaged learners.

## *The First Pillar: Independence, Flexibility, and Freedom*

> *Freedom to choose pacing and space*
> *Freedom to discover, explore, dig deep*
> *Freedom to make mistakes*
> *Freedom to switch gears*
> *Freedom to interact*

Freedom is an innate human desire—an innate human need. Humans have searched for freedom since the dawn of history. We have pushed borders and boundaries, political restraints, and governmental policies. We desire life in a world in which our decisions matter and each of us is treated as an individual with value. Children are no different—they need guidance, but they are perfectly capable of managing independence and freedom. Children thrive in a flexible environment that offers them independence and freedom.

## ORSCH...CUTTING THE EDGE IN EDUCATION

Orsch has shown that an educational environment that offers its students independence, flexibility, and freedom in much of its academic programming will enjoy intrinsically motivated students who have genuine ownership in their learning. Children want to learn. They want to develop skill. They desire knowledge and valuable experiences. Freedom leads to purposeful learning, much more so than an environment that offers no choice to its students. Children who feel independent in their academic choices also have a great advantage toward the development of the essential skills described in Chapter 9. Furthermore, current research concludes that learning environments require flexibility if they are to serve each student's cognitive development.

In contrast, restrictive environments minimize opportunities to develop essential skills. A restrictive environment limits the development of decision-making and choice-making skills. It limits the opportunity for leadership to flourish and critical thinking to take place. Authentic work ethic is impossible to develop without independence and freedom. If they are told at every turn exactly what to do, students become nothing more than cogs in a machine. And lack of freedom can lead to underdeveloped communication skills or fabricated social interactions.

Restrictive environments also invite unwanted challenges and rebellious feelings in their students. Even very young children fight restriction that they don't understand. On the other hand, if children understand a school's necessary restrictions, they are generally happy to oblige. An

## THE FIRST PILLAR: INDEPENDENCE, FLEXIBILITY, AND FREEDOM

example is traffic safety—children agree with the restrictions placed upon them about traffic danger. They understand that it is in their best interest to steer clear of the street unless crossing appropriately. However, they don't understand some of the other restrictions placed upon them. Some schools are so full of rules and restrictions that children experience little independence. Lack of freedom feels frustrating and stifling; it is one of the factors present in behavioral issues.

I am not suggesting that children should have free rein to bumble around making chaotic choices throughout the day with no direction from adults. They would not benefit from, nor would they enjoy, such an existence—nor would it actually feel *free*, as I'll explain in the following sections. Again, students desire knowledge and productivity. They are eager to engage in purposeful material and in learning. They will generally make appropriate choices, especially if they are skilled decision makers.

## *Boundaries = Freedom*

It is important to explain my, and Orsch's, definition of *freedom* and to recognize the importance of adult guidance. I have long said that boundaries equal freedom for children. Their desire for freedom is powerful, but they do not actually *feel* free without boundary lines. When children clearly know their boundaries, they feel free to express themselves and shoot for the moon within them. For example, students in Orsch are welcome to work on anything academic during Academic Options. They have plenty of other things on which they would love to spend time, such as tossing a football or running around in the courtyard, but they know that these options are not available to them during the Academic Options portion of the school day. The term *freedom* is relative in this sense—it does not mean *no* boundaries. Because students know that their choices during Options must be academically based, they feel liberated in their ability to make choices about academics. If they had complete freedom during these moments of the day, they would end up feeling overwhelmed and would not feel productive, as their choices without boundaries would likely not be productive choices. In addition to the importance of boundaries, appropriate adult guidance offers students support in their independence. They are not yet fully mature, nor are they able to perfectly choose wisely—they need adult guidance in many of their choices. Boundaries equal freedom, and guidance enhances responsible independence.

Consider a child whose parents let him run wild in a toy store. This child grabs things off shelves, tears open packaging, makes loud noises, and runs from aisle to aisle. The child causes an embarrassing scene for all the shoppers present as well as for his parents. The child acts this way everywhere he goes—he has no boundaries. He experiences no real freedom, only chaos. In contrast, a child who respects acceptable toy store boundaries that are laid out for him, including polite behavior and not opening packages until they are purchased, will enjoy his experience and

## THE FIRST PILLAR: INDEPENDENCE, FLEXIBILITY, AND FREEDOM

feel free to browse respectfully. Wreaking havoc isn't actually any fun. The child who runs around crazily and behaving obnoxiously doesn't really enjoy that time. He is likely seeking some boundaries that make sense to him, and he tests his parents to find them. He is probably seeking some guidance and direction. Within appropriate boundaries, he will find satisfaction.

When my own children were babies, they had one cupboard in the kitchen that they could open up and rummage through—this is a common form of entertainment for babies and toddlers. Some parents choose to put child locks on every kitchen cupboard door. Some parents struggle throughout the baby years, continually keeping their children out of cupboards. We chose to offer a safe, accessible cupboard full of plastic containers and wooden spoons. We didn't lock any of the cupboards, not even the dangerous ones. We showed our toddlers which cupboards were unsafe or off-limits, and we invited them to play in the safe, available cupboard. We experienced many positive toddler moments of harmonious kitchen time and never did either child venture into the other cupboards. They understood this boundary—it made sense to them. Had we restricted every cupboard yet utilized the cupboards ourselves in their presence, our children would have pushed and questioned those boundaries. Had we not offered a safe option, we would have continually battled their desire to pillage through every kitchen cupboard. Our toddlers knew that they were able to act with complete freedom within safe choices offered to them. Boundaries = freedom.

## ORSCH...CUTTING THE EDGE IN EDUCATION

Orsch students have a "Create Room." They are allowed to go into the Create Room when they have time or when they need materials or tools for a project. The room is filled with craft items, art tools, and seemingly endless boxes and drawers of materials. Students are permitted to use most of the materials with complete freedom. There are, however, a few items that students are asked to not use, such as "teacher-only paintbrushes" and acrylic paint. Students value and respect the free rein they are offered in the Create Room and regard the restricted areas with respect. They feel free and unencumbered while working in the Create Room; it is one of their favorite elements of their school experience. The Create Room is also our most valuable carrot—if your work is completed, you will likely get to head in there. Boundaries = freedom. If students didn't have Create Room parameters, the Create Room would feel like an out-of-control free-for-all that would not satisfy. It would end up in shambles, and acrylic paint would head home on the skirts and T-shirts of every child. It would not be a pretty scene, and instead of freedom, we would likely default to restriction.

Even adults enjoy boundaries—they offer us freedom as well. For example, if we had utter freedom to lie around all day, we would feel lazy and aimless; we would not have the positive feelings of productivity. Likewise, if we had no boundaries about our eating habits, we might gorge on unhealthy food all day, leaving us feeling awful in many ways. And if we didn't have boundaries for our spending habits, we would quickly run out of money, experience no freedom to purchase wisely, and the items we purchased would likely lack meaning. Boundaries offer freedom; when we have guidelines to follow, we are free to make all the choices we want within them.

## *Academic Independence, Flexibility, and Freedom*

Academically, students are capable of making many of their own choices. Schools need to realize that students inadvertently choose their own pace, regardless of a teacher's objectives. Teachers can motivate students with awards and offer consequences for lack of performance, but ultimately students choose how fast they will work and at what pace they will learn, even given rigid requirements—*you can lead a child to lessons, but you cannot make him learn.* Interestingly, when they are given the independence and freedom to choose pacing, students seem to work harder and move faster than they would have otherwise. Intrinsic motivation is a powerful thing; at Orsch, we have found that the very route to intrinsic motivation is through independence and freedom of choice. The best lessons offer a variety of approaches, and the best assignments offer multiple options. Students innately want to learn most new concepts and are naturally engaged in new material. When they are allowed to make choices about how best they learn and how they prefer to practice a new skill, they find their own best way. Ultimately, a student's own best way is the most efficient route to understanding. Students choose appropriate programming, learning options, and levels. You will read more about this in "The Third Pillar: Variety in Innovative Approaches to Knowledge and Experience."

Sometimes, students simply need to change gears or have a "brain break." A well-run program with engaging lessons and invigorating activities very rarely has students who lack focus; however, when focus is just not there or a concept is just not sinking in, students should have the opportunity to communicate this to their teachers and should have valuable options that help keep them from wasting their time.

Students need freedom to explore, to discover, and to dig deeply into concepts and interests. Most school schedules are set up so tightly that just when a student gets really involved and really interested in a concept or experiment, he or she must move on to the next scheduled event. Scheduling issues are a reality in any educational program and in life in general. Scheduling is a challenge no matter how you slice it, but if time to explore, discover, choose activities, and dig deeply into concepts is largely absent, students miss out on a significant piece of their ability and desire to learn. Freedom to choose subject matter and choice of activity are important elements to add to a child's school day.

During Academic Option time each day, Orsch students may finish up an activity from the previous class, work on extensions, or tend to ongoing assignments and projects. During this time, they are welcome to find space that best

**THE FIRST PILLAR: INDEPENDENCE, FLEXIBILITY, AND FREEDOM**

fits their mood and project. Sometimes, students choose to sit alone; sometimes, they prefer a group setting. Sometimes, they desire a quiet space; sometimes a vibrant, active part of our school. All students love Academic Options, as it is a time to make choices and work toward personal goals and deadlines. Most students feel motivated to start and accomplished when work is complete. And for the few students who are still working toward and discovering intrinsic motivation, this is their chance to find in themselves what works and what doesn't.

## *Logistical Independence, Flexibility, and Freedom*

*Good judgment comes from experience; experience comes from bad judgment.*

—Jim Horning

Logistically, students thrive given simple choices, such as when to use the restroom and when to grab a snack, where to sit, and when to walk across the room to grab a pencil. Yes, some of them will take advantage of this, but those who do take advantage have some important lessons to learn about mutual respect and time management. A setting that trusts children to make good choices will facilitate lessons of mutual respect and time management much more effectively than a setting that eliminates such an opportunity. Students appreciate being trusted to make good decisions. Personal responsibility is a rewarding and motivating feeling to those who have mastered it, and it is an important goal for students who have yet to master it. Again, independence leads to essential skills.

Students need freedom to make mistakes in a supportive and forgiving environment. When their environment is supportive, children feel freer to take risks and more comfortable making mistakes. Mistakes come in all shapes and sizes, but they are inevitable. Some children deal better with mistakes than others. Some make more mistakes than others. Some make big mistakes with real-world consequences, and others make little mistakes with small consequences, but everyone, especially children, makes mistakes. An environment where mistakes are seen as an everyday mode of learning and growing offers children the ability to learn from experience and develop good judgment. An environment that has little tolerance for life's inevitable mistakes leaves children feeling fearful and hesitant to take chances—chances that stand to add character, talent, skill.

Students are quite capable of switching gears when they need a brain break or a change of pace. The ability to switch gears is a powerful tool in a productive student. Each of us has our own tolerance for intense focus, and each of us has a unique attention span. Further, students may have a large attention span one day and lack focus the next. A child may have a large attention span prior to lunch and have almost no focus by two o'clock. Each individual has his own

## THE FIRST PILLAR: INDEPENDENCE, FLEXIBILITY, AND FREEDOM

capacity for focus. Each individual's capacity for focus can change day to day, hour by hour.

As I've discussed, many factors play into a child's ability to focus on a given task or lesson. Much of it depends on her teacher's approach and the available activities offered, but we have found that when children are in touch with their own ability to focus and have the freedom to switch gears as needed, they are highly productive individuals. Consider the resources of time and processing capacity as described in Chapter 7—if a child lacks focus in a given activity at ten thirty in the morning, he will waste precious time if he is forced to continue. However, if he is allowed to express his lack of focus to his teacher, if he knows he has the freedom to tackle a more engaging project or to take a small brain break, he will switch his own processing gears to a more productive moment. Critics will say that a child needs to learn to persevere in these moments. Agreed. A skilled, intrinsically-motivated child will do so naturally and will benefit from the experience. A child who lacks intrinsic motivation will feel the lack of productivity in the activity in which he lacks focus. He will recognize this and move one step closer to avoiding it in the future, as all productive people do.

Students come in all shapes, sizes, and personalities—some are studious, while others are goofballs. Some love to sit properly in desks, and some do not. At Orsch, we have several students with Sensory Processing Disorder and many students on the gifted end of the spectrum.

## ORSCH...CUTTING THE EDGE IN EDUCATION

We have students of all sorts. Every child must learn to operate within the real world, no matter what type of learner, sitter, or listener he is. When children have freedom to make their own decisions about learning, space, and pacing, they learn to operate within a real-world setting. A couple of our students cannot sit still for more than a few minutes. We see nothing wrong with their need to hold and play with a soft object during instructional time. We use sensory processing tools, such as a band at the bottom of a chair, to allow students to use their feet muscles while sitting.

The best part about our ability to offer such freedom to students is that they are developing tools and skills to understand themselves, their behavior patterns, and what works best for them. Ned is one such student. Ned must wiggle. He is content and attentive, as long as he's wiggling or playing with something. I often think about how much he would struggle in a conventional environment where he would be forced to sit still. He would be miserable and grumpy. He would not learn the academic content as would be expected of him, so he would be pulled out and shipped off to special classes where the material might sink in, but he would not have the opportunity to learn how to manage himself in the real world. Because he has the freedom to choose his style of learning and fulfill his need to wiggle, he is respectful, attentive, and engaged, and he is also visibly and verbally appreciative that he is allowed the freedom to be who he is. Ned loves school. His parents continue to tell us how much he loves school; this same little boy would not love school in a restrictive environment, nor would he learn academic material as effectively as he is able to in a flexible environment.

## *Social Freedom*

Finally, students benefit immensely from the freedom to interact with their peers and with their teachers. Again, students are quite capable beings. They enjoy a vibrant and healthy social life within their school day, just as much as adults enjoy a social life within their workdays. Students in independent, free, flexible environments develop the necessary skills to interact responsibly. We must provide students with the ability to learn these essential skills—if we don't allow development of authentic social skills, students develop fabricated social relationships that are not based in reality. Peer pressure is a concept our society has been discussing for generations. In many of these discussions, peer pressure seems a necessary evil to a child's school career and beyond. *Negative peer pressure does not need to exist.* Orsch has a thriving environment where it is absolutely nonexistent. Positive peer pressure, on the other hand, is flourishing. Group ethics are strong. I believe we can come to a place where negative peer pressure is essentially nonexistent in school settings. In order to establish such a culture, students must be given the freedom to interact naturally with each other and with their teachers. Some examples of natural and healthy student interactions are: working in self-selected groups or pairs; student-initiated group activities, such as projects and clubs; student-initiated performances, such as skits and musical productions; students helping each other on assignments and teaching each other concepts, solving problems together, and communicating with each other during school projects and outside of school projects; planning events together.

Students who feel free to interact do not need to one-up each other or display inappropriate behavior to feel accepted. Many factors play into healthy social interactions, and specific systems can be established to enhance individuality, collaborative skills, tolerance, etc., but none of these strategies will work without allowing students specific flexibility and some freedom in their social interactions.

A flexible environment that offers its students independence and freedom in much of its logistical systems and social aspects will enjoy students who gain essential skills. Children love to learn. They understand justice and desire a harmonious community. If they have ownership in the logistical and social choices they make, they will become self-driven, competent citizens.

# *The Second Pillar: Creativity*

> *We are creative beings.*
> *Creativity must be encouraged and accepted in all that we do.*
> *Creativity must reign in assignments, projects, answers, questions, discussions, vision.*
> *Creativity must have no limits.*
> *Creativity can be modeled and taught, but mostly it must simply be...*
> *allowed to flourish.*

My contention is that creativity, now, is as important in education as literacy and we should treat it with the same status.

—Sir Ken Robinson

## ORSCH...CUTTING THE EDGE IN EDUCATION

Some think creativity must be defined as a product or an outcome. Some think that it must be taught. Some think that creativity is a gift given to a lucky few and a skill of which others are deprived. Orsch sees creativity as a natural mode of being. As I touched on in Chapter 9, our studies with children lead us to believe that creativity is as naturally human as language or affection. Creativity is present from the beginning. It need not be taught. Every human civilization has benefited from ingenuity, and ingenuity requires creativity. Creativity is not missing from our culture—quite the contrary. Creativity is in the chair in which you sit, the infrastructure within the building where you work, and in the clothing you are wearing. Creativity is in the packaging on your cereal box and existed in the process you used to purchase your last cup of coffee. Even today's toothpaste caps are superior to, or at least fancier than, those of yesteryear. Fuel-efficient vehicle designs and development in advanced technologies exist because of creative and inventive thinking.

As the musician Paul Simon sings, "The thought that life can be better is woven indelibly into our hearts and our brains."[27] We invent. We create. We think about the world around us and about how we can improve it, enjoy it, or make it more efficient. Children are the most inventive, creative beings among us. Why? Because creativity is an innate human tool and an innate human skill.

*Creativity* is a word and a concept that is commonly misused and misapplied. Creativity does not just reign in art

## THE SECOND PILLAR: CREATIVITY

projects and in colorful presentations. It is not simply a product of artists, pop culture, or the entertainment industry. Creativity is a mind-set that is present in each of us. Creativity exists in good problem-solving techniques. Creativity exists in new ways of thinking about systems. It exists in the interactions we have each day. It exists in the way we interpret the world.

The more creativity we allow into our minds, the more successful our thinking, whether we are trying to solve small problems that arise or understand the outcome of a tragedy. If each of us restricted our thinking to only the things we are accustomed to thinking (i.e., nothing creative), we would not change or grow—we would not progress or develop new understanding.

Think of the last real-life problem you were forced to solve—think of the ways in which you approached it creatively. As I write these words, I am cruising west on I-70 in a twenty-eight foot RV. We are on a big family road trip, but I must meet the deadline I have set to finish this book. The "Vessel" is bumping along. I-70 is not very smooth here in Indiana. Before I got creative, typing was very cumbersome—letters were popping up in places they shouldn't have, and my work seemed to cut and paste itself. Then I thought about the problem and realized that if I added a pillow underneath the keyboard, some of the shocking highway bumps would be absorbed by the pillow. Voilà!

I would guess that I solve in excess of ten problems by noon each day. I would guess you do as well. If milk spills, we figure out a way to clean it up—if no towel is in the midst, a sock will work. When schedules become difficult to maneuver within a family unit, the family gets creative and charts new options.

Creativity is not something that each of us must train for or learn—it is innate. However, in some settings—a stifling workplace, or a rigid school structure—creativity can be *flattened* or essentially eliminated because of monotonous ways of thinking. If there is no flexibility in thought, if there is no flexibility in modes and in methods, then we forget to be creative and allow the status quo to lead us. If we exist in an environment where creative thinking is a norm—where problems are seen as solvable and new ways of thinking are encouraged—then creativity flourishes. I just typed at twice the speed, thanks to this here pillow!

## *Fine Arts*

A strong arts program is critical in educational programming and is tied to decades' worth of research. Visual arts, performing arts, music, and dance are all linked to improved test scores, gains in critical thinking, cognitive ability, verbal skills, motivation, concentration, confidence, teamwork, improved self-regulation, as well as

## THE SECOND PILLAR: CREATIVITY

equitable opportunity for disadvantaged students. Links to specific studies and research efforts can be found on the National Arts Education and Public Awareness Campaign pages of the Americans for the Arts website (www.americansforthearts.org). In an informative article in *Edutopia*, "Why Arts Education Is Crucial and Who's Doing It Best,"[28] Fran Smith presents solid evidence that state mandates, tight budgets, and the pressure to raise test scores have reduced schools' time devoted to the arts. Although NCLB includes mandates for arts instruction, Smith argues that because the arts are not tied to *testing outcomes*, schools have traded the arts in favor of core subject academics.

Orsch enjoys the positive effects of a strong arts emphasis firsthand. Children are natural artists and flourish within all of the arts. We include the arts in almost everything we do, from allowing students to present their work artistically and creatively to staging performances and musical jam sessions. Students are immersed in art throughout their day. When students work within an artistic realm, they are focused, calm, engaged, joyful, and motivated. Although specific arts instruction and time to develop skill within the fine arts is critical to a high-quality, well-rounded education, schools can also integrate art into their daily practices and core subjects. Below is a perfect example of a child's ability to represent meaning artistically. Students were asked to define the word *monotonous*. This is Dalton's (age eleven) definition:

# ORSCH...CUTTING THE EDGE IN EDUCATION

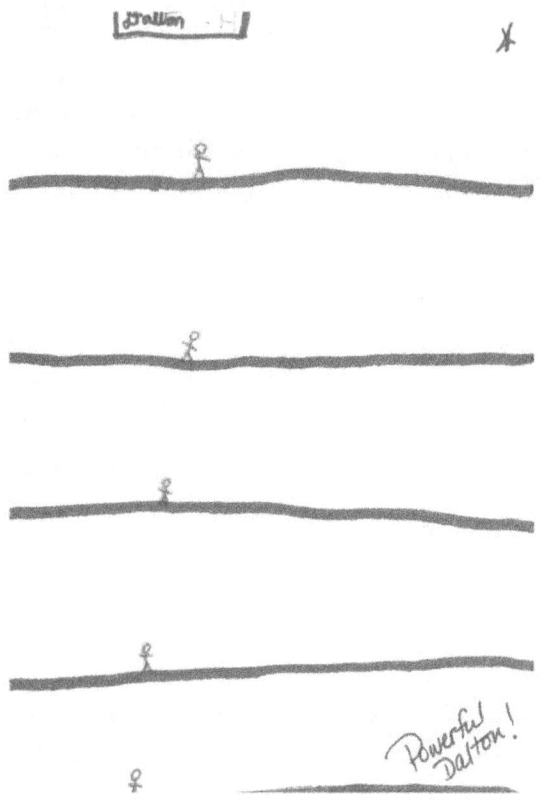

## A Creative Environment

Obviously an art studio, art classroom, or a performing arts school is a creative environment in which its residents are immersed in independent thinking and ingenuity, but every workplace and every school has the ability to allow creativity in its everyday operations. Imagine working for Google—do you think they employ people who cannot

## THE SECOND PILLAR: CREATIVITY

stretch their thinking? Do you think they start out each day saying, "This is the way it will be done—it has been done this way for as long as we can remember, so you will do it just so..."? Imagine working in a setting full of children—unique individuals, overflowing with creative, inventive thought and curiosity. Imagine being told that you must follow a curriculum pacing guide because each of them must literally be on the same page at the same time.

A creative environment is not just an environment full of colorful walls and crayon drawings. A creative environment is one in which thinking is dynamic and fluid. It is an environment in which each of the individuals is encouraged to use innate thinking skills to solve problems and adjust as necessary. It is a place where everyone's suggestions are considered, and the best paradigms succeed. It is one in which children are free to fail and are not judged by teachers or peers for having done so but rather encouraged for having tried. A creative environment is fulfilling, invigorating, motivating, engaging, and inspiring. A creative environment is one of the key elements of a thriving community, because each member feels he or she can give input and has ownership in outcomes, systems, and methods. A creative environment is accepting; as new ideas are celebrated, more new ideas are born, and inventive thinking is honored—appreciated—useful. A creative environment, by nature, will be on the cutting edge, as each person in its community continually seeks a better way—a more enjoyable or efficient way.

## ORSCH...CUTTING THE EDGE IN EDUCATION

In a school setting, creativity should be an integral part of the system. Administration should be willing to adjust procedures based on classroom needs and feedback—they should tackle all problems with creative and innovative thinking. Teachers should be allowed to differentiate, individualize—create better ways to reach their students. And students should absolutely be able to utilize and improve upon their inventive, creative minds.

Do you remember learning to "head" your papers in elementary, middle, and high school? My family moved frequently throughout my school years, so I had to adjust to each new school's paper-heading system. Sometimes my name was to go up above the lines, with the date below, the name of the class below that, and the teacher's name below that. Some schools preferred I write my name on the first line, followed by the date specifically written in digit form. I attended one school that required my name be written on the left side and another school which required the right side. I have been pondering this since—it has baffled me how much emphasis can be placed on such a trivial matter. So, of course, when I became a teacher, I allowed students to "label" their paper however they wanted. Many students responded with utter shock. My first year of sixth-graders had never been allowed to head their papers any differently than the determined norm. Another year, I taught in a pull-out program where students came to my classroom for a portion of their day. I had a couple of first-graders who desperately wanted to write their names in cursive; their classroom teachers forbade this. Knowing that I would likely

## THE SECOND PILLAR: CREATIVITY

allow something creative, these two little girls asked me if they could please learn their names in cursive. I asked them to try on their own. They linked each letter at its bottom—a child's first signature. They were thrilled, motivated, and excited. They felt like they were breaking the mold, and molds are quite fun to break! I was forced to tell them that they should follow the rules outside of my classroom; they were giggly and agreed to oblige.

During our first year of Orsch, a dear friend of mine, who is a college professor of literature, taught a month-long poetry unit for us. She is a person who is full of creativity and flexible thinking, which is why this story sticks out. At the end of the unit, all the final drafts of poetry were turned in. Shelley brought the stack to me before reading them. "None of these have names," she said. She placed each poem on the desk in front of me one by one. I was taken aback looking through the stack with her—had she lost her mind? I waited patiently until she got to the end of the stack, watching each paper fall as she illustrated her point. Each child had signed his or her name at the bottom of the poem, as poets do. Shelley was looking in the upper-right-hand corner for a heading. We shared a good laugh, and a fun and meaningful conversation followed.

Creativity can be in a signature. Creativity can be present in a choice of paper or a personal style. Creativity should be present in our methods and approaches to teaching and learning. We have a student in Orsch who prefers to make the majority of his products giant. His name is

## ORSCH...CUTTING THE EDGE IN EDUCATION

Nelson. He is possibly the most unencumbered creative thinker I know. He thrives in Orsch, because we try to say yes. When the others in his group made their paper fraction sundaes with eight scoops (eighths) and twelve scoops (twelfths), Nelson created a giant construction paper fraction bowl with sixty-four scoops of ice cream. He loved every minute of it. He created an entire wall's worth of multiplication facts when asked to find a means of studying his facts. Instead of using one sheet of normal paper to make a writing web, Nelson will likely use chart paper; if no chart paper is available, he'll tape together as many sheets as necessary to fulfill his creative needs. I often think of Nelson's similarities to Christo and Jeanne Claude[29]—he may become a grand installation artist himself. In this, Nelson's creative side motivates him; he is excited to complete his assignments because he can add his own flair. He is not particularly drawn to math, but he sure can conceptualize fractions now. He probably thinks about fractions every time he eats ice cream.

That is not to say that every child needs to be given free rein to wreak havoc in the classroom, creating giant projects. It is to say that when we trust children's creative ideas and allow them a creative outlet, mundane tasks become invigorating. Not to worry, children respond beautifully to guidelines, especially if the list of allowable means is appealing to them. So schools should not fear lack of order as they allow more creativity. On the contrary, the genuine engagement that comes from allowing creative options

## THE SECOND PILLAR: CREATIVITY

far outweighs the small amount of trouble spent gathering chart paper for their Nelsons.

Because most children love color, cutting, and pasting, at Orsch, we often copy basic skills worksheets onto colored paper and allow students to create art out of them. Where a child would have struggled through a worksheet with seemingly boring math problems, he is now content to snip and paste away to create his math-practice robot picture. He is engaged the entire time. He barely notices that he is practicing a math skill over and over again as he chooses the next problem to paste onto his picture. Similarly, we encourage students to add art and/or color to anything they wish—this has shown to be motivating in multiple ways to most students. Some students are motivated to finish a task or an assignment simply so that they can color it; they enjoy making an assignment aesthetically appealing and love to develop their artistic skills. They enjoy personalizing their assignments and take pride in a well-presented product.

In addition to the fun and motivating elements that art offers, it seems that some students use artistic additions as a sort of brain-break—they enjoy adding a creative border or colorful heading. Doodling is an effective way to take a break from a tedious or challenging task; students who are encouraged to decorate their work have built-in doodling at their fingertips. We have found this option to be motivating and ultimately more efficient than simply assigning tasks, and we have also found that doodling or coloring does not have an age limit—even students into high-school age enjoy adding color to their products.

Students who are allowed the flexibility to use their minds the way that best works for them get an immense amount of work done. It is easy to relate if we put such ideas in the perspective of ourselves—think about what you do during your day-to-day requirements to get small brain breaks. Personally, on a big writing day, I throw in chores, such as laundry and closet organization. I need time to process, time to think, and time to ponder. Students need this time too.

Socialization is an added benefit of adding art and/or color to their assignments. A very common scene in our school is a table full of students engaged in authentic conversation while adding color to a final product.

Finally, adding art and color to assignments further extends the notion of individuality. Students show pride and self-fulfillment when they add a personal flair to their schoolwork. They become more and more confident in their own product presentation skills and continually develop new skill as well.

## THE SECOND PILLAR: CREATIVITY

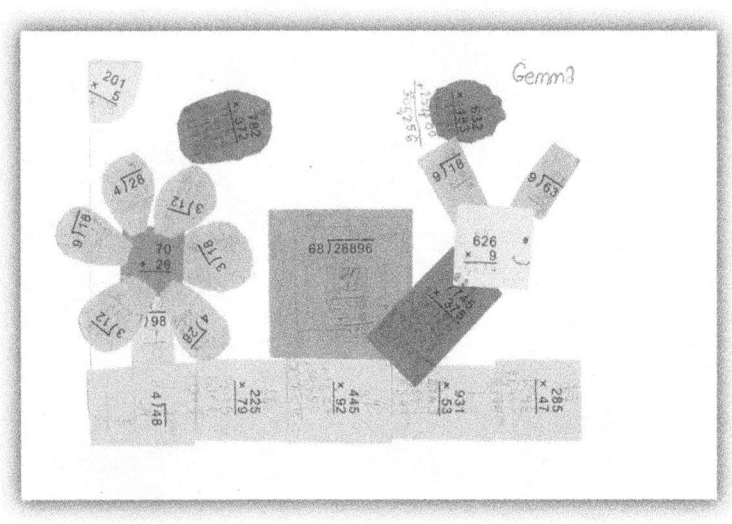

 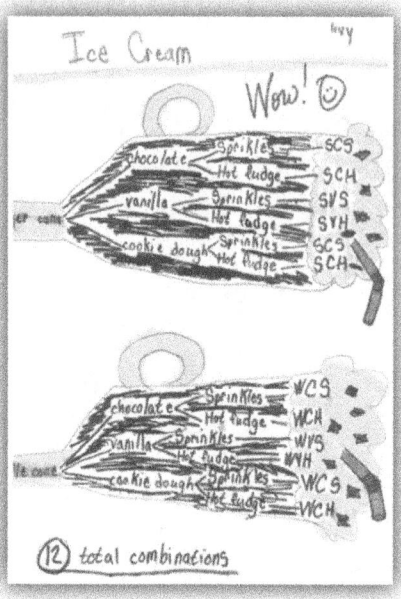

Creativity doesn't need to involve color or giant paper sundaes—creativity in student assignments comes in various forms. When students are accustomed to creativity, they use interesting phrasing in their writing or design their own graphic organizers. Sometimes, a flow chart just doesn't flow, but a student's own mind map is just the thing to link her thoughts together. Often, creativity flourishes when students are asked to *show they know*. For assessment purposes, Orsch students are often asked to show proficiency in a given skill or concept. Students are generally permitted to show they know in any format they like. We

## THE SECOND PILLAR: CREATIVITY

have seen PowerPoint presentations, skits, essays, books, dioramas, posters, poems, videos, speeches, art projects, collages, student-led lessons, songs, and all of the everyday methods, such as classic worksheets. Students who are accustomed to approaching assignments and requirements creatively find their own best approach, their own most efficient or enjoyable way.

Of course, students need adult guidance to be successful in the arena of creativity, since it is easier for experienced adults to foresee a project's potential depth and required level of effort. It is often necessary for teachers to offer guidelines to creative options within a consideration of time, space, or materials. However, for the most part, experienced students who are accustomed to a creative environment seem to naturally balance their choices. For example, if a student chooses to create a diorama to show proficiency in subject-verb agreement, she will likely not choose such a labor-intensive product the next time—she will try a PowerPoint presentation or a poem. Furthermore, students learn valuable lessons about time, space, and materials as their choices become experienced and wise—competent *creators* are the result.

In addition to product creativity, creative thinking and creative questioning are innate human skills that thrive when nurtured. They need *not* be *taught* to be nurtured. Children who are allowed and encouraged to think for themselves are natural creative thinkers. Creative thinkers naturally seek solutions to problems and question deeply, because they know their thinking is allowed to be inventive and mistakes are a necessary part of the process. Creative thinkers ponder their world in very important ways. Creative thinking is among the significant elements that lead to *critical thinking*. If a child is encouraged and allowed to think creatively about a problem, a concept, or a situation, he begins to think critically about it. He ponders a problem from many angles and considers it from multiple perspectives. The more accustomed he is to thinking creatively, the more he will apply unconventional ideas and critique potential solutions.

Creative thinking becomes exciting and vogue in a creative environment, and the whole community benefits. Students appreciate the eclectic nature of each person's individual thoughts, products, and solutions. In the first year of Orsch, I watched my students transition from a group of kids afraid to express themselves, unable to think outside of norms, to a group of kids thriving in creative thought, appreciating more and more the ideas and unique products of their peers. New ideas quickly became the norm—creativity is infectious.

Furthermore, when new ideas and creative thinking is the norm, a group of individuals thrives and gels (I would guess working for Google feels a bit this way). In addition to the positive group dynamics that result from a creative group of people, each individual within the group appreciates the ability to have his or her own unique thoughts without risk.

**THE SECOND PILLAR: CREATIVITY**

A sense of creativity plays a significant role in a child's sense of individuality, especially when creativity is accepted and genuinely appreciated within a group. In contrast, an environment of sameness simply cannot benefit from the positive outcomes that a creative environment offers to both its individuals and to its community as a whole.

To offer a truly successful program for students, a school's administration and teaching staff must be creative as well. An environment in which procedures and systems are stagnant cannot grow and change as necessary. If you have already dismissed this idea as you read it, ask yourself why. Was it a response based on tradition? Based on a single experience? Based on a few experiences? Should you spend more time assessing the viability of variations on this idea?

As stated early in this book, education evolves too slowly. It is likely that part of the reason for this is that we have rigid structures set up, which we do not question or ponder creatively. When Orsch teachers struggle with any aspect of their classes, they have the freedom to improve their situation. When the mind-set of an institution or company allows for creative improvement and it is willing to adopt or at least experiment with new ideas, it becomes cutting edge. I would guess that we, at Orsch, improve the lives of our students every single day by implementing new ideas and better systems. We are always willing to bail on the ideas that don't work, but we never stop looking for better approaches, more efficient uses of our space, smoother transitions, more high-quality uses of our students' time, and overall improvement of our program.

Teachers thrive and enjoy their jobs when they have the ability and the freedom to be creative in their approaches. As I've said before, teachers are people who work hard to offer the best to their students. If teachers have the freedom to adapt a lesson to a more teachable moment or to link their students' understanding to a relevant current event, or to adjust the schedule within their classroom to enhance engagement, they will have more successful students who ultimately learn more. Teachers who are stuck in stifling or suppressive work environments do not have the opportunity to reach their own potential, nor do they offer their best to students.

Ponder how many teachers in our public education system would be more inspirational, more motivating, more effective if allowed some flexibility in programming and in creative individualization for their students. You probably know a wonderful person who is a wonderful teacher but is extremely frustrated about his or her current setting. He or she is likely forced to adhere strictly to the curriculum in an effort to meet benchmarks and standards, ultimately getting his or her students to test day. But rigid requirements are counterproductive—a flexible, creative environment stands a much better chance of reaching those benchmarks.

Too many schools today are devoid of creativity for both their students and their teachers. Because of rigid

## THE SECOND PILLAR: CREATIVITY

standards, unbending procedures, and required benchmarks, creativity lies dormant. Retroactively, our culture is beginning to notice the lack of creativity in our school systems. In some schools, "creative thinking" is a special class or is often a targeted aspect of gifted and talented programs. Many creative thinking books, workshops, and activity options are available to teachers. It seems we are beginning to see the significance of creativity in our culture and the importance of *adding* it to our school structures. It is terribly ironic to watch our educational community prevent creative thinking while it simultaneously struggles to implement it.

Although Orsch utilizes all the wonderful activity books and enjoys attending the workshops to help teach creativity to students, we have yet to meet a child who does not naturally think or question creatively. I have, however, met many children who do not realize that thinking creatively is a natural ability or who are sadly out of practice. It is pure joy to see such children open up to their own ability to think creatively. Students display obvious elation as freedom of thought begins flooding in. Creative thought becomes a motivating, thrilling use of processing capacity. As we begin to let creativity slip into our nation's school settings on a grand scale—which we will inevitably do—it will be a thrilling and vibrant transition to watch; creativity will motivate, inspire, and breed more inspiration and more effective methods. We will begin to see education evolve at a pace fitting for such an institution, an institution built on the ideals of progress and human potential.

## ORSCH...CUTTING THE EDGE IN EDUCATION

Orsch has proven that to create an environment rich in creative thought, rich in creative programming—an environment overflowing with systems and tasks that are more enjoyable and more efficient—we need only allow it. Individuals will naturally do the rest. Creativity must simply be *allowed* for it to flourish.

## *The Third Pillar: Variety in Innovative Approaches to Knowledge and Experience*

It is hard to argue with the advantages of *student-centered learning* or *child-centered learning*. The concept of student-centered learning[30] is well studied and is based on decades of research. In essence, it considers the needs of the student first, rather than starting from academic objectives or outcomes established by teachers or administrators. Student-centered learning encompasses *active learning*[31] with an emphasis on deeper learning and authentic understanding. It is surprising that given its wealth of positive attributes, student-centered learning is not more utilized in our educational system.

Its lack of presence in our educational system is likely due to its seemingly intensive commitment to time and workload for teachers. In a traditional school setting, student-centered learning requires that a teacher differentiate and individualize for his students. Individualizing and differentiating for each student is by far the best means of reaching him and meeting his academic, affective, and social needs. However, conventional methods say that to effectively differentiate, a teacher must consider multiple intelligences and learning styles, interests and aptitudes, readiness and prerequisite skills. Teachers must preassess and then tailor a child's learning plan to his needs. But teachers don't have time to cover the content they are required to cover each school year, let alone differentiate for every learner in this manner.

"As we start a new school year, Mr. Smith, I just want you to know that I'm an Abstract-Sequential learner and trust that you'll conduct yourself accordingly!"

Many schools opt to hire specialists and send students to remedial classes or gifted and talented classes in an effort to help students meet academic benchmarks and standards or to serve their exceptional needs. I suppose a specialist, a remedial class, or a gifted program is an attempt to individualize for a student, but it requires funds that many schools don't have and such practices remove students from the heterogeneous grouping[33] that is also supported in decades of research. Ultimately, schools and districts waste resources with this method. Instead, they could offer an effective student-centered environment to their students.

Orsch has discovered the ease with which student-centered learning is a reality—it is simply to offer students ample variety in approaches to learning and to teach them to utilize their own time, space, materials, and available resources, including teacher guidance. There is an investment here—the students must learn to use the powerful tool of self-direction—but it is a wise investment. *Learning left in the hands of the learner is more meaningful, more enjoyable, and therefore more effective.* Our job as schools, teachers, parents, and advocates of children is to provide them with a wealth of experiences and opportunities. Learners will reach higher than our expectations or limitations would have allowed otherwise. As I've emphasized many times, children are natural learners. When our adult view of the world and all its order and rigidity is placed upon young learners, we stifle them and waste resources while doing so.

In traditional settings, academics are too often characterized and presented as something that will not be appealing to young minds. It is my observation that to children, academics are equally as playful and exciting as jumping and running around a park, unless we convince them they are not, unless our delivery is mundane and unbending. Children have important interests and goals, such as learning long division, engineering blocks, mixing colors on paper, role-playing, studying bugs, and developing skills in literacy, music, art, and geography.

Again, learning is energizing and motivating in itself, but our attempt to shove knowledge into children and frame their education into limiting boxes, columns, and categories is literally erasing their natural ability to seek it themselves. We cannot hope to cover every detail of a child's interests and abilities. We cannot test, inventory, and chart adequately enough to serve him or her appropriately. To adequately craft a child's learning plan, we must trust the child to take the reins himself, standing by to offer guidance, experience, and the necessary tools.

How do teachers create an effective and true child-centered classroom? Offer plenty of variety in lessons, programming, and explorative options, and then let the child choose. Nobody, no test, no battery of tests, no data, no results know better than the student, especially when this choice is appropriately nurtured, guided, and encouraged and especially when the child has developed the skills necessary to make valuable decisions. Efforts to categorize learning styles and aptitudes and then craft an individualized plan are an inefficient and insufficient method to individualization.

## THE THIRD PILLAR: VARIETY IN INNOVATIVE...

The following scenario is an example of a typical Orsch approach to teaching a given concept. The lesson: Finding Common Denominators for Fractions

Students arrive at the lesson on time—they are excited and genuinely love to learn a new concept. Ms. Elizabeth has planned carefully—she knows she must include at least three different approaches to her lesson. She chooses to use fraction bars, whiteboard drawings, and the lecture available on khanacademy.org.[34] She presents the concept in each format. Students know that if they don't grasp the concept within her first approach, she will offer another angle. Throughout the lesson, they are patient but eager; their readiness for learning is heightened. After her lesson, which offers several examples, she allows students to express how the concept strikes them. Students take turns at the front of the room showing each other how they think about fractions with unlike denominators, drawing their own thinking on the whiteboard. Within twenty minutes, students have a grasp of this concept and are ready to tackle it hands-on. The subsequent practice session offers many options as well. Elizabeth offers differing levels of practice problems from which students can choose. She offers several hands-on tools (fraction bars, fraction pies, paper/scissors). And students know that they can access more resources and information online as needed. Students practice the concept for the next half hour. Some choose to draw on whiteboards or build each problem with hands-on tools. Some choose to get creative and build a colorful scene out of their practice problems. Some choose to head right to their personal Khan Academy account (www.khanacademy.org) to officially show proficiency of the concept. The room is a place of vibrant, active learning.

As the concept is better grasped by each child, he or she is engaged and completely, intrinsically motivated to dig deeper. At no time do students feel they are "behind" or struggling. At no time does a child feel he is waiting for others. Levels are inherently appropriate when the child is permitted to choose. Furthermore, children naturally challenge themselves in this environment. Their learning is not lazy or despondent; it is fueled by invigorating feelings of new knowledge and understanding. That feeling of "I get it!" is motivating and rewarding. Students of all types, abilities, and backgrounds seek this feeling all day when their environment offers it.

Students are then allowed to show that they know the concept in a variety of formats, ranging from accomplishing a set of problems to writing a short "how-to" pamphlet. Students are accustomed to the assessment "show you know" options available to them and are also accustomed to inventing their own from time to time. We see no reason to limit their ability or desire to show their knowledge the way they best see fit. Students, in turn, have a great deal of ownership in their learning and in their confidence to present knowledge and understanding of a concept.

**THE THIRD PILLAR: VARIETY IN INNOVATIVE...**

## Variety in Programming

> *Knowledge and Experience*
>
> Independently sought. Taught. Offered.
> Invented. Encouraged. Guided.
> Hands-on. Project-based. Using technology.
> Collaborative. Innovative. Interactive. Lived.
> Acted. Sung. Created. Heard. Visualized.
> Sculpted. Dreamed. Drawn. Danced...
>
> And ways we haven't even thought of yet.

The reason that variety in programming is key to a successful student-centered program is that students are complex little people whose learning inventories[35] change day by day, minute by minute. It is good to consider Howard Gardner's Multiple Intelligence Model[36] in an educational setting, but to attempt to craft each child's learning plan to his or her specific intelligence style adequately is not possible—the child is too complex. We have learned that a child may be a kinesthetic learner at nine o'clock in the morning and a musical learner at one o'clock in the afternoon. The same child will prefer a more visual approach to spelling one day and a more audio approach the next. Children need variety, and they thrive within novelty. Students are all multi-intelligent and change throughout the year, week, day, and minute.

*If there is a constant within the realm of K-12 academics, it is variation.*

A true student-centered program can be a reality in any school environment. It is possible. Using the wealth of inexpensive resources they have, teachers can easily plan lessons that offer engaging content and a variety of approaches. Students will come to value their lessons, as they are not mundane. In an effective student-centered classroom, students know they can count on a bit of novelty and guaranteed engagement. If one approach does not strike them, they know that their teacher will present another approach—and another. Their readiness is heightened, because they trust that their teacher will deliver valuable content in a way that makes sense to them. At Orsch, students can generally count on learning a new concept from at least three angles. Then, to practice, delve into, or explore the concept, teachers offer a variety of levels and options. Students know that the explorative and practice portion of their learning will offer engaging, meaningful activity as well.

Our experience has shown that each student does not seem to gravitate to the same practice method each day. This is partly how we know that students prefer variety. One day, a student will practice word families by creating a poem; the

## THE THIRD PILLAR: VARIETY IN INNOVATIVE...

next day, the same student will prefer an online game to practice the skill. We have found that students do not need endless choices—they are completely satisfied with two or three options to practice a skill. When given choices, they sometimes stick with one practice option throughout the time period, or sometimes try two or three variations. This simple structure combats classroom sameness and leaves each child feeling successful, confident, and capable. The ability to choose from a variety of options also offers ownership to students' learning, making learning more meaningful and more purposeful.

To approach teaching and learning with variety is not more work for the teacher. On the contrary, as I've emphasized previously, *recognizing each child as an individual is easier than trying to make all of them the same.* Curriculum guides offer plenty of options for teachers and students, since curriculum companies know the value of differentiation and individualization. Extensions, hands-on ideas, and multiple avenues for practice are elements of every good research-based curriculum guide. Teachers also have online resources, supplemental books on their shelves, and their own innovative ideas—sometimes their own ideas are the most effective. Teachers are generally very creative, and they welcome a classroom with more variety and flexibility, especially if they know that this approach will more effectively engage their students.

An added benefit of ample variety in a school setting is that students begin to learn what works for them as learners.

For example, Christopher very much prefers to use tangible tools to tackle subtraction with regrouping. He uses the base-ten blocks for every problem, carefully trading a ten rod for ten ones and then eliminating (subtracting) the units one by one. He understands subtraction in this manner. If this option were not available to him, he would struggle to grasp the abstract approach to regrouping on paper. He will move to the abstract when he is ready to do so, but he is not yet ready. He appreciates the ability to work at his own pace with tools that make sense to him. He may finish five problems while another student finishes fifteen problems, but each student is practicing this skill within his level of understanding and within his chosen method.

Christopher doesn't mind that he has only done five problems and Michael has done fifteen. At Orsch, students have become accustomed to not comparing themselves to each other. Some students are able to grasp abstract mathematical concepts right away; some students need to use manipulatives (objects that they can hold and work with) to solidify understanding. If each child knows that a hands-on option is available to him, he will feel confident tackling problems with the tools he knows will work. And if the environment encourages student choice of tools that will facilitate understanding, students will feel confident making appropriate choices, ultimately conquering concepts much more efficiently.

In contrast, if a lesson is presented in only one manner and a child does not understand, he is then left to feel behind or frustrated and then will likely lack confidence. Lack of confidence snowballs and builds, leading to less academic potential. On the other hand, the confidence that comes from the ability to choose effective tools and methods leads to increased academic potential and increased skill. *The more you can put in the hands of a child, the more authentic his lessons will be.*

When students are given the ability to choose from tools and methods that work for their individual styles, they begin to gravitate toward their own passions and interests with more purpose. They show signs of intrinsic motivation to tackle new topics and dig deeply into areas of interest. These are the students who will yearn for higher-level math or nineteenth-century European history in high school or may end up brilliant musicians with real potential.

Not every subject matter or skill will be intrinsically motivating to students. Some memorized facts and basic skills simply must be mastered, so that a student can move to the next level. A perfect example is multiplication facts. A student cannot succeed in learning all of the steps involved in long division if his multiplication facts are not easily accessible. Sometimes, students are not necessarily motivated to memorize facts without some extrinsic motivation—there is nothing wrong with a sticker chart or a public award to celebrate mastered skills. However, students who are proficient at knowing their talents and learning styles are able to seek mastery and attain these skills much more efficiently than if we tried to craft their plan for them.

## ORSCH...CUTTING THE EDGE IN EDUCATION

My son had been studying piano for seven years. Until last November, he had yet to memorize the notes on his written music; rather, he played by ear and got by. I kept him with a traditional teacher through the ups and downs, because she contrasts him beautifully. If left to his own teachings, music would flow freely to him. He would express this art with talent and grace his whole life long. But that was not good enough for his mother, who knows his talent exceeds this. He struggled to learn to read music. Pam, his piano teacher, insisted; she begged, instructed, suggested flash cards, teased, tried humor, tried gadgets—nothing. Seven years into this and nothing. Until it hit me: I'm the expert in this realm...I know what to do! Finally, after seven years of after-school struggles, I said, "Sam, how do you think you would best learn these [darn] notes?" I offered a few suggestions to get the creative juices flowing. "If you do it by Monday, I'll give you twenty bucks!"

Suddenly motivated, Sam knew what to do. He created a piece of art and came up with a crazy song relating the art to the note he naturally hears. On Monday, I tested him. I was impressed, but I needed verification from an informed judge. He would have to wait until Friday to earn his reward.

On Friday, Pam told me that he was a different student—forever changed, learning his songs in unprecedented time and now reading music.

Sam is smart, but he is no prodigy. He is musically talented, but it is not his main focus. In one weekend, seven years of traditional attempts were clobbered with a child's genuine view of himself and the methods of learning *he* knew would work. In one weekend, he merged his talents with the benefits of reading a classical language. He knew what was best for him—he just needed to be given the independence to choose its route and reasonable purpose.

Sam is clearly proficient at choosing his way, his method, and it is because in his learning environment, he is given the freedom and encouragement to do so. He is good at choosing his methods, as anyone is good at a practiced skill. It took a while to get him there, and I'm sure he has not reached his full potential for success in learning, but he is a giant step ahead of the average American student who has no choice in his path.

Note: I am not suggesting we offer students money to learn, although I have been known to offer some creative incentives. A student gets extremely motivated with the promise of a lunch date, but other reward systems, such as proficiency charts and celebratory public recognition, are sufficient.

## *Variety in Skill Level*

Part of the problem we face in our current educational climate is the negative results of single-grade classrooms and the same skill level in which they attempt to operate. Graded classrooms, *in theory*, contain students of relatively similar ability levels. But in reality, they don't. Humans do not develop at the same rate. Each person exists in a unique set of circumstances (family life, nutrition, experiences, cognitive conditioning[37]), and each person is born with unique potential. Because human development is so complex, it should be obvious that children of the same age will not display similar ability levels.[38] American classrooms contain a very broad range of abilities.

The first semester of Orsch, our student body was made up of twenty-two students from kindergarten through seventh grade; I was their only teacher for all core subjects. I was often asked how I managed to teach each of them. My answer: "Every classroom in America has this range of ability levels; they're just not willing to accept it." And how did I manage to teach each of them? With ample options in approaches and skill levels.

Eliminating age-based classrooms would go a long way toward solving our problems. However, similar to the test-driven climate in which most students exist, graded classrooms are so entrenched that they will be around far into the future. However, we can begin seeing groups of children as the complex and diverse groups they are, offering them varied and dynamic approaches that are as varied and multileveled as the students themselves.

Variety in skill-level options is an extremely important element of a student-centered program. The success and effectiveness of a good multiage[39] program is due, in

## THE THIRD PILLAR: VARIETY IN INNOVATIVE...

large part, to the dynamic approach required to reach multiple age groups in one setting. Variety in skill-level options allows students in the same classroom to move at their own pace. And students are quite efficient level choice makers. Students who are proficient at choosing their own level know exactly which level fits them and have no qualms about backing up a level as needed. Nor do they stay stagnant. It seems that it is human nature to challenge oneself academically when allowed to do so. Having come from a traditional teaching environment, I was conditioned to preassess every student to find where I should start his programming. When I started Orsch, I tested each child and set out to individualize his or her programming appropriately. Although I'm grateful for the data, I now see that preassessments for programming purposes were largely a waste of time, for the most effective and efficient way to find what skills a student possesses and at what level he should be working is to allow him to choose himself.

I'll use a lesson I taught last year as an example. The lesson's objective was to learn the distributive property of multiplication. For example: using 375 multiplied by 7. Students were instructed to multiply 300 x 7, add its product to 70 x 7, and then add its product to 5 x 7. Some students took to the idea right away, and some students needed extra help. Students who really understood the concept were encouraged to take on bigger numbers. Students who were hesitant were able to choose smaller numbers.

## ORSCH...CUTTING THE EDGE IN EDUCATION

Each child ended up understanding the distributive property of multiplication, but none of the students in that lesson felt underwhelmed or overwhelmed by the concept.

Had I taught even a broader range of students for this lesson, I could have let beginners explore the idea of expanded notation and simple multiplication, as those concepts are prerequisite skills for the use of the distributive property. And I would have included multidigit multiplicands for those with more prior knowledge. The following lesson and the work examples illustrate each of Orsch's three pillars. First, during the initial lesson, the concept was presented in multiple ways with multiple examples (I used base-ten blocks and hundred grids and also showed the conventional algorithm on a whiteboard). Students actively participated in work examples and took notes as they saw fit—they have the freedom to take as many notes in whatever format they would like in their math journals. Then students were given the independence and freedom to choose the manner and the numbers with which to practice their skill. A variety of numbers were available, as were the manipulatives used to teach the lesson. Then students had the opportunity to present their understanding as creatively as they wished. As you can see, the colorful collage style quickly caught on that day.

# THE THIRD PILLAR: VARIETY IN INNOVATIVE...

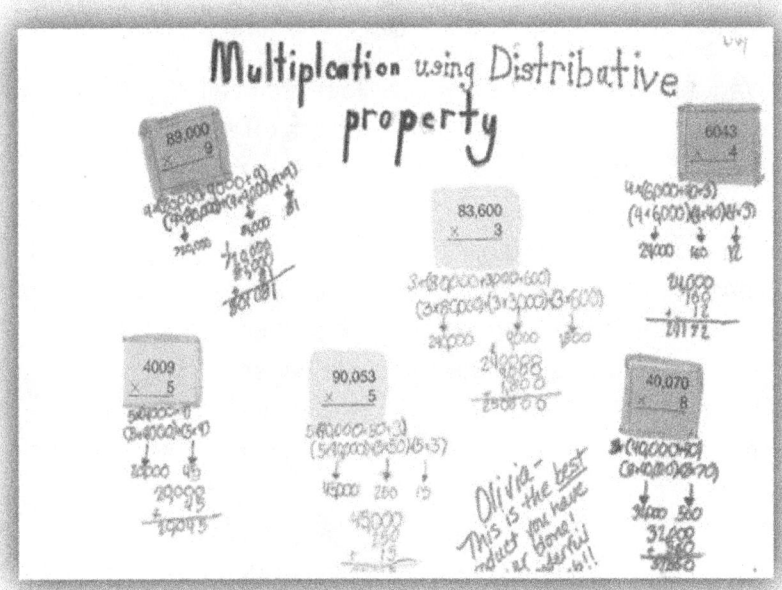

## ORSCH...CUTTING THE EDGE IN EDUCATION

Variety is key because one size does not fit all, nor does one method fit all. Students will learn more effectively from multiple approaches and various ways to practice and develop their skills. They will learn what works best for them and will develop new strategies for learning along the way. They will learn how to effectively choose their own level and will soon realize that they prefer to challenge themselves. Students will remain engaged, given ample variety in the methods we teach. They will develop deeper understanding from the active learning they experience, given ample variety in exploration and practice.

Traditional education has too many students struggling to meet benchmarks and standards without the creative or flexible means necessary to do so. There are also too many students wasting time waiting for others. Our educational system has yet to launch into student-centered learning on a broad scale, but it really has no excuse.

The pendulum swings. The search endures. Blended Learning,[40] Brain-Based Learning[41], phonics instruction versus Whole Language.[42] The answer surely lies in a grand combination of all approaches. Student *needs* are as varied as students themselves. Students tire of monotony and they require a dynamic environment in which to learn. While those in the field of education endlessly debate the benefits and detriments of each new educational fad, the

## THE THIRD PILLAR: VARIETY IN INNOVATIVE...

latest approach, or path to accountability, students wait in classrooms eager to try all of them, ready to choose appropriately, ready to dig in to engaging material. And effective approaches—solid, research-based approaches—all of them—are waiting in the wings, ready to help our students soar.

# Conclusion—In My Dreams

I constantly dream of fifty years from now. And yesterday I contemplated whether or not I should adjust each year. If I dream of fifty years from *today*, I might be able to see it. But if I continue to set my sights at fifty years, I'll never see it. Shall I begin counting down? When I dream of fifty years into the future, I see myself at ninety-two in awe of a world of compassion and empathy and less sickness, hunger, and war. I want that. But if I personally hope to see it, must I dream of progress in diminishing increments—forty-nine years, forty-eight years, forty-seven years from now?

Orsch student Lolo at age five (December, 2010): "Ms. Jackie, did you know that at the turn of the century, I'll be ninety-five?"

Me: "Wow, Lolo…How old will I be?"

Lolo: "Well, how old are you now?"

Me: "Thirty-nine."

Lolo: "Oh, you'll be dead!"

## ORSCH...CUTTING THE EDGE IN EDUCATION

I am still laughing about that adorable conversation—so pure and logical in the eyes of a five-year-old.

Fifty years from now, will we still label our children and place them in illogical, irrelevant categories that take ten years to establish, another five years to discover and diagnose, and then even more years to treat, or will we take ten minutes to understand a child and never send him or her down that road? Will we find answers to our most burning questions? What will heal? What can cure? What can bring harmony rather than conflict between races, genders, preferences? What will prevent unnecessary devastation of people? Anyone with hope and the desire to progress seeks these answers innately.

Each day, another question enters. Quests will remain. Answers lead to more answers, and fifty years will never come, and fifty years is here.

My most burning question: With all of the potential of fifty years from now and the knowledge of fifty years in the past, how can anyone fight progress? How can anyone logically adhere to a broken paradigm? Progress is a human truth. Humanity, systems, paradigms, and technology are ever changing, while adapting to the inevitable challenges of change. Progress is messy and change often feels uncomfortable, but progress will take place.

Orsch began year five this week. Summer's end was bittersweet to me. I had not been able to complete my final edit,

## CONCLUSION—IN MY DREAMS

although I was desperate to do so after my confidence reinstilling meeting with Shelley Read, my editor and friend. I had dreams of systems and programs I was sure I'd have ready for the new school year. The girls' bathroom was going to be so beautiful that they would *want* to keep it clean. I was to be finished with the book—have it available and in parents' hands by October and be able to focus on lesson planning and school logistics. But it's September 6, 2013, tonight and we just finished our first week—the very best week.

I had realized early this summer that I had to teach in the classroom again. Last year, I was happy to be relieved of some of my many hats. I was happy to have somewhat of a home life for the first time in many years, and I was the one staff member available to zip to the post office or answer the school phone. It was a relief not to run a school *and* plan and grade *and* answer a million e-mails each night and deal with inevitable issues that arise when so many humans are in the mix. I thought I had reached a breathing level. I took a deep breath—I think it was September 4 of last year. That was the last peaceful breath I got. The school year was busy and chaotic (in hindsight we were adapting to more progress). During all of it, I yearned to teach. I yearned to be in the children's lives, because that is what I love. I realized that I could prevent more problems than I could solve, and so it is that I am thrilled to be back in the classroom. The very best year.

This week reignited purpose and relationships with students and even more progressive thoughts about education and lessons and people. Productive new paradigms are emerging like never before, and I am full of good feelings for the school year and the future. We are a team of dedicated teachers and staff. We unite in harmony about our mission, and we iron out our difficulties and problems. We create. We invent. We oversee sixty-eight children this year of mixed abilities and mixed ages, and they are each progressing at an astonishing rate already. Only one sheet of paper went home this week in students' Friday folders, but the knowledge, understanding, and learning that took place cannot be measured. We had discussions with children that will last a lifetime. We kept track of, not grades, but quotes—brilliant things students said. We listened to a couple of parent concerns and jumped on them immediately. We guided a few friendship troubles and attitude adjustments with a loving approach. We celebrated individuals and pointed out differences with genuine appreciation. We laughed—a lot! We enjoyed our students. They *grew*, and we *knew*—even though there is only one piece of paper to show it.

Fifty years from now, grade levels will not exist; they are one of the worst ideas ever. Fifty years from now, students will be able to choose courses of study at fairly young ages, given they are fluent in communication tools, such as numbers, letters, and technology. Fifty years from now, Eastern medicine may have merged with Western medicine, because both worlds stand to learn from and teach each other. Cures for sickness and disease and poverty will have made significant strides. Our politicians will finally have the skills that many of today's sixth-graders already possess. Fifty years from now—oh goodness, what will the MTV Awards bring us? Fifty years from now, if we are still contemplating big data and test-driven educational practices, progress in this incredibly significant field will have been much too slow. I will be ninety-two, and I will wish you would have taken action long ago, because fifty years is already here and another one is unveiling.

## *The Very Best Year*

This is already shaping up to be the very best year. We began the year with the perfect schedule—one that offers the answer to skills classes and one that offers the most up-to-date paradigms we know to benefit our students. It's interesting how often discovering the perfect paradigm feels like "duh!" I remember the very moment I finally nailed this year's schedule. I had been scratching different versions of the whole-school schedule on various pieces of paper for weeks, contemplating the many schedules of yesteryear that did not meet our needs. I estimate that I was about thirty hours in at the moment epiphany struck—actually, *five years* and thirty hours, to be more accurate. The schedule needed to offer ample time for whole-school interaction, multiage interaction, skills-based classes, open-ended projects, honors classes, student independence, guided learning, and collaborative options. It also needed to serve our littlest students who are not yet literate and do not benefit from projects that require reading instructions independently. The schedule had to offer diversity in grouping—because we are a small community, we must be careful to allow students to interact and collaborate with a wide variety of classmates. And the perfect schedule would bend to philosophy, not the other way around.

I have often said that in the lab called Orsch we make nine mistakes for every one thing we get right. As tough as it is, I am comfortable with that. This is a *lab*, and we must be brave and be willing to find out what doesn't work. We're very good at finding out what *doesn't* work. Nine failed attempts for every success. One of my teachers disagrees. She says it's more like six to four. But with all due respect, and said with a smile, she's not the one creating the schedule!

Any administrator knows the difficulty of scheduling. A schedule is a framework with unbending parameters. It requires columns and rows, and it requires that others comply with its boundaries. A schedule is particularly difficult in an environment that claims "flexibility" as its middle name. And so it is that I spent five years and thirty hours on the perfect schedule. On August 10, on a family trip, I came running into the camper. "I've got it! I've figured out the schedule puzzle! Here it is…What do you guys think?"

"Yeah, Mom. Great! It really sounds perfect, but I coulda come up with that in about five minutes!" When the perfect paradigm strikes, it feels like, "Duh!" Every time I have

## CONCLUSION—IN MY DREAMS

shared some of our more successful structures and solid paradigm discoveries with interested individuals, the conversation feels like, "Duh!" But these developments and epiphanies are only "duh" in hindsight. Years and hours of failure must go into the perfect answer. Any lab, any inventor, knows that to be true. I don't fully understand why simple, perfect paradigm shifts are so hard to conjure, but I know that there is only one way to find them. We must be open to evolution of thought, and we must be willing to be wrong, again and again. We must be brave and progressive, even though it feels uncomfortable.

There is no reason we can't say "the very best year" every year. Every year we learn more. Every *day* we learn more. Our lab solves problems every day. Teachers come up with new ideas. Kids come up with new ideas. We implement every feasible idea and even some that don't seem so feasible—sometimes those are among the most brilliant ones. We become better, and I think that each and every one of us, students and teachers alike, would *wilt* without the opportunity to do so.

Every school community can learn, grow, and evolve. Every year, *the very best year* is possible in every school and in every district. Every school can learn from others, and every school can share its discoveries with a vast community; collective knowledge will increase educational evolution exponentially. Consider the potential of collective knowledge working toward innovative paradigm shifts in the field of education, and then consider the students who will benefit

## ORSCH...CUTTING THE EDGE IN EDUCATION

from innovative programming and collective evolution of thought. Consider the future when these children grow to lead and invent new paradigms themselves. World peace and the end of suffering will become a realistic vision... lucky kids! And fortunate are the people who will see it. I see it in my dreams.

I shall not think in fifty, forty-nine, forty-eight, nor shall I think about ninety-three, ninety-four, ninety-five. *The only answer for anyone who cares about the future is to take steps toward it today.*

Orsch will continue to evolve and invent. We will continue to refine, and we will certainly continue to share our vision and our results (the ones that didn't fail) with you. We will continue to publish thoughtful ideas and new paradigms. You are welcome to keep an eye on our website and our blog. I invite you to take part, to question us, and to offer input. I encourage you to be inventive and brave. Think big and begin. Share your discoveries and your ideas. Share your hopes for your children and your students. Be heard. The world of education needs you. The world of education needs millions of minds thinking about tomorrow. *What Could Be?*

# *Philosophy from a Parent's Perspective—Parent Essays*

What follows are unaltered parent essays that were submitted in recent years as part of a scholarship application. I am greatly encouraged and rewarded by the sentiment and expression in these essays. Prior to these submissions, I did not realize to what extent Orsch parents recognize and appreciate the environment in which their children learn. I have included these essays because they offer another perspective, a parent's point of view, about what constitutes a well-rounded and high-quality education. It is likely that these essays reflect what all parents want in their child's education. These essays include personal stories and references to specific outcomes and hopes. I am amazed to find that parents so highly value some of the intricate pieces of our philosophy and that our philosophy does, in fact, result in tangible, recognizable outcomes. I am moved to tears every time I read these essays. Thank you to all our scholarship applicants. The reward is mine; my gratitude is immeasurable.

ORSCH...CUTTING THE EDGE IN EDUCATION

## IMHO...Why Choose ORSCH? By Debbie

Parents are the guardians of the future. Their children ARE the future. What is your child's future? All children begin as free thinkers. It is the experiences in the world around them that mold them into who they become. Children who are spoken to from babyhood learn, understand and grasp the language. Children who are hugged and loved learn affection and a sense of belonging. Children who are treated with respect, respect themselves and others. Children learn from what surrounds them. What surrounds your child?

Orsch is what all schools should aspire to be. Orsch is a vision. Orsch is a model. Orsch is unique. Orsch is an inspiration.

Orsch, at its core, is a community within a community. Communication is key. A sense of belonging is key. Respect for self and for others is key. In that community setting, children are comfortable in learning. They thrive. They grow a desire within themselves to learn. They grow a desire within themselves to help others to learn.

"Standard" academic excellence, unfortunately, encompasses a rather narrow scope of life. While the three R's are indeed important, we severely limit ourselves when they are our only focus. A child's natural sense of curiosity is a far more important area of learning to develop. With practice, anyone, at any level, can recite facts and figures. Anyone can memorize songs or poems or paragraphs from a book. Not all people can make that book come alive. Not all people can breathe life into a poem. Not all people can inspire joy or despair through music. These things are not learned techniques. They are inspired. Inspired many times, by those around us.

# PHILOSOPHY FROM A PARENT'S PERSPECTIVE—PARENT ESSAYS

Learning is an essential part of living. We learn things every day of our lives. So do our children.

What are our children learning at Orsch? They are learning life's lessons. To be a part of a bigger world. To be comfortable in their own skin. To be free to use their own voice. To reach out for the impossible. To explore and to question. To laugh and to sing and to play. To be a friend and to have a friend. To discover a limitation and to overcome it. To be the person they were meant to be. And... to recite the alphabet.

As a parent whose child has attended Orsch since its inception, the possibilities opened to my child for her future are, quite simply, amazing. At thirteen, I believe if she never attended another day of school, she would excel in all she does. Not because of a vast accumulation of knowledge, facts, or excellent test scores. But because of the person Orsch has helped her to become. She is, even now, a confident, bright, giving, and caring inspiration in life. She reaches for the stars and the moon and the depths of the oceans of knowledge and learning, not because she is required to but because she loves it. Because she is surrounded by people who love learning and inspire others to be the very best they can be. Her sense of possibilities and accomplishment knows no bounds. She knows who she is and what her place is in the world around her. And for all this I am so very grateful.

All children begin as free thinkers. If we put them in a box, they will think within the walls of the box. If we set them free, who knows what they can achieve?

IMHO...there is no choice but Orsch.

## Why My Child's Attendance at Orsch Is Important to Me. By LeeAnne

Orsch is where my child thrives best and comes home happiest. When Ingrid attends Orsch, I don't worry about supplementing her at home to fulfill her thirst for knowledge. I know she is getting what she wants, needs, and desires in her education. She doesn't come home complaining about wanting more math, nor does she complain about how "so and so" is holding up the entire class with misbehavior. She comes home happy and satisfied with her day. To me that is worth everything. I see the difference. She enjoys education buffet style and self-served, as opposed to force-fed. Ingrid enjoys being a teacher and leader to the younger kids—a role she would not experience otherwise. This educational system works for her. She loves Orsch. She can't imagine her life without it. I had great educational situations growing up and I had miserable situations. I know how it feels. Knowing that my daughter is receiving a proper education, and having an awesome time all day is why her attendance is so very important to me.

Although I am not the one attending, I also have my own personal reasons why I love Orsch. I like the fact that my daughter is not trained to pass standardized tests, and pressured to achieve higher marks so that her school looks better. At Orsch, she is Ingrid, not a statistic. Her report cards are painstakingly created, and reflective of her progress, not an average of arbitrary numbers. Work is done over until it is done correctly, as it should be. I appreciate the level of communication experienced at Orsch, as well as the speed of change this fosters. It is a "problem solved" sort of environment, no red tape, no hoops...I like the simplicity of that. If an issue arises, or an adjustment needs to be made, one e-mail, phone call, text, or conversation, and there are instant results. I like that we are in control of attendance. In my opinion, many experiences are educational and if I want Ingrid to draw her education for the day from an out-of-school opportunity, I simply write an e-mail and take her out. Our educational experience is just that..."OURS."

I also love the feel of the environment when you walk in. It is not stifling and regulated, it is humming with energy, happy kids, and interactions. I see it as flowing, pulsing, amoeba-like, learning in process, its own little system and everyone doing their part. I do feel that a parent must have a certain amount of trust in this system, but that's just it...I do! I don't feel the need to be hyper-vigilant and concerned, as I have in other situations. I trust in Orsch. I trust that my daughter will have a great day and receive an educational and school experience that is just as unique, creative, and special as she is!

These are the major ones for me, the ones I most appreciate at this very point, but there are countless other and constantly emerging points that make me further appreciate the educational experience my daughter is fortunate to be a part of.

## What Constitutes a Good Education for My Child? By Lauren

A good education for my child is just that...it is a designed for MY CHILD, not just any child. Yes, she should be able to read, write, and do arithmetic, but it should be more than that, too. [A good education] is reflective of her goals, interests, aspirations, and aptitudes. It improves her weaknesses and fortifies her strengths. Her education should tease her curiosity, and fuel her inner fire. She should be happy and satisfied with her accomplishments at the end of the day, and long to do it all over again. Her education should include social aspects, teach her to be a leader, a team player, accomplish common goals with others, and to get along with those who are both easy and difficult. [Her education] should build her confidence, and teach her to push through struggles toward success.

At the end of high school, I want her to be ready to embark on her personal journey, and have the tools and knowledge to be successful. It is also important that this is a happy, generally stress-free and pleasant process, as it should be. For what good is a splendid amount of knowledge, derived from a process resulting in an individual resentful of the first eighteen years of her life experience.

Yes, individuals have their own personalities and draw their own experiences from an education, but if they have a positive learning environment, I could safely say, the results will end in a happier individual. For me that is key: Do you have the required intelligence and education to be happy and successful (by your own definition) in life? And, do you accept your life as a continuous education? I found it interesting that although my daughter and I have never had a conversation about the meaning of education, in her project she used the word "life" foremost in her statement about education. I try to embrace every teachable moment in life, and was pleased she was on board in her own way.

## What Constitutes a Good Education for Our Children? By Steve and Randi

Wikipedia defines learning as acquiring new, or modifying existing, behaviors, skills, values or preferences and may involve synthesizing different types of information. It does not happen all at once, but builds upon and is shaped by what we already know. To that end learning may be viewed as a process, rather than a collection of factual and procedural knowledge.

Human learning may occur as part of education, personal development, schooling, or training. It may be goal oriented and may be aided by motivation. Learning may occur as a result of habituation, classical conditioning, seen in many animal species or as a result of more complex activities such as play, seen only in relatively intelligent animals.

## PHILOSOPHY FROM A PARENT'S PERSPECTIVE—PARENT ESSAYS

When we ask our children what learning means to them, they both offer a different perspective. We imagine this to be true for all people. Therefore, it is clear that the acquisition of new information is relative to the individual acquiring the knowledge. The way we learn is as unique to us as individuals as our genetic code. So we must ask ourselves: How can sameness in education produce success on any level? Putting people together based solely on things like age and perceived ability seems like an abuse after having had the Orsch experience. In our opinion, children thrive in a multiage environment where their learning is tailored to their individual needs whether they are advanced in one area, challenged in another, or just walking to the beat of their own drummer.

A good education for our children takes this individuality into account on the highest level. We are learning that what constitutes a good education for our children is as evolving of a process as they are as individuals. This concept grows and changes with each passing year, sometimes each passing moment. We as humans and we as a society are constantly changing. The universe is dynamic, not static, and with that our learning environment must be also if we are to meet the individual needs of our children and continue progression. When something is not working there needs to be enough flexibility and judgment to course correct and make changes.

To us education is not purely academic. Success is determined on the product as a whole, which is the sum of numerous parts. To be well rounded there are certain life skills that must be present. They need to understand the principles of being a good person. Sometimes this is challenging to accomplish when a child has little other contact other than with his or her own age group. A group lacking in diversity can translate to a child with the same lack. We value the environment at Orsch because it provides our children with diversity in interaction. Some they like and some they don't. This is an exercise that is more in tune with the reality of our adult world. We want them to learn to be problem solvers and freethinkers. We believe it is important to question things and find out for themselves if something fits. Not just because someone "said so." That translates to a sense of independence and confidence in decision making. It is important for them to develop a work ethic. This work ethic needs to come from within. There needs to be an intrinsic reward in it for it to develop into habit or become part of who they are. Many of these qualities translate to happy, healthy, productive adults who take pride in what they do and who they are.

A good education allows them to fulfill various roles, from teaching and mentoring, to working with others in groups or partnerships, and independently. This exposure allows them opportunities to develop leadership skills, but also to follow directions from another and to contribute parts to make up a whole. A dynamic that allows for a child to play multiple roles is valuable. In life we don't get to just interact with people who are all the same. There is immeasurable value in our children operating within an environment ever-changing in its interaction landscapes. It is important for people to know how to undertake an independent project and be accountable to themselves to finish, just as it is valuable to be able to work in pairs or teams and to come together to reach the common goal, being accountable to others for your part of the product.

A good education is a culture of success, not just academically but emotionally as well. A child who is a success on the inside is also on the outside. A sense of confidence and drive that propels them through the world they create for themselves, allowing them to achieve their wildest dreams. It is a safe haven for them to create themselves without being conformists, thus allowing them a truer sense of self. It is a culture that not only embraces but also nurtures their individual spirit and praises them and promotes internal reward for who they are. Children who feel safe and confident in their surroundings are free of emotional roadblocks that can hinder their learning regardless of environment. We have seen what lack of confidence can create with respect to roadblocks in learning.

Our hope is that they are in an environment that allows them to meet their full potential and be so engaged and excited about it that they don't consider it work but a pleasure. Alli may have said it best: "We play when we are learning and learn while playing. Sometimes it all feels like the same thing." Quality education incites a zeal and enthusiasm far beyond our wildest dreams that will carry on into their twilight years, so that they may enjoy the world around them and everything it has to offer, by being lifelong learners and sponging up every experience life throws at them.

For us, as parents, a quality educational experience brings peace of mind, a full night's sleep free from worry, reassurance that our children are getting everything they need in arenas we don't feel qualified to tackle. It gives us a village. A village of likeminded parents, educators, and friends to lean on when we need support or reassurance, or just a kind word and a friendly face. It is a place where we feel heard and safe in knowing that what we say matters with a sense that "we are all in this together."

Most of all, at the end of the day it means happy, healthy children who can't wait for what is next and possess the will and desire to chase after learning as if it is an adventure they never want to end. Confident and empowered in who they are and what they know to conquer wherever they find themselves. We are pleased to say that Orsch is accomplishing this for us, and we are confident that it will be as ever-changing in its methods as our children are.

## "What Constitutes a Good Education for Your Child?" By Nella and Craig

Often times it is forgotten that there is much more to education than academics. Kids spend so much of their day preparing for state-mandated testing to determine how well their school is doing. Kids are stuck at desks all day, they are taught at the same pace, they all learn the same lessons, and individuality is lost. Bullying is running rampant, teachable moments are lost, and kids are not learning critical life skills.

A good education embraces individuality. Educators should acknowledge that just because kids are in the same age group in the same classroom they are not the same. It is unrealistic to expect all eight-year-olds to be at the exact same level, read at the same pace, and do the same math problems as all of their peers. They should be taught at their own pace, be proud of what they can accomplish and not focused on what they are not yet able to do. This demand for sameness creates a system where kids are unnecessarily labeled and put into categories. These kids will all get there in their own time. There is no need for pressure, stress, and labels. Learning should be fun!

Another critical component of a good education is teaching kids skills that are not found in textbooks. Communication skills, problem solving, conflict resolution, and empathy are all so important in creating well-rounded citizens. Parents can't always provide guidance at the time it is needed so when conflicts arise at school, kids look to teachers for guidance. Often times kids are told, "It's no big deal" or "just ignore it." This does not teach kids how to problem solve or help them resolve issues. When children are given a safe place with a trusted teacher to help resolve issues, skills are learned and confidence is grown in their own abilities.

Another important component of a good education for my child is flexibility. There should be flexibility in their schedules. If kids are really enjoying a lesson it should not be cut short to move on to the next lesson because the clock says it is time to. There is a lot of learning to be done in impromptu moments. Kids should be allowed flexibility in their seating arrangements. Kids are not hardwired to sit still for long periods of time. Kids should be encouraged to get up and move. By allowing students flexibility in their academics you are allowing students to take ownership of their education.

## PHILOSOPHY FROM A PARENT'S PERSPECTIVE—PARENT ESSAYS

Orsch provides all the things that we consider to constitute an amazing education for Andrea. She is receiving a foundation that will carry her into her teen years with confidence in herself and her abilities. This scholarship would help tremendously to continue to provide Andrea with an outstanding education that encompasses all that we believe to be important. In the two years that she has been there we have seen her blossom. She is proud to be part of the Orsch family and so are we.

## Why It Is Important for Rachel to Attend Orsch? By Steve and Randi

Prior to attending Orsch, Rachel was a "good" student. While we were grateful for this, we knew she had potential to be a great student. We knew this because we would often see glimpses of it, but there was no consistency. As the years came and went we started to see a pattern emerge. She was learning how to skate by. She was discovering, through no fault of her own, that she could do "just enough." We feared that if it continued to go unchecked, this would translate into a state of being and a characteristic of who she may become. It was beginning to feel like laziness.

When we addressed our concerns with her educators we were dismissed. It felt like they had bigger problems to worry about...and we are sure they did. Who complains about a "good" student? We began to wonder if our standards were too high. We now know their standards for her were too low. We could see that she needed something to motivate her. She needed to be inspired. Orsch has done just that. It has taken time and some frustration, patience and perseverance on her part and that of her teachers; perhaps mostly her teachers. Orsch flipped the switch for her. When that light bulb finally went off she couldn't have shined brighter, and she knew it. We have seen a miraculous change in Rachel's approach to her learning and consistency in her work ethic. She gives her endeavors her all because she values the final product and has begun to understand the power of intrinsic rewards. It is imperative that Rachel remain in this environment so that she may continue to be inspired to take ownership in her learning and chase after it like a child chases a butterfly, with excitement and enthusiasm.

We are seeing what we knew was there all along. With the right guidance and support she will continue to learn how to harness this potential and use it to her advantage. She now knows she has it within her. The task ahead is for her to continue in a way that nurtures this potential and allows it to take root so that it becomes an integral part of who she is and becomes automatic. She must turn these wonderful gifts into habit. We believe this will allow her advantages and opportunities in her later learning years, i.e., high school and postsecondary education. It goes well beyond her education into how she will thrive within the workplace as well. We believe that only Orsch can offer her the support and guidance, beyond ours as parents, that she will need during these formative years. Rachel is completely enamored with school. We will be forever grateful that, as parents, we have the opportunity to experience our children being enchanted by education.

Rachel has always had a huge capacity for love. We deemed her early on as our child with "extra feelers." She has a sensitive spirit and can tune in very quickly to what goes on around her. We have often said that she can find the good in anyone. It is something we often praise her for. (Truthfully, it often gives us something to aspire to.) We have found that this does not always work to her advantage. With this has come some tough lessons. Life is full of these, to be sure. We all have to learn what kind of people we want to surround ourselves with, sometimes by trial and error. We value the small student body of Orsch and its multiage dynamic for this reason. We also value the fact that it has diversity in its student population. There is a diverse group of needs, personality, and backgrounds. This provides our children with lessons in acceptance and the embracing of individuality. Not only allowing for the development of their own individuality, but also that of their peers. It has taught us many lessons in acceptance of diversity as well. Our wish is that, continuing in this learning environment, Rachel will have more time to develop a strong and unshakable sense of self that will serve her in years to come. The tween and teen years are hard. Sometimes it seems like it can be especially hard for girls. We know we cannot protect her forever, but we really want Rachel to stay at Orsch through her middle school years, giving her every opportunity to develop confidence in who she is, both physically and emotionally, and value for those she surrounds herself with. We want her to feel so safe in who she is that she can inspire the same in others and avoid the pitfalls of being a follower. It is important to us that she develops strong leadership so that she can confidently make good choices and avoid the danger of negative peer pressure.

The freedom and independence coupled with personal responsibility that Orsch encourages is reinforcing the idea that we are in charge of our own destiny. This is something that we can't place enough emphasis on in our family. Rachel must know that she has the power to be and do whatever her mind and heart can dream of. It is important that she be in a place where she is empowered to make decisions. This grows confidence in her ability to make good choices so that when choices become bigger, along with their potential outcomes, she will have been given opportunity to practice. It allows for them to be accountable for their own actions and responsible for their outcomes. This is a life skill that is very valuable. When given the opportunity to master it at a young age they are all the more prepared for what life can bring.

When it is all said and done, Rachel is happy at Orsch, she is fulfilled and engaged and embraces any experience she can get her hands on. She is head over heels in love with learning and has finally found out how much fun reading can be. She sees the world as full of possibility and has an optimism to be rivaled. We feel this is the only place that she has all of the tools at her disposal to be who she now knows she can be, and we don't want anything to stand in her way.

## Why Is It Important For Alli to Attend Orsch? By Steve and Randi

That Alli had a rough finish to her first year of public education is a well-known fact at Orsch. This is known to some degree because she was not the only one from her class who found her way there. There are so many feelings when we think of how grateful we are that she has had this opportunity, we are not sure they can all be put into words. Looking back on who Alli was in her kindergarten year, who she has become so far is a surprise to us. We always saw her as this quiet, shy, potential follower. We worried that we would forever have to peel her off of one of us and that she would not embrace change or new experiences. How wrong we were. Who knew that she just needed the right environment? We have seen her blossom into an independent leader who relishes a new experience and can't wait to ask: what, who, how, and why. She questions everything, but more importantly, she seeks out the answers because she sees learning as an opportunity not an obligation.

Orsch has provided her with the opportunity and environment not only to allow her to become her own person but to embrace the process of it. It has helped her grow her confidence in all arenas, but especially to be a capable learner. Without Orsch, we have to wonder where she would be. We fear she would have been held back in every subject based on her level of reading at the time. For Alli, this would have been devastating. She gets bored. If she is not engaged and interested, she is checked out.

The Orsch dynamic has allowed her to excel in subjects individually, not be categorized as a whole based on the performance in a single subject. This has translated to increasing her confidence in reading, because she can see that she is capable of learning and excelling. We believe that math specifically has created an opportunity for her to improve her reading, because, in her own words, "it makes me feel smart." When she knows she can be good at one thing, she knows she can be good at others. We feel she must stay in this environment to further improve her reading and her sense of self (to a point these two things were tied together for a time). Improve is a relative term. This is anything from actual fluency and testing to generating a love for what it can do for her and the world she can travel to via books. We would love to see her develop a passion for reading.

The individualized approach that Orsch has offered us allows Alli to grow into the learner she is meant to be. The diversified approach allows her to be engaged all around. In areas where she excels it is important for her to continue to do so. There have been times when Alli has felt held back, or complained that she was "bored." Orsch is a safe place where she can express those concerns and feel like they are not only heard but also acted upon, specifically in math. This child could not wait to learn multiplication. It was the greatest day ever when they "finally" started. Looking back on our own educations this idea seemed absolutely crazy to us. Who gets that excited about multiplication? Kids who go to Orsch do...they get excited about everything. Our children simply must be exposed to their education in the fashion that everything is this exciting. We see the difference that type of engagement makes, and it has become as necessary as feeding them a healthy diet. This is the diet for their mind.

The multiage dynamic is a wonderful gift in so many ways. From a character building perspective the bounty is beyond our expectations. Alli has been given the gift of freedom. Freedom to choose who she wants to be and the support to embrace her individuality with guidance toward being a motivated self-starter and a sense of personal responsibility. There is so much more than academics going on. Orsch is helping us raise "good people." We have seen so many positive changes in the pride she takes in her schoolwork and zeal and enthusiasm for learning. Her commitment to a job well done is astounding. We are looking forward to this translating to the same consistency in her work ethic at home. She has not yet managed for her school persona and her home persona to merge. We are looking forward to this in the coming years as her confidence grows and she sees increasing value in consistent performance.

Our fear is that if we were to return her to public school these aspects of individuality and growth would become lost and perhaps irrelevant in the learning process. We are building "whole" people here. It is important to take into account their individual needs and attributes without casting them into a mold of sameness due to age or level of performance in a single subject. It is paramount that she be given the opportunity to further solidify who she is and develop a strong sense of self and confidence in learning, so that she may reach her full potential and maximize her educational opportunity. It is so important to us that she learns good habits, takes ownership of her education, and values diversity in the world she inhabits. These are things we believe she will only get in their entirety at Orsch.

## What Constitutes a Good Education for My Children? By Charles

I have two children who currently attend Orsch, Angie and Nick. I demand excellence in my children's education, and put simply, Orsch has delivered. I have tried to live my life by striving to always exceed expectations, and I have tried to instill this value in my children as well. Orsch is a perfect example of this philosophy. At each Orsch event I attend, and with each Orsch teacher I meet, I walk away positively impressed, and usually with a feeling of "Wow! I wasn't expecting that."

## PHILOSOPHY FROM A PARENT'S PERSPECTIVE—PARENT ESSAYS

For my children, there are three components I believe are critical to a successful educational experience. First, the educational environment must instill my children with self-confidence. When Angie first started at Orsch, her confidence had been crushed. She did not believe in herself, and therefore, she had no idea what she could achieve. She was scared to try, scared to fail, and miserable inside. She cried each morning before school. Her teacher described Angie to me as simply an average little girl.

Well, my Angie is a star. She was born a star and she will always be one. But she had forgotten that. Slowly, Orsch began building that self-confidence back up. It took time, but by the end of her first year, she was shining again. She believed in herself. She wasn't scared to try or fail anymore, and she practically glowed with joy by the time she came home from school each day. Orsch gave Angie her confidence back, and with it, her ability to reach her potential.

Second, my children's educational environment must embrace creativity and individuality and encourage both. Nick is unique, and though he was doing well in a traditional educational setting, I saw the rigid structure (both educational and social) of public school squelching his creative potential and his personality. Understandably, he wanted to fit in, be one of the guys, complain about school (because everyone else was), do only what was required.

When he came to Orsch, it was like watching a bird who had only hopped from branch to branch take off and soar into the clouds for the first time. Nick is a leader, not a follower. And being in a safe, comfortable educational environment that allows (and encourages) him to follow his creative instincts has been fun to watch. I thought I was pretty cool for being able to walk the dog with a yo-yo. Now I know better. Nick's passion is infectious, and consequently, the 2011-2012 Orsch school year could rightly be labeled the year of the yo-yo. Oh, and he wrote a book, at twelve. I can't wait to see what's next.

Third, and perhaps most importantly, my children's educational environment has to instill in them a love of learning and teach them how to learn. Although it sounds simplistic, in my opinion, a child (or adult) who loves to learn, and knows how to learn, will learn; it really doesn't matter what the subject is. I believe this to be true whether the child is eight learning to read or in college studying astrophysics. Orsch is teaching my kids how to learn, and they are loving every minute of it. How could you ask for anything more?

Well, I can because I am greedy, and as I said, I demand excellence from my children's educators. On top of everything else, Orsch is teaching my kids to be kind and tolerant and supportive and cooperative. They are part of a community, and they know this; they feel this. At Orsch, they depend on others, and in turn, others depend on them. They are loved, and they love in return. Experiencing such interconnectedness during such formative years is—in my opinion—invaluable, because at the end of the day, that is what it is really all about. You can try and go it alone in this world, but I don't think you'd get very far, and you certainly won't go as far as you could by accepting help and helping others along the way.

## Why My Child's Attendance at Orsch Is Important to Me. By Ellie

In early January of 2011, I walked my first-grade daughter, Alexis, to her classroom, the same as I had done every morning that year. When we reached her classroom she buckled her knees and refused to enter the room. As compliant a child as anyone has ever been, I was astonished at her resolve in the fact that she refused to walk through that threshold and into her class. I had never seen her defy any authority in her life; and I was both amazed and alarmed when she looked at me, and adamantly refused to do as I said.

# PHILOSOPHY FROM A PARENT'S PERSPECTIVE—PARENT ESSAYS

"I won't go in there, Mama," she cried. "I will not ever go in there again," Alexis proclaimed. And she never did step foot in that classroom again.

Staunch public school education fundamentalists, my husband and I had never really considered putting our children in private school. That option was for extraordinarily rich people, whose beliefs led them to think they couldn't/wouldn't mingle with the masses of mainstream society, right? Even though my son's favorite teacher had left his school to start her very own new and exciting school, it wasn't the right option for us, right?? My husband and I were both public school educated. Both my parent-in-laws were public school teachers. Pulling our children out of public school was teaching them that they are better than the rest of the world, right??? Right????

Yet, here we were. Since the start of her first grade year under the guidance of an exceptionally inflexible and borderline cruel teacher, I had watched my beautiful, passionate, self-confident little girl turn into a withdrawn, sad emotional wreck (and all at the ripe old age of six).

Enter Orsch.

Although not accepting new students at the time, Orsch said that they couldn't and wouldn't turn their back on my daughter. They found a spot for her and she started attending shortly after the New Year. By the third week of January, she started making eye contact with adults again. By Valentine's Day, she was putting on an act, on a stage, in front of the whole school. By snowmelt, she was standing up for herself at home, with her friends, and speaking her mind at school. The winter had found my little Alexis wilted and closed in on herself, by spring she was blooming with pride and confidence.

Meanwhile, my son, Noah, was catching on to what a different approach Orsch had to education and philosophy on learning. An independent thinker, and lover of learning, Noah was quick to find a pull to Orsch and its hands-on approach. Noah started attending the first year of his middle school years, and has grown so much as a person, a writer, a dream chaser, and an overall thinker.

Education comes in many forms. In a society founded on rules and traditions, it is hard to see outside of the ideas, and dreams, you think you want for your children. But because life threw us a curveball, and because we were fortunate enough to be forced to change our path, a whole new world was opened up to us.

What started out as a nightmare-looking situation, ended up being a huge blessing. It has also caused me to take a real and deep look into what "education" is, and about how I hope for my children to be able to obtain an "education." I have come to decide that most traditional academic advancements can be made at most any age or stage of life. A person wanting to learn a specific skill or ability can most likely obtain their goal with a certain amount of follow through and access to the materials needed to learn that skill.

What I think is so much more important for my children is the basic and fundamental ability to be themselves, to be confident in themselves, to enjoy who they are, to learn to enjoy (at least some) of the attributes of those around them, and to learn to learn in a way they enjoy and find beneficial. This is the education that attending Orsch is giving them, and this is the most important aspect to me.

## Why Elliot Attending ORSCH Is Important to Me. By Robin

There are many reasons that I am so thankful for Orsch and everything that has come from it. Elliot has had many struggles in his life that were mostly inflicted by my lack of parenting skills as a very young parent. As I have grown, I have realized that my children's education, skill set, exposure level, experiences, etc. are all the responsibility of the parent and the harder I work, the more of those things my children can have. While this may be a simple notion, it is a full-time job all in itself that as a young parent I was unaware of, as well as having priorities that were out of order.

Orsch has given my son the opportunity to be himself without being punished for who he is at his core. He is creative, and energetic… not ADHD. He is friendly and passionate…not an inconvenience to those around him. While he may have faults, everyone does and I love that Orsch praises his accomplishments rather than harping on his faults. Also, when issues arise they are addressed appropriately and effectively. Rather than avoiding the situation and sending him to a confined space, the Orsch teachers try and get to the root of the problem to increase his success in the future.

Overall, the Orsch community is the most enlightening experience my son has ever had. Also, it is the first educational institution that has given him the chance to learn, which he has been denied previously due to lack of understanding and variety of learning methods. My son is loving, caring, endearing, yet somewhat misguided at times. He has many things in his life that I wish he had not experienced at his age, however, he has and must learn how to process all of the information while receiving the loving attention he so much deserves as well as the opportunity to be everything he can be. Thank you for everything!!

## What Constitutes a Good Education for My Child? By Rebecca

A good education for my child would include the following:

1. A safe environment for my child to learn.

2. An environment where my child is not bullied.

## ORSCH...CUTTING THE EDGE IN EDUCATION

3. Teachers who take individual time with the child to individualize the learning experience.

4. Teachers who focus on the success of the children rather than the end of the quarter.

5. An environment where my child has the opportunity to express himself without fear of punishment.

6. Learning in different ways to expand the mind and allow him to learn in areas he may not otherwise have the opportunity.

7. Coming home and feeling as if he has learned something.

8. A place where he is excited to learn because the experience is made fun.

9. A good education for my child is going to Orsch! Where my son comes home and can't wait to tell me all about what he learned.

While I always remain open minded to new ideas to benefit my child, I am certain Orsch is where my son will receive them. Ethan loves coming to school and comes home excited to tell me about his day. He does not feel like an outcast and is excited every day for the possibility of a new experience. I want to give a large thank you to Orsch, the teachers, and all of the wonderful students who have welcomed my son with such an open heart.

# PHILOSOPHY FROM A PARENT'S PERSPECTIVE—PARENT ESSAYS

## What Constitutes a Good Education for Your Child? By Beth and Randal

A good education is one that develops lifelong learners. When the innate curiosity of children is encouraged in a safe environment, great ideas are spawned. For my children, I wish them to be in an environment that provides creative input and embraces creative output. The children should have the opportunity to ask questions about the world around them and encouragement to explore various answers in an analytical manner. A typical school day should include academics focusing on reading, writing, math, science, arts, and music, and structured and unstructured play. A good education in a nurturing environment fosters independence and self-confidence. It is also important to me that my kids have a sense of being part of a community and have the support of their teachers and peers.

An unanticipated benefit to our family for having both Becka and Shelton at Orsch is the effect it has had on their relationship with each other. They have always been close, and having so many shared experiences and people in their day has deepened their bond with each other. I feel so privileged to be a part of the Orsch experiment and have seen for myself that these elements are part of my children's daily life at Orsch. Thanks for all you do.

## Why Is Shelton's Attendance at Orsch Important to Me? By Beth

Shelton was made for Orsch and Orsch was made for Shelton. He is a very creative kid and is excelling in the creative environment of Orsch.

Shelton is shy and it takes time for him to trust people and open up to them. The relationships that Shelton has developed at Orsch, especially with Miss Erica and his fellow Mid Littles, has enabled Shelton to open up, be himself, and even share some of his ideas. This foundation in his early education will be the rock he builds on as he gets older. He also benefits from having older kids, notably the older boys, to look up to and show him that learning and creating is "cool," bullying is not. I have noticed a big change in Shelton this year in his relationships with younger kids as well, especially his relationship with his younger niece and nephew. He has much more patience with them and takes pride in showing them "big boy" stuff. For example, he taught his little nephew Simon how to chew gum this summer.

## Why Is Becka's Attendance at Orsch Important to Me? By Beth

Becka's presence at Orsch initially was the result of Shelton's attendance and experiences at Orsch. Through Becka's experiences I have seen that the program is personalized for each student. Becka's ability to work at her own pace and explore areas of math that challenge her academically has been instrumental in creating an excitement for learning that carries over into her other subjects. The multiage environment has been beneficial to Becka in that she has discovered her love for teaching others. I also see her gaining self-confidence in sharing her ideas with peers and older students, which will be a great asset to her in the future. I feel another year in this environment and Becka will show even more improvement in this area. Mostly, I want Becka to be appreciated for the sweet, caring, compassionate young lady that she is.

PHILOSOPHY FROM A PARENT'S PERSPECTIVE—PARENT ESSAYS

## "Why Is Your Child's Attendance at Orsch Important to You?" By Nancy and Carl

There are so many reasons why Anna's attendance at Orsch is important to us!

Orsch has created an environment where learning is fun and Anna wants to learn! Orsch recognizes that all kids are not the same, do not learn the same, and should not be treated the same.

Orsch has provided Anna an environment where she is free to be herself. Kids at Orsch have the amazing freedom to be themselves. They are encouraged to embrace what makes them unique and are not allowed to compare themselves to others. Orsch provides a safe environment where kids are not teased or bullied. There is no greater gift to a child!

Orsch has given Anna a voice. She is not afraid to express herself. She is comfortable and confident with her peers and her teachers. She knows she can express her thoughts and feelings without judgment. She communicates so effectively that sometimes I forget she is only eight.

Growing up can be difficult and Anna has had some issues with peers. When she needs guidance navigating these issues she knows that she is surrounded by caring adults who are there to help her. Her feelings are validated and she is given problem-solving skills that she will benefit from the rest of her life. It makes her feel so good to be able to "call a meeting" and resolve an issue.

Orsch provides Anna with thoughtful, caring, supportive adults who listen, nurture, and know her well enough to know when she needs an extra hug, or two. When Anna lost her great-grandma and was feeling sad she received so much love and support from the teachers at Orsch. It was just what she needed to help her through a tough time.

Anna has occasionally been known to be lazy in her school work. Her teachers recognize this and know that if they challenge her, she will rise to the occasion. She loves a challenge! Anna was so proud when she earned her reading wings.

## ORSCH...CUTTING THE EDGE IN EDUCATION

The teachers at Orsch are always available to assist parents too. Carl and I have been so grateful for the insight and support provided by Jackie, Erica, and Elizabeth. We have been able to sit down and talk and make a plan. These amazing teachers have helped us navigate difficult times, given us ideas and lots of support.

We strongly believe that Anna would not be the same kid today had she not attended Orsch. We are so grateful that she is surrounded by teachers who are passionate and are committed to education.

It is possible for all parents to feel their child is receiving such programming. Let us dwell in possibility.

# *Acknowledgments*

What follows is not just a list of names, but a brief record of stories that brought Orsch to life and the acknowledgment of those who contributed to all we have discovered and learned.

First, I would like to thank my parents, Peggy and Glen Padilla, for offering me a nurturing environment in which to grow and allowing me to pursue my dreams, hopes, and passions throughout my life. Thank you for the supportive, flexible upbringing you offered. I grew up feeling like anything was possible.

Secondly, I am forever grateful for the memorable teachers and professors throughout my life who inspired me, pushed me to be my best, and left a lasting impression. Your contributions to your students' lives will live forever.

As I entered my teaching career, I was lucky enough to begin under the inspiration of principal Dr. Susan Lebow-Tollefson; she valued innovation, creativity, and the engagement of students above all else. Thank you, Dr. Lebow, for your encouragement and belief in me as a young, wide-eyed, very green teacher. Your support led to everything this book is about. And thank you for staying in touch—it means the world to me. To my first teaching partner, Robin Weidemueller, thank you. We were a great team; I will always value those years and the innovative ideas we implemented together. And thank you, Barb Haas, for being that person in the hallways to whom I could tell my dreams, schemes and plans. Thank you for encouraging me to keep going and for telling me that the expense of a copy machine was a surmountable obstacle. You were right; it worked out.

Thank you, Sam Burt, for keeping the dream alive by knowing that a fun place to learn was possible and knowing that somehow we could make it happen. Thank you for being the reason I could not give up. Thank you for the advice, the support, and the love. Thank you, also, for always testing us and letting us know when we don't offer you the best—you make us better teachers. Thank you, Emma Burt, for being so loving, supportive, and helpful, and thank you for attending Orsch—I will be forever grateful for your presence, by my side every day. Thank you for your continued reminders that it is all worth it.

As Orsch became a reality, several people contributed greatly to its success—first and foremost, my husband, Ashley. At every turn, he was there to keep us moving forward with positivity, hard work, and solid strategy. He has supported our mission and vision from day one and continues to be as passionate about Orsch as I am. He has supported the writing of this book with countless hours of discussion, conceptual structure, editing detail, and, more

## ACKNOWLEDGMENTS

than anything, has been a source of positive feedback that gave me faith in this project throughout.

The biggest thanks goes out to all Orsch students and families. Students, thank you for showing us the way, for speaking up, and for suggesting new ways of thinking. Your input is invaluable. Thank you for the mountains of joy you have added to our lives. Parents and grandparents, thank you for putting your trust in us, especially in year one, when the paradigm was untested. Your support and feedback have truly built this program. Thank you for believing in and supporting your children and their dreams, passions, interests, and potential. Thank you for always showing up at our parties, performances, and workdays. You are the most wonderful group of people and your children are amazing.

A sincere thank-you goes out to Bob Teitler, whose generous donation allowed Ms. Beth to teach with me for ten hours per week in year one. Somehow, having another adult around for even a small fraction of time helped me feel like I had a team of people on my side. And thank you for all of the kind and positive words you have spoken about Orsch throughout the years. Your support was instrumental. Thank you to BK and Michael Bleakley, who have generously supported our scholarship program, supporting those who would not have otherwise been able to attend Orsch.

Thank you, Beth Jenkins, for everything. Thank you for believing in our program—your support was instrumental, as your wealth of experience in education added such validity to what we are doing. Teaching with you was unforgettable. You and your children will forever remain one of the foundational blocks of this program.

To the first follower, Miss Elizabeth Weiss, thank you for falling into our lives. You landed in just the right spot. You have offered me endless support, both moral and pure workload. You have become an adored and effective teacher; you are an incredible teammate and friend. Thank you for believing in everything we do, and thank you for keeping all of us centered in purpose. Thank you for bringing Erica to us.

Thank you, Stacy McPhail, for the endless volunteer hours you gave as a parent, and then for rescuing me in year two so that I didn't have to study for ten hours to teach our students one hour of science. You remain a rock, an incredible teammate, and the most engaging and effective teacher I have ever known. We owe our students' 100 percent engagement in scientific inquiry and love for science to your methods and approach to children. You are such a valued and supportive friend; this has been a fun journey together. I know that Orsch would not have survived without your presence and I would have wilted without you.

Thank you, Miss Erica Bendixen, for choosing to teach at Orsch instead of taking a job with a handsome salary and health coverage. You truly do work for passion. You are such a dedicated and wonderful teacher and employee. Thank you for everything you give to your students and for all of

## ACKNOWLEDGMENTS

the wisdom, perspective, and solid thinking you offer our team.

Thank you, Miss Erin Angle, whom I met at the top of a mountain peak. Thank you for not thinking my approach was too strange as we passed each other on that trail; I somehow sensed you would be as amazing as you are. I will be forever grateful that I hiked back up that peak to introduce myself and ask for your number. We are so very lucky to have you. You bring peace, warmth, and complete joy to our lives while keeping your little monsters happy as can be.

Thank you to Miss Jordan Cooper—the most teachable teacher I know. You came to us with a traditional mind-set and have now found your own creativity. You are flourishing and are such a testament to what a creative environment can offer a teacher. Your connection with students and your ability to learn and grow have been such positive attributes to our team. Thank you for all of your dedication, hard work, and many hours to become a truly amazing teacher. I know you will flourish in your new endeavors.

Miss Jenny Hill, your inspiration will live in Orsch forever. You have shown so many students their musical talents and passions and have connected deeply with so many—they will forever have the inspiration you gave to them. You offered us so many smiles and so many opportunities to laugh. You have been a loving and cherished member of our team, and we are so grateful that you decided to stay!

## ORSCH...CUTTING THE EDGE IN EDUCATION

Travel the world when you are ready; follow your heart and your passion, and never look back.

Thank you Stephanie Hicks. When you waltzed through the door, it was as if we had never spent a day without you. Your presence in Orsch fills a place that would otherwise be a gaping hole in our lives. Your gentle nature and optimism transfers instantly to the students you touch and to all of your colleagues. Thank you for landing back in Gunnison where your heart lives and thank you for dedicating your days to Orsch for much less salary than you deserve.

Sierra Logan, we can't imagine a school without you. Thank you for filling every moment with productive, cheerful help to all of our students and teachers. You have become an integral part of our team. And to Robin Norton, thank you so very much for giving the love of music to our tiniest members. They will forever have rhythm and style in their musical endeavors.

To all of our other teachers and various volunteers, thank you for all of your unpaid and underpaid hours and your dedication to students.

To my wonderful friend. mentor, and editor, Shelley Read. You and I have had hundreds of significant conversations over the years. Our endless discussions have led to many of the key points in Orsch philosophy and your input has given me hope and faith in Orsch's message. Thank you for continuing to help me combat my deepest fears. And thank

## ACKNOWLEDGMENTS

you for the diligent editing that you provided to this book; it would not have been solid without you.

Finally, thank you to Matt Burt and Allen Ivy for capturing the essence of us so beautifully in your photos. Please enjoy all of our smiling children and fun events recorded by Matt and Allen, which are available on Facebook. And a wonderful shout-out and thank you to Emily Edwards, producer of our *Try to Say Yes* minidocumentary (accessible on our website). You represented us beautifully!

# *Bibliography*

Başar, Erol. *Memory and Brain Dynamics: Oscillations Integrating Attention, Perception, Learning, and Memory.* Boca Raton, FL: CRC, 2004.

Berger, Kathleen Stassen. *Invitation to the Life Span.* New York: Worth, 2010.

Bonwell, Charles C. "Active Learning: Creating Excitement in the Classroom." *Active Learning: Creating Excitement in the Classroom.* http://www.ntlf.com/html/lib/bib/91-9dig.htm.

Browning, William. "Learning Styles." www.browningwrite.home.comcast.net Accessed July 16, 2012.

Carroll, A., S. Houghton, R. Wood, K. Unsworth, J. Hattie, and L. Gordon. "Self-Efficacy and Academic Achievement in Australian High School Students: The Mediating Effects of Academic Aspirations and Delinquency." *Journal of Adolescence* (2009): 797–817.

Cline, Foster, and Jim Fay. *Parenting with Love and Logic: Teaching Children Responsibility.* Colorado Springs, CO: Piñon, 2006.

"Clonlara School Homeschool Program and Campus Program." *Clonlara School Homeschool Program and Campus Program.* http://www.clonlara.org/.

Costa, Arthur L., and Bena Kallick. *Learning and Leading with Habits of Mind: 16 Essential Characteristics for Success.* Alexandria, VA: Association for Supervision and Curriculum Development, 2008.

"Education." The White House. September 16, 2012. http://www.whitehouse.gov/issues/education.

Ellis, Nick C. "Constructions, chunking, and connectionism: The emergence of second language structure." *The handbook of second language acquisition* (2003): 63-103.

Evans, Robert. *The Human Side of School Change: Reform, Resistance, and the Real-life Problems of Innovation.* San Francisco: Jossey-Bass, 1996.

Florida, Richard L. *The Rise of the Creative Class: And How It's Transforming Work, Leisure, Community and Everyday Life.* New York, NY: Basic, 2002.

Fullan, M. *Choosing Wrong Drivers for Whole System Reform.* Seminar series 204. Melbourne: Centre for Strategic Education, April 2011.

Fullan, Michael. *All Systems Go: The Change Imperative for Whole System Reform.* Thousand Oaks, CA: Corwin, 2010.

## BIBLIOGRAPHY

Gladwell, Malcolm. *Blink: The Power of Thinking without Thinking.* New York: Little, Brown and Company, 2005.

Hoff, Syd. *Barkley.* New York: Harper & Row, 1975.

"Home | StopBullying.gov." *Home | StopBullying.gov.* September 16, 2012. http://www.stopbullying.gov/.

"Howard Gardner, Multiple Intelligences and Education." *Contents @ the Informal Education Homepage.* http://www.infed.org.

*The Incredibles.* Directed by Brad Bird. Written By Brad Bird. 2004. DVD.

Johnson, David W., Roger T. Johnson, and Edythe Johnson. Holubec. *Cooperative Learning in the Classroom.* Alexandria, VA: Association for Supervision and Curriculum Development, 1994.

*Kagan.* http://www.kaganonline.com.

Kieves, Tama J. *This Time I Dance: Creating the Work You Love.* New York: Jeremy P. Tarcher/Penguin, 2006.

Koo, Grace S. "Targeting Boredom in School, in Life." *Philippine Daily Inquirer.* July 4, 2011

Kriete, Roxanne. Turners Falls: Northeast Foundation for Children, 1999.

*Learning Styles Links.* 2007. http://www.oucom.ohiou.edu/fd/learning_style_inventories.htm.

McAvoy, Donna. "Heterogeneous Grouping of Students and Its Effects on Learning." November 15, 1998. http://ruby.fgcu.edu/courses/80337/McAvoy/HETERO~1.html

McLeod, Saul. "Carl Rogers." *Simply Psychology*. http://www.simplypsychology.org/carl-rogers.html.

McLeod, Saul. "Lev Vygotsky." *Simply Psychology*. http://www.simplypsychology.org/vygotsky.html.

McQuillan, P. J. "Possibilities and Pitfalls: A Comparative Analysis of Student Empowerment." *American Educational Research Journal* (2005): 639–70.

"Ministry of Education and Culture." *OKM*. http://www.minedu.fi/pisa/piirteita.html?lang=en>.

O'Niell, Geraldine, and Tim McMahon. "Student-Centered Learning: What Does It Mean for Students and Lecturers?" *Student-Centered Learning: What Does It Mean for Students and Lecturers?* (2005). http://www.aishe.org/readings/2005-1/oneill-mcmahon-Tues_19th_Oct_SCL.html.

"Parent Involvement." *NEA*. www.nea.org/tools/17360.htm.

Robinson, Ken, and Lou Aronica. *The Element: How Finding Your Passion Changes Everything*. New York: Viking, 2009.

Robinson, Ken. *Out of Our Minds: Learning to Be Creative*. Oxford: Capstone, 2001.

# BIBLIOGRAPHY

Rutherford, Paula. *Instruction for All Students*. Alexandria, VA: Just Ask Publications, 2008.

Sahlberg, Pasi, and Andy Hargreaves. *Finnish Lessons: What Can the World Learn from Educational Change in Finland?* New York: Teachers College, 2011.

Sarason, Seymour Bernard. *The Predictable Failure of Educational Reform: Can We Change Course before It's Too Late?* San Francisco: Jossey-Bass, 1990.

Smith, Fran. "Why Arts Education Is Crucial, and Who's Doing It Best." *Edutopia*. January 28, 2009. http://www.edutopia.org/arts-music-curriculum-child-development

Smith, Mark K. "John Dewey." *Contents @ the Informal Education Homepage*. http://www.infed.org/.

Sousa, David A., and Carol A. Tomlinson. *Differentiation and the Brain: How Neuroscience Supports the Learner-Friendly Classroom*. Bloomington, IN: Solution Tree, 2011.

Strauss, Valerie. "Ravitch: Why Finland's Schools Are Great (by Doing What We Don't)." *Washington Post*, October 12, 2011. http://www.washingtonpost.com/blogs/answer-sheet/post/ravitch-why-finlands-schools-are-great-by-doing-what-we-dont/2011/10/12/gIQAmTyLgL_blog.html

Swindall, Clint. *Engaged Leadership: Building a Culture to Overcome Employee Disengagement*. Hoboken, NJ: John Wiley, 2011.

Tomlinson, Carol A. *The Differentiated Classroom: Responding to the Needs of All Learners*. Alexandria, VA: Association for Supervision and Curriculum Development, 1999.

Wagaman, Jennifer. "How to Teach to Multiple Ability Levels." Suite101.com. http://suite101.com/article/how-to-teach-to-multiple-ability-levels-a80811.

Wagner, Tony, and Robert A. Compton. *Creating Innovators: The Making of Young People Who Will Change the World*. New York: Scribner, 2012.

Wagner, Tony. *The Global Achievement Gap: Why Even Our Best Schools Don't Teach the New Survival Skills Our Children Need—and What We Can Do about It*. New York: Basic, 2008.

Wagner, Tony. "Rigor-Redefined." *Educational Leadership* (October 2008): 20–24. http://www.ascd.org

"Welcome to Bullying Statistics." *Bullying Statistics*. September 16, 2012. http://www.bullyingstatistics.org.

Wenzel, Thomas J. "AC Educator: Cooperative Student Activities as Learning Devices." *Analytical Chemistry* 72, no. 7 (2000): 293 A–95 A.

*Worldpeacegame.org*. www.worldpeacegame.org.

# Notes

## (Endnotes)

[1] Robinson, Ken, and Lou Aronica. *The Element: How Finding Your Passion Changes Everything*. New York: Viking, 2009: xi.

[2] Wagner, Tony. *The Global Achievement Gap: Why Even Our Best Schools Don't Teach the New Survival Skills Our Children Need—and What We Can Do about It*. New York: Basic, 2008: xxvii.

[3] Resnik, LB. "ERIC - Tests as Standards of Achievement in Schools., 1989-Oct." 1989. http://eric.ed.gov/?id=ED335421

[4] www.ed.gov/esea/flexibility.

[5] http://www.whitehouse.gov/the-press-office/fact-sheet-expanding-promise-education-america

[6] Bill Evers, Jay P. Greene, Greg Forster, Sandra Stotsky, Ze'ev Wurman, et. al. "Closing the Door on Innovation. *Heartland Institute*," May 2, 2011. http://heartland.org/policy-documents/closing-door-innovation

[7] http://www.edreform.com/issues/teacher-quality/#what-we-believe

[8] http://www.edreform.com/issues/standards-testing/#what-we-believe

[9] www.corestandards.org/Math/Content/3/MD.

[10] www.corestandards.org/Math/Content/3/NBT.

[11] "Driving Miss Data—or Is Big Data Driving Schools?" *St. Louis Beacon*, July 7, 2013, https://www.stlbeacon.org/?_escaped_fragment_=/content/31517/voices_inda_data_062013.[9] www.ets.org.

[12] www.ets.org.

[13] "Standards for Educational and Psychological Testing," The American Psychological Association, 1999, Accessed July 7, 2011. http://www.apa.org/science/standards.html.

[14] Strauss, Valerie. "Ravitch: Why Finland's Schools Are Great (by Doing What We Don't)." *Washington Post*, October 12, 2011. http://www.washingtonpost.com/blogs/answer-sheet/post/ravitch-why-finlands-schools-are-great-by-doing-what-we-dont/2011/10/12/glQAmTyLgL_blog.html

[15] Sahlberg, Pasi, and Andy Hargreaves. *Finnish Lessons: What Can the World Learn from Educational Change in Finland?* New York: Teachers College, 2011: 5.

## NOTES

[16] Jonassen, David H, and Lucia Rohrer-Murphy. "Activity theory as a framework for designing constructivist learning environments." *Educational Technology Research and Development* 47.1 (1999): 61-79.

[17] Sahlberg, 35.

[18] M.L. Loukola, "Education for sustainable development in Finland" (2006), http://www.minedu.fi/export/sites/default/OPM/Julkaisut/2002/liitteet/opm_340_89ktpo.pdf.

[19] "Program for International Student Assessment (PISA)—Overview," National Center for Education Statistics (2002), August 2012, http://nces.ed.gov/surveys/pisa/.

[20] "OKM—The Results of PISA 2009," Ministry of Education and Culture, Finland (2010), August 10, 2012, http://www.minedu.fi/pisa/2009.html?lang=en.

[21] Sahlberg, 124.

[22] "Why Education in Finland Works," YouTube, accessed August 10, 2012, http://www.youtube.com/watch?v=ntdYxqRce_s.

[23] "Why Education in Finland Works," YouTube, accessed August 10, 2012

[24] "Experiential Learning" (2011), August 10, 2012, http://www.instructionaldesign.org/theories/experiental-learning.html.

[25] "NEA - Research Spotlight on Parental Involvement in Education." 2009. http://www.nea.org/tools/17360.htm

[26] "What Is Cooperative Learning?" (2005), accessed August 24, 2012, http://serc.carleton.edu/introgeo/cooperative/whatis.html.

[27] Paul Simon, "Train in the Distance," in *Graceland*, Warner Bros, 1986 http://www.paulsimon.com/us/music/paul-simons-concert-park-august-15-1991/train-distance.

[28] "Americans for the Arts News." *Americans for the Arts*. September 16, 2012. http://americansforthearts.org.

[29] "Christo and Jeanne-Cluade." *Christo and Jeanne-Claude*. September 16, 2012. http://christojeanneclaude.net.

[30] "Student-Centred Learning: What Does It Mean for Students and…" (2005), http://www.aishe.org/readings/2005-1/oneill-mcmahon-Tues_19th_Oct_SCL.html.

[31] "Active Learning: Creating Excitement in the Classroom," http://www.ntlf.com/html/lib/bib/91-9dig.htm.

[32] http://4.bp.blogspot.com/_CZCC_EW7viw/TNH9OeW0z8I/AAAAAAAABE/U1XwKdVkS2I/s1600/Learning+Styles_gif.jpg.

[33] "Heterogeneous Grouping of Students and Its Effects on Learning," http://ruby.fgcu.edu/courses/80337/McAvoy/HETERO~1.html.

[34] www.khanacademy.org.

[35] "Learning Style Inventories" (2007), accessed August 7, 2012, http://www.oucom.ohiou.edu/fd/learning_style_inventories.htm.

## NOTES

[36] "Howard Gardner, Multiple Intelligences and Education" (2002), http://www.infed.org/thinkers/gardner.htm.

[37] Wayne A. Wickelgren, "Chunking and Consolidation: A Theoretical Synthesis of Semantic Networks, Configuring in Conditioning, SR Versus Cognitive Learning, Normal Forgetting, the Amnesic Syndrome, and the Hippocampal Arousal System," *Psychological Review* 86 no. 1 (1979): 44.

[38] "How to Teach to Multiple Ability Levels: Teaching Above and Below," http://suite101.com/a/how-to-teach-to-multiple-ability-levels-a80811.

[39] S. J. Stone, "The Multi-Age Classroom" (2005), http://www.pac.dodea.edu/edservices/educationprograms/Research%20article.pdf.

[40] http://www.christenseninstitute.org/blended-learning-3.

[41] http://www.funderstanding.com/theory/brain-based-learning/brain-based-learning/

[42] "Reading Wars: Phonics vs. Whole Language … - Reading Horizons." 2010. 9 Dec. 2013 <http://www.readinghorizons.com/blog/post/2010/09/07/Reading-Wars-Phonics-vs-Whole-Language-Reading-Instruction.aspx>

www.ingramcontent.com/pod-product-compliance
Lightning Source LLC
Chambersburg PA
CBHW051645040426
42446CB00009B/986